THE THEORY OF INTERNATIONAL TRADE

JAMES R. MARKUSEN
JAMES R. MELVIN
University of Western Ontario

HARPER & ROW, PUBLISHERS, New York
Cambridge, Philadelphia, San Francisco, Washington,
London, Mexico City, São Paulo, Singapore, Sydney

1817

Sponsoring Editor: John Greenman
Project Editor: B. Pelner
Cover Design: Michel Craig
Text Art: ComCom Division of Haddon Craftsmen, Inc
Production Manager: Jeanie Berke
Production Assistant: Paula Roppolo
Compositor: ComCom Division of Haddon Craftsmen, Inc.
Printer and Binder: R. R. Donnelley & Sons Company
Cover Printer: R. R. Donnelley & Sons Company

THE THEORY OF INTERNATIONAL TRADE

Library of Congress Cataloging in Publication Data

Markusen, James R., 1948–
    The theory of international trade.

    Portions of the book were originally published: The theory of international trade and its Canadian applications. Toronto : Butterworths, 1984.
    Includes bibliographies and index.
    1. Commerce. 2. Canada—Commerce. I. Melvin, James R. II. Title.
HF1008.M37 1988   382.1'04   87-27001
ISBN 0-06-044212-3

        90 91 9 8 7 6 5

CONTENTS

To the Instructor

This book is intended primarily for a conventional half-year course in international trade at the undergraduate level. Its secondary purpose is to serve as a basic text and reference book in graduate courses. The analytical exposition is largely in terms of geometry, with the necessary tools being developed in Chapters 2, 3, and 4. A half-year course in intermediate microeconomics would be a helpful preparation, but we have not assumed that it is a prerequisite for the course.

We have tried to maintain a uniform level of analysis throughout the book. A few sections, which are marked by an asterisk, are more difficult than the standard treatment of the Heckscher-Ohlin model, and may be skipped without loss of continuity. One reason for writing this book is our perception that competing books tended to treat certain topics such as Heckscher-Ohlin on a fairly formal level and then resort to informal and anecdotal treatments of other topics such as scale economies, imperfect competition, factor mobility, and multinational corporations. In many of the relevant books, such topics are not treated at all. We have included all of these topics and many others at a level of analysis that is approximately equal to that used in the standard development of the Heckscher-Ohlin and specific-factors models. Furthermore, we have attempted to use the same basic "tool kit" over and over to avoid the costs of developing and learning new analytical constructions for each new topic.

As just indicated, we believe that our book differs significantly from its competitors on the criterion of breadth. We have devoted entire chapters to important topics that are dealt with superficially or not at all in other texts. They include:

1. A chapter that presents a full analytical development of the specific-factors model and that relates that model to the Heckscher-Ohlin model (Chapter 9).
2. A chapter devoted entirely to imperfect competition and domestic tax distortions. The effects of these distortions on trade flows, welfare, and factor prices are discussed. The important notion of procompetitive gains from trade is developed (Chapter 10).
3. An entire chapter devoted to scale economies. External economies, internal economies, and monopolistic competition are all examined. This material is considered important for understanding questions of industrial strategy and for explaining North American-EEC-Japanese trade. The implications of scale economies for the gains from trade, the direction of trade, and the pattern of production all receive attention (Chapter 11).

4. A chapter on demand determinants of trade that includes discussions of nonhomogeneous demand, the Linder hypothesis, and the product cycle (Chapter 12).
5. An expanded analysis of tariffs, especially their relationship to and effects in the presence of other taxes. Export subsidies are also analyzed (Chapter 14).
6. An entire chapter devoted to quotas and nontariff barriers to trade. Recent work on the nonequivalence of tariffs and quotas is incorporated (Chapter 15).
7. A chapter on strategic trade policy in the presence of scale economies and imperfect competition. Possible welfare gains from the strategic use of production and export subsidies are demonstrated. Key assumptions are analyzed and it is shown, for example, that free entry of firms leads to very different conclusions from those forthcoming from a simple duopoly model (Chapter 16).
8. A much expanded analysis of portfolio factor movements, which incorporates a great deal of new theoretical literature. Welfare effects are carefully analyzed and the relationship between commodity trade and factor trade is discussed in detail (Chapter 19).
9. An entire chapter devoted to direct foreign investment. Recent formal theories such as technology transfer, multiplant economies, and preemptive entry are presented. The welfare effects of multinationals on host countries are emphasized (Chapter 20).
10. A chapter on growth and the intertemporal gains from trade. Much new theory is presented and old concepts such as the Prebisch-Singer hypothesis, immiserizing growth, and export-led growth are analyzed in the light of that theory (Chapter 21).

James R. Markusen
James R. Melvin

one

TECHNICAL CONCEPTS AND THE GAINS FROM TRADE

chapter *1*

Introduction

1. WHAT IS THE "THEORY OF INTERNATIONAL TRADE"?

Let us begin by situating the study of international trade within the discipline of economics. International economics is a subset of the economics discipline and therefore deals with the same kind of questions with which any student of even introductory economics is already familiar. In the most simple terms, international economics is concerned with how economic units behave. The important distinction between it and other branches of economics is the economic unit that is being studied. International economics, rather than being primarily concerned with questions such as how producers maximize profits, or how consumers maximize utility, is concerned with the question of how *nations* can maximize some measure of collective well-being. That is not to say, of course, that the theory of the firm and the theory of consumer behavior are unimportant in the study of international economics; indeed, as we will see, these traditional economic problems will play an extremely important role in our analysis. However, rather than being the subject of this book, such traditional problems will be the building blocks on which our analysis rests.

International economics can be conveniently divided into two parts: *real analysis* or trade theory, and *monetary analysis* or international finance. Real analysis, with which this book is entirely concerned, assumes that all transactions are carried out through barter. That is, it is assumed that commodities are exchanged for one another without the use of money as a medium of exchange. While such an assumption is clearly unrealistic and very much at variance with the way in which transactions are actually carried out in the world economy, and while it is clear that in some circumstances the introduction of currency would affect some of the conclusions reached, the complications that would arise if money were explicitly introduced into the model would not justify the increase in realism that would thereby be attained. It must always be kept in mind that abstractions from reality are not in themselves undesirable; indeed, the whole notion of theory rests on such abstractions. The important question is always whether the simplifications of reality that we make in order to render a problem tractable significantly affect the conclusions that are reached. For present purposes, the introduction of money as a medium of exchange would not substantially affect any of the conclusions. Indeed, those readers who feel uncomfortable with the assumption of barter exchange are free to assume the existence of a neutral money that is used for all transactions.

The types of problems treated by the two branches of international economics are quite different. Real analysis (trade theory) concerns itself with such things as the reasons for which trade takes place, the implications for commodity and factor prices of changes in real variables such as the stock of capital and the supply of labor, the analysis of the benefits that accrue from international trade, and the welfare effects of such things as tariffs and custom unions. International finance, on the other hand, is concerned with such issues as the determination of equilibrium exchange rates, the comparison of fixed and flexible exchange-rate systems, the relationship between internal and external balance, the effects of devaluations, and the question of the form that an efficient international monetary system should take. As well as these differences in subject matter, the two branches of international economics also use quite different methodologies. Trade theory is very much in the tradition of neoclassical economics, where full employment is assumed and where, in general, all markets are assumed to clear. International finance, on the other hand, is mainly in the tradition of macroeconomics; it is concerned with such things as the price level and the level of unemployment. International finance typically assumes a single aggregate output and an aggregate price level, whereas trade theory assumes at least two commodities and is concerned with relative rather than absolute prices.

Although these two branches of international economics have developed more or less independently, so that it is possible to study one branch without explicit reference to the other—as is done in this book—nevertheless, it is clear that a complete understanding of the international economy requires an appreciation of both the real and the monetary sides of the model. The reader is, therefore, cautioned that the material contained in this book represents only one part of the whole story.

2. WHY "INTERNATIONAL" TRADE?

The subject matter of this book essentially concerns the trade in commodities that takes place among nations. A question that naturally arises is, Why is it seen to be necessary to distinguish trade between nations from trade between regions, or even trade between individual consumers? Several arguments have traditionally been used. First, a distinction is usually made with regard to the mobility of labor. It is argued that although it is reasonable to assume that *within* a country labor is completely mobile because of such things as language, religion, social customs, nationalism, and government regulation, labor mobility *among* countries is severely restricted. Indeed, it is usually assumed that labor is completely immobile among countries. Much of the theory of international trade also assumes capital to be immobile among countries, and although such an assumption may not seem as reasonable at first glance, it should be recalled that "capital" means physical equipment that is being used for production. Thus, while trade in capital equipment is common, this trade takes place *before* the equipment has become part of the capital stock of the countries under consideration. It is not common to observe trade in capital stock after it is in place and being used to produce commodities. As we will see, the assumption of the international immobility of factors is not necessarily a severe restriction on our model, for under certain conditions it can be shown that trade in commodities can be a substitute for factor mobility.

A second justification for considering trade among nations as a distinct branch of economics is simply that, in many situations, nations do behave as if they were a single economic unit, and interact with one another very much as would a group of consumers or a group of firms. Countries impose tariffs against one another and set up various other forms of restrictions on the flow of commodities. They severely limit the free flow of factors of production, particularly labor, from one country to another, and in certain circumstances they even adjust domestic policies so as to change the pattern of international trade. Such activities are virtually unknown among regions within the same country and, indeed, in many countries would actually be against the law. Furthermore, because almost all sovereign nations have their own currencies, the value of international transactions is easily determined, and, particularly in recent years, many countries have found themselves in either a debtor or creditor position with regard to the rest of the world. These situations are inevitably due to international transactions of one kind or another; thus international transactions of all kinds are brought into sharp focus.

Although a variety of arguments can be presented to justify considering international trade as a distinct branch of economics, these arguments must be kept in proper perspective. It has been suggested that factors are immobile internationally and completely mobile within nations, and although this is probably a better assumption than any alternative, at least if one is restricted to consideration of polar (i.e., extreme) cases, it is easy to think of situations in which such a proposition would be difficult to defend. In Europe in recent years, for example, there has been a considerable degree of labor mobility among various countries. In the case of Canada it seems quite probable that there is more labor mobility between, say, Ontario and New York than there is between Ontario and Prince Edward Island. It has also been suggested that the international flow of commodities, and particularly the deficits and surpluses generated by such flows, gives rise to a distinction between international and, say, interregional transactions. Such a sharp distinction, however, may not be warranted, for the same kind of deficits and surpluses may, in fact, exist between regions in the same country, but because these regions use the same currency, such imbalances are difficult to detect. However, the fact that these deficits or surpluses are not easily observable does not mean that they are unimportant, and it can be argued that much more attention should be paid to such internal imbalances. All this, however, does not mean that the study of international transactions is in any sense inappropriate; rather, it suggests that the scope of the analysis should perhaps be broadened. Perhaps we should take a cue from Bertil Ohlin, one of the founders of the modern theory of international trade, who entitled his book *Interregional and International Trade.*

3. THE IMPORTANCE OF INTERNATIONAL TRADE

The identification of something called "international trade" does not, by itself, justify a careful examination of this phenomenon; we must also convince ourselves that such trade is an important part of the overall activity of the economy. For many countries this is easily done, particularly for smaller countries such as Australia, Canada, and many of those in Europe, for international trade makes up a significant proportion of their gross national product (GNP). In Canada in 1981, for example, exports were approximately 20 percent of GNP, and thus, as an aggregate variable, were larger than such things as gross investment. But even in countries where trade is less important in relative terms, international transactions still have an extremely important influence on the overall level of economic activity. This point was very clearly emphasized by the mid-1970s energy crisis in the United States. Although at the time less than 5 percent of the United States' consumption of petroleum products originated in the OPEC countries, restrictions on the supply and increases in prices brought about extreme disruptions in the American economy; indeed, it seems quite clear that this energy crisis was one of the important causes of the ensuing recession. We have also seen numerous cases in which, because of an imbalance in international transactions, international monetary markets have been thrown into chaos, with various adverse effects on the domestic economies of the countries involved. In short, it seems quite clear that international transactions have a very important influence on the domestic economy.

Perhaps the most important aspect of international transactions from the point of view of the domestic economy is that, to a considerable extent, the influences are exogenous and therefore not under the control of the domestic economy. The OPEC oil embargo of 1973–1974 is again a case in point, but even in less extreme cases it is clear that a country that relies heavily on international trade is susceptible to the transmission of all kinds of international instabilities.

If international trade can give rise to such difficulties, why do countries participate in it at all? A little thought quickly brings one answer to this question: If the interference of international trade in certain commodities can have such a marked effect on the domestic economy, then it must be clear that this international trade forms a very important element in the overall activity of the economy. Indeed, many countries could not enjoy their present standard of living except for the existence of international trade. If Canada was not able to export commodities such as wheat and other grains and natural resources, Canadians could not enjoy their present high standard of living. Japan imports raw materials and exports final products, and without such imports and exports the standard of living in Japan would be significantly lower. Even large and diverse economies such as the United States depend on foreign trade to supply a significant proportion of essential commodities such as petroleum. Thus, while disturbances in trade patterns can result in serious domestic disruptions, this is the price that must be paid for the substantial advantages that accrue from international trade.

A second answer to the question is that the ability to trade may help insulate the economy against disturbances that are domestic in origin, such as a bad crop or an industrial strike. In each case trade allows the country to obtain the temporarily scarce commodity rather than go without.

4. THE UNDERLYING CAUSES OF INTERNATIONAL TRADE

It has been argued that international trade is an important phenomenon in the world, and it is now time to comment briefly on why this international trade exists. This is a complex problem; indeed, a major part of this book will be dedicated to the careful analysis of just this question. The brief discussion here can, in fact, be thought of as an introduction to Part Two of the book.

Some insights into the reasons for international trade can be gained from considering the question of why trade takes place among individuals within a country. In standard consumer theory it is usually supposed that individuals trade in order to reach the final equilibrium position; our question is why this exchange between individuals is necessary. At a superficial level the answer is obvious; trade takes place because the two individuals differ in some respect. Perhaps the first difference that would come to mind would be differences in endowments. If we imagined a very simple world in which the only two commodities were apples and bananas, and if we further supposed that one individual were endowed with the entire supply of apples while the other individual had all the bananas, then we would expect that, if exchange were allowed, there would be trade between the two individuals, so that in the final equilibrium both individuals would consume some of both commodities. In this case a difference in the initial endowments has resulted in trade.

But, one could argue, suppose the individual endowed with bananas likes bananas but dislikes apples, and suppose that the individual endowed with apples likes apples but dislikes bananas. In such a case it is possible that there would be no trade. Thus implicit in our simple example was an assumption about the tastes of the two individuals; in particular, we implicitly assumed that both individuals liked both of the commodities. Now imagine a situation in which we have the same two individuals, one of whom likes bananas, the other of whom likes apples, but where we now assume that the initial endowment of apples and bananas to the two individuals is identical. Again, if exchange is allowed, we would expect some trade in apples and bananas to take place; in this case, however, trade takes place because of demand differences and not because of differences in endowments. Thus it is clear that fundamental differences in people's preferences for commodities can be a reason for trade.

So far our model with the two individuals has been very simple, for we have assumed that the endowments of the commodities were predetermined and that no production takes place. Suppose we now assume that the two individuals are each required to produce commodities that will ultimately make up their endowments. A question that now arises is why these two individuals will not produce precisely the amounts of the two commodities that they wish to consume. Two reasons immediately come to mind. First, it may be that the two individuals have inherently different skills, or that one possesses technical knowledge that the other individual lacks. If this is the case, then it might well be profitable for individuals to specialize in producing the commodities for which they have special skills or about which they have special knowledge. In terms of two countries, trade might be generated if these countries possess different technologies. But even if both of our individuals possess the same skills and the same technical know-how, it may still be profitable for them to specialize if there are economies of large-scale production. Such economies could be exploited by specialization, the end result being that both individuals would have larger amounts of both commodities to consume. The same argument can apply to nations; if significant economies of large-scale production exist, it may well be profitable for specialization and trade to take place.

5. THE IMPORTANCE OF PRICE DIFFERENCES

What is the link between production and consumption differences and the actual trade in commodities that takes place? The correct answer is the obvious one; these differences will be reflected in price differences. This point, although a simple one, is of fundamental importance. Trade, whether it takes place between individuals or between countries, must ultimately be due to price differences. Only if the price of a commodity is higher in some foreign market than it is domestically will it ever be profitable to export that good, and, similarly, only if the domestic price of a commodity is higher than the price of the same commodity elsewhere will it ever be worthwhile importing that good.

It is now easy to see the connection between the underlying causes of trade, which we discussed in the last section, and the actual exchange of commodities. Consider Figure 1.1, in which we show the simple partial equilibrium demand and supply situation for some commodity X in two countries, H and F. We initially assume that the demand and supply conditions in the two countries are such that the price is the same in both markets. Note that this need not imply that the demand and supply curves are identical. Now suppose that for some reason there is a shift in preferences in country H toward commodity X. In Figure 1.1 this will result in the demand curve in market H shifting to the right, resulting in a higher price p' for commodity X in that market. Prices in the two markets are now different, so there is a basis for profitable exchange. We would now expect some consumers in country H to buy commodity X in the foreign market where prices are lower, or, alternatively, we can say that some

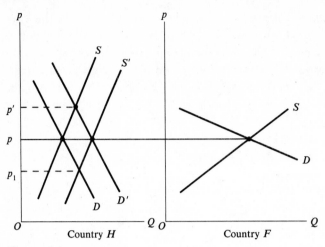

Figure 1.1

producers in country F will now prefer to sell their commodities in the market in country H. This, of course, would tend to again equalize the prices in the two markets.

Now, returning to the initial situation in which prices are the same in the two markets, suppose that in country H a more efficient technique of production was developed. This shifts the supply curve to the right, resulting in a lower price p_1 for commodity X in the home market. Again, trade would be expected, only this time country H would export commodity X to country F.

Although it would be possible, albeit somewhat more difficult, to illustrate how endowment differences and returns-to-scale differences would result in price differences in the simple partial equilibrium diagram of Figure 1.1, the two examples given are sufficient to illustrate the point. Underlying differences in supply and demand conditions in the two countries result in price differences in the two markets and these, in turn, produce the possibility of profitable international exchange. Although illustrative of the causes of trade, the simple partial equilibrium diagram of Figure 1.1 is not appropriate for the analysis of the aggregate model that we wish to develop. Instead, we will want the aggregate counterparts to the demand and supply curves of Figure 1.1. It is to this task that we will turn in Chapters 2 and 3.

6. PLAN OF THE BOOK

The theory of international trade deals, in the main, with two broad kinds of questions; the first is the causes or determinants of trade, and the second is the welfare implications of this international exchange. While these two questions cannot be completely separated, Part Two of this book will focus primarily on the question of *why* trade takes place. Chapter 5 of this first part will examine the welfare effects of free trade versus no trade (autarky). Part Three will then turn to a consideration of welfare questions, and in particular, to the question of how the welfare of the countries involved in trade will be affected by restrictions on the free flow of international exchanged commodities. The topics examined in Part Four are factor movements, direct foreign investment, and growth. But before addressing any of these questions we need, as has already been suggested, to develop some of the analytical tools that we will use throughout; it is to this task that we turn in the next several chapters.

chapter 2

The Production Possibility Curve

1. PRODUCTION FUNCTIONS

The basic building block of the supply side of our model will be the production function, as represented by equation (2.1):

$$X = F(K, L). \qquad (2.1)$$

This equation is just the algebraic way of representing the fact that commodities are produced with certain primary factors and certain technical knowledge or technology. Thus equation (2.1) is simply a shorthand way of saying that given a certain technology as represented by F, an amount of capital represented by K and an amount of labor services represented by L can be combined to produce some quantity of output represented by X.

The production relation described by (2.1) contains three variables: the level of output and the levels of inputs of capital and labor. Geometrically, it could be represented by a three-dimensional surface; diagrammatically, it can be illustrated as in Figure 2.1. The production surface can be thought of as a hill, with the origin representing the ground level. At the origin there is no labor input nor capital input and therefore no output. With positive amounts of both capital and labor there will be a positive level of output of X, and as we add more of either capital or labor, or both, the output of X increases.

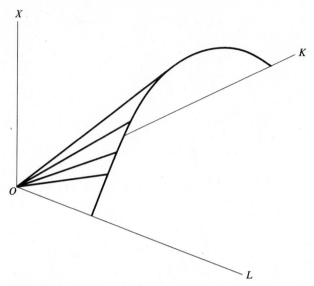

Figure 2.1

Three-dimensional diagrams are awkward to draw and are not very useful in illustrating economic phenomena. Economists have traditionally found it more useful to convert three-dimensional diagrams, such as the one shown in Figure 2.1, to two dimensions by considering one of the three variables to be fixed. Reexamining equation (2.1), we see that there are three possibilities open; we could fix X, L, or K. First, suppose we fixed the level of output at some amount $\bar{X}$ and considered the combinations of K and L that are consistent with this level of output. In terms of Figure 2.1 we can imagine taking a slice through the production hill at a height $\bar{X}$ above the plane KL. Looking down on the plane KL from above, the edge of the slice could be represented by the line $\bar{X}$ in Figure 2.2. Note that this line $\bar{X}$ is completely analogous to a contour line in a topographical map. It represents the locus of points of equal height above some arbitrarily chosen reference plane. In terms of our production model, it represents the locus of output points distance $\bar{X}$ above the origin.

Loci such as $\bar{X}$ of Figure 2.2 are called *isoquants,* and show all possible combinations of capital and labor that could be used to produce the level of output $\bar{X}$. There are, of course, many such loci, and indeed, one such locus can be drawn for every possible level of output. In Figure 2.2 the locus X_0 represents a level of output $X_0 < \bar{X}$, while X' represents a constant level of output greater than $\bar{X}$.

Now, suppose that rather than fixing the level of output in equation (2.1), we fix the level of one of the inputs. In particular, suppose we assume that the level of input of capital is fixed at the level $\bar{K}$, and investigate the

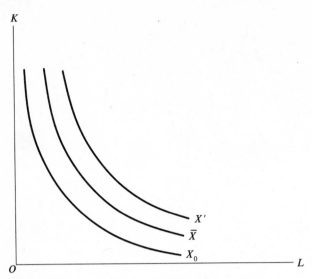

Figure 2.2

relationship between varying amounts of the input L and the output X. This would give the locus shown in Figure 2.3, known as the *total product curve*. There are several characteristics of this curve that are of interest. Note, first, that we have drawn the curve starting at the origin. This implies that no output is possible unless there is a positive amount of labor used as an input; although not necessary for our analysis, this assumption seems quite reasonable. It will also be noted that the total product curve of Figure 2.3 has been drawn to curve toward the labor axis. Thus, although additional units of labor input are assumed to result in additional units of output, the rate of increase of output is assumed to diminish as more and more labor is added. This is an illustration of the *law of diminishing returns,* and we have the following definition.

Definition

The law of diminishing returns is said to hold if, as increasing amounts of one factor are added to a constant amount of the other factor, output increases but at a decreasing rate.

Figure 2.3 shows only one total product curve, but it is clear that there will be a different total product curve for every different level of capital stock that is assumed. For fixed amounts of capital larger than $\overline{K}$, the total product curve will lie everywhere above the one shown in Figure 2.3, while for smaller capital stocks the total product curve will lie everywhere below the one shown. It is also clear that rather than fixing the amount of capital,

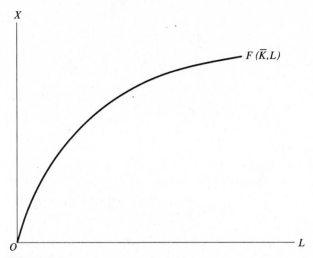

Figure 2.3

we could have assumed the labor supply to be fixed and drawn the relationship between X and K. This would have given a figure completely
analogous to Figure 2.3, and again, of course, a whole family of curves
could be drawn, depending on the quantity of labor assumed. Note that
just as the isoquants of Figure 2.2 can be thought of as the loci formed
by taking a slice through the production hill parallel to the KL plane, so
the total product curve of Figure 2.3 can be thought of as the locus of the
production hill found by taking a slice parallel to the XL plane.

2. RETURNS TO SCALE

Equation (2.1) is a convenient algebraic summary of production conditions, but it is a very general expression, and to make it useful for economic analysis, we must impose several restrictions. Such restrictions
have been implicitly assumed in drawing Figures 2.2 and 2.3, and before
proceeding, these must be introduced explicitly. Specifically, it is assumed
that all isoquants are smooth, and that, for any level of output, the set of
all combinations of capital and labor that would yield at least that much
output is convex.[1] It should also be noted that the law of diminishing
returns, referred to in the last section, is assumed. Although this last
assumption will be made throughout most of our analysis, production
functions in which this condition is not satisfied are easily constructed.

Another characteristic of production functions such as (2.1), which
is particularly important from an economic point of view, relates to the
response of output to equiproportional changes in *both* of the inputs. A
very common assumption in economics is that of *constant returns to scale,*

namely, that proportional changes in all inputs lead to the same proportional change in output. This assumption is referred to somewhat more formally as *homogeneity of the first degree,* and it is such an important concept in economics, and in the discussion of this book, that a formal definition seems worthwhile.

Definition

The function $X = F(K, L)$ is said to be homogeneous of degree k if for any λ, λ constant and greater than zero, we have that $\lambda^k X = F(\lambda K, \lambda L)$. If $k = 1$ the function is said to be homogeneous of degree 1, or to be linear homogeneous.

This definition is easy to interpret. Suppose, for example, we double both K and L. If the function is homogeneous and if k is equal to 1, then the output will also double. With k greater than 1, called *increasing returns to scale,* a doubling of both factors will result in more than the doubling of the output. Similarly, for $k < 1$, called *decreasing returns to scale,* a doubling of both inputs will result in output less than double.

The returns-to-scale assumption can be illustrated by the isoquant diagram of Figure 2.4. Consider first the isoquant X_0 where it has been assumed that the level of output is equal to 10. There is an infinite number of combinations of capital and labor that, when combined with the assumed technology, would give this level of output, namely, all the points on the curve X_0. One such point is A, which shows that 10 units of output can be produced using 6 units of labor and 7 units of capital. Suppose we now double the inputs of both factors and move to point B. Since the capital/labor space is "full" of isoquants, there must be one that passes through point B. The question now is, What is the level of output associated with that particular isoquant? The answer must clearly depend on the assumption we make about the degree of homogeneity of the production function. If k is equal to 1, so that we have constant returns to scale, then it is clear that the level of output associated with point B must be 20 units, twice that associated with point A. If, on the other hand, k is greater than 1, implying increasing returns to scale, then although we do not know the precise number to be attached to isoquant X_1 we know that it will be greater than 20. Similarly, for decreasing returns to scale, where k is less than 1, the level of output associated with X_1 would be less than 20.

Another characteristic associated with the concept of homogeneity relates to the slopes of the isoquants as we move along a ray from the origin, such as K/L of Figure 2.4. It can be shown that for any such ray,

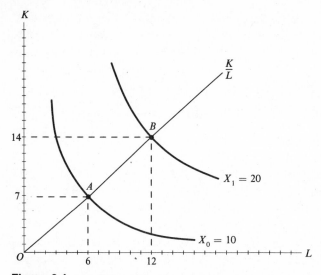

Figure 2.4

and for production functions that are homogeneous of any degree, the slopes of the isoquants at all points such as A and B are identical. This characteristic will be very important in the analysis, for it means that once one isoquant is known, all other isoquants can be derived. In terms of Figure 2.4, if isoquant X_0 is known, then at point B, where $OB = 2OA$, there will be another isoquant with exactly the same slope. For any other ray, other points on this new isoquant can be found in the same way. Furthermore, since $OA = AB$, and since this production function has been assumed to be homogeneous of the first degree, the level of output associated with this isoquant will be equal to 20, twice that associated with X_0.

   Note that there are two important characteristics associated with the preceding assumptions of homogeneity. First is the fact that the functions are assumed to be homogeneous, and this implies that the slopes of the isoquants along any ray from the origin are equal. This is true regardless of the degree of homogeneity. The second part of the assumption relates to the degree to which the functions are assumed to be homogeneous—that is, the value of k—and this assumption determines the spacing of the isoquant in Figure 2.4.

   Observe that there is an important difference between the law of diminishing returns discussed in the last section and returns to scale discussed here. With the law of diminishing returns we are fixing the input of one factor and varying the inputs of the other and observing how this changes output. For returns to scale we are varying *both* factors in the same proportion and examining how this changes output. It should be noted that there is no conflict between the assumption of constant returns to scale and the law of diminishing returns; indeed, almost all of the production functions that we use in this book will be assumed to satisfy both conditions.

3. EQUILIBRIUM FOR A SINGLE PRODUCER

To this point, attention has been focused entirely on the physical characteristics of the production functions; no behavioral assumptions of any kind have been made about our producers. This section presents a very brief summary of those parts of production theory that will be central to our discussion. The behavioral assumptions for an individual producer can be stated in either of two entirely equivalent ways: The producer can be thought of as maximizing output subject to a cost constraint or as minimizing costs subject to a production constraint. We will employ the first approach, but the equivalence of the two will become obvious as we proceed.

It is assumed that the producer, having access to a technology represented by equation (2.1), wishes to maximize output, subject to the condition that he must spend no more on inputs than an amount C_0. It is assumed that the wage rate, w, and the rental on capital equipment, r, are known to the producer. It is further assumed that the individual producer is too small to have any influence on the price of his inputs, so that w and r can be treated as constants regardless of his level of output. The first task is to describe all possible combinations of K and L that the producer could purchase with the fixed amount of money represented by C_0. Two such points are easily found. Since the price of K is r, if the total amount were spent on purchases of K, he could hire $K_0 = C_0/r$ of capital services. Similarly, if all expenditure were made on labor, he could hire $L_0 = C_0/w$ of labor services. Both of these points are shown in Figure 2.5. Now suppose equal amounts are spent on both factors. Since prices of capital and labor are constant, this implies that one-half K_0 and one-half L_0 can now be purchased, giving rise to point A in Figure 2.5. It is obvious that point A must lie on the straight line joining K_0 and L_0, and furthermore, that all allocations of C_0 between expenditure on capital and labor must lie on this line. Thus the line K_0L_0, sometimes referred to as the *isocost line,* represents the cost constraint that this producer faces.

We now add the technological information by imposing on Figure 2.5 three representative isoquants from equation (2.1). The producer could produce a quantity of output X_0 by allocating expenditures between labor and capital as represented by point C, or alternatively, he could produce the same quantity by purchasing the capital and labor services

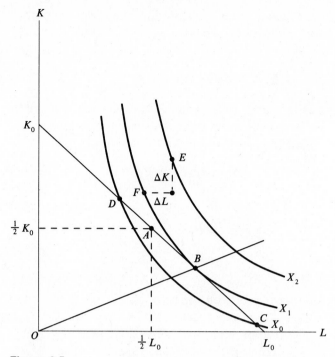

Figure 2.5

associated with point D; but it is clear that neither of these allocations would be efficient. For the same expenditure, the larger output associated with X_1 could be achieved by producing at point B. Furthermore, while production at points such as E on isoquant X_2 would be preferred to B, it is clear that this output is not feasible, since it implies a larger input of labor and capital than is possible, given the firm's cost constraint. It is thus evident that output is maximized by producing at point B, the point at which the highest isoquant is tangent to the cost constraint.

From Figure 2.5 it can be seen that the slope of the cost constraint is the distance K_0 divided by the distance L_0. But K_0 equals C_0/r and L_0 equals C_0/w, implying that the slope of the cost constraint is equal to w/r, the wage-rental ratio. Thus the individual firm is in equilibrium when the wage-rental ratio is equal to the slope of an isoquant. It is also possible to derive an expression for the slope of an isoquant. Consider any two points in factor space such as F and E in Figure 2.5. We can express the change in the output of X in going from F to E as the change in L times the additional output of X for each unit of L plus the change in K times the additional output of X associated with an additional unit of K. The additional unit of output associated with adding one more unit of an input is called the *marginal product* and is written as *MP*. In Figure 2.3 the marginal product is the slope of the total product curve for any labor input. Thus our expression for the total change in X can be more formally written as

$$\Delta X = \Delta L \cdot MP_L + \Delta K \cdot MP_K \qquad (2.2)$$

where Δ is defined as the change in a variable. Now suppose that both points are on the same isoquant. From the definition of an isoquant this means that $\Delta X = 0$, and thus equation (2.2) becomes

$$0 = \Delta L \cdot MP_L + \Delta K \cdot MP_K.$$

Rearranging, we obtain

$$\frac{\Delta K}{\Delta L} = \frac{MP_L}{MP_K} \qquad (2.3)$$

where the right-hand side is positive since ΔK and ΔL have the opposite sign. But as we consider two points on the same isoquant, and as these two points become closer and closer together, it is clear that $\Delta K / \Delta L$ becomes a closer and closer approximation to the slope of the isoquant. Indeed, in the limit $\Delta K / \Delta L$ is the slope, and thus the slope of any isoquant is equal to MP_L / MP_K, the ratio of the marginal products. We showed that the slope of the isocost line is w/r, and thus the condition for output maximization, namely that the slope of the isocost line be equal to the slope of the highest attainable isoquant, is given by equation (2.4):

$$\frac{w}{r} = \frac{MP_L}{MP_K}. \qquad (2.4)$$

In the last section it was noted that for production functions that are homogeneous, all isoquants have the same slope along any capital-labor ratio. This implies that for a given capital-labor ratio, the wage-rental ratio will be constant regardless of the level of output. Thus for any wage-rental ratio, all production points will lie along a line such as OB extended of Figure 2.5. The wage-rental ratio is thus a function of the capital-labor ratio only and does not depend on the level of output. An even stronger condition can be derived when production functions are homogeneous of degree one; that is, when production functions exhibit constant returns to scale. Not only is the *ratio* of marginal products constant for any capital-labor ratio, the individual marginal products are constant as well. This in turn implies that the family of total product curves derived for a given input of the fixed factor (one such curve is shown in Figure 2.3) also has a constant slope along any ray from the origin. These results will prove to be useful in Chapters 8 and 9.

4. THE TWO-GOOD, TWO-FACTOR MODEL

In this section the simple general-equilibrium model that will be used throughout most of the book will be developed. We assume that two commodities, X and Y, are produced using two factors, capital and labor, with technologies described by production functions (2.5) and (2.6):

$$X = F_x(K_x, L_x) \tag{2.5}$$

$$Y = F_y(K_y, L_y). \tag{2.6}$$

Note that subscripts are now being used to distinguish the two production functions and the inputs used by each. These production functions are assumed to be homogeneous of the first degree, and are assumed to be increasing functions of both inputs. It is further assumed that positive outputs imply positive inputs of both factors. The economy is assumed to have fixed total supplies of both capital and labor, and these two constraints are represented by equations (2.7) and (2.8):

$$\bar{K} = K_x + K_y \tag{2.7}$$

$$\bar{L} = L_x + L_y. \tag{2.8}$$

As well as showing the allocation of the two factors between the two production processes, the equality sign in these two equations also implies that these two processes use all the available $\bar{K}$ and $\bar{L}$. Full employment is, therefore, implicitly assumed. Also implicit in our analysis is the assumption that both factors of production are completely divisible and are homogeneous in the sense that all units are identical.

An assumption central to the analysis is that the commodities, X and Y, differ in the sense that the production functions differ. Representative isoquants Y_0 and X_0 for the two industries are shown in Figure 2.6. While it is clear from the diagram that these two isoquants have been derived from different production functions, it will be useful to describe the differences in a somewhat more formal manner. Consider an arbitrary wage-rental ratio equal to the slope of the line $K_0 L_0$. With these relative factor prices, production in industry Y would take place somewhere along the line OA, and production industry X somewhere along the line OB, these being the points where the wage-rental ratios are tangent to the respective isoquants. It is clear that the capital-labor ratios for industries Y and X, represented in the figure by k_y and k_x respectively, differ. We thus have the following definition.

Definition

Production functions are said to differ if, for the same wage-rental ratio, the capital-labor ratios differ.

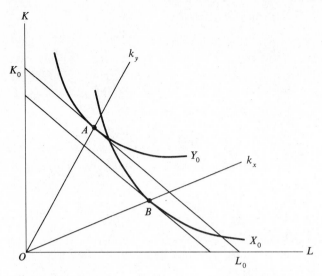

Figure 2.6

From Figure 2.6 it is evident that k_y is greater than k_x, and thus commodity Y is said to be capital-intensive relative to commodity X. Of course, a completely equivalent statement is that commodity X is labor-intensive relative to commodity Y. For the time being, we assume that commodity Y is capital-intensive relative to commodity X for all wage-rental ratios. This is known as the *strong factor intensity hypothesis*.

5. THE SHAPE OF THE PRODUCTION POSSIBILITY CURVE

The production possibility curve, as its name implies, is a locus that shows all possible efficient production points. It is important to note that two kinds of efficiency are being assumed here. The first, which we might call engineering efficiency, implies simply that for either of the production functions and for any bundle of inputs, output is as large as it could possibly be. In other words, we are assuming that there is no waste involved in the production process. The second kind of efficiency, which we could call market efficiency, is concerned with the way in which factors are combined in the production processes. More will be said about this second efficiency criterion subsequently.

The specific task now faced is to construct, from the technological information given by the production functions (2.5) and (2.6), and the constraints on factor use given by (2.7) and (2.8), the production possibility curve. This locus is also called the *transformation curve*. Two points on this locus are easy to find. Suppose that all the labor and all the capital were allocated to the production of commodity Y, so that in equation (2.6), K_y and L_y are replaced by $\bar{K}$ and $\bar{L}$. This will give us a well-defined level of output for Y, which we can call $\bar{Y}$, and this point is shown in Figure 2.7. Note that since all factors are being used to produce Y, the output of X must be zero. Similarly, allocating all of the capital and all of the labor to the production of X would give a point such as $\bar{X}$ in Figure 2.7.

A slightly more difficult task is to find the various points on the production possibility curve that allow some output of both commodities. To obtain some idea of where this curve might lie, construct the straight line joining $\bar{Y}$ and $\bar{X}$, and consider whether points on this line are possible production points. Recalling the assumption of constant returns to scale, we see that all such points are indeed possible. Suppose, for example, that one-half $\bar{L}$ and one-half $\bar{K}$ are allocated to both production functions. Because of constant returns to scale, half the inputs results in half the output, so we have the two points ½ $\bar{Y}$ and ½ $\bar{X}$ shown in Figure 2.7. This gives point A in output space, and it is obvious that this point lies on the straight line $\overline{YX}$. All other points on the line $\overline{YX}$ could be generated in a similar fashion. If three-quarters of all of the capital and labor were allocated to the Y industry, leaving a quarter of both factors to be allocated to X, then we would obtain the outputs indicated by point B in Figure 2.7.

We have shown that points such as A and B in Figure 2.6 are possible production points. The important question, however, is whether these points are efficient or, in other words, whether there are possible produc-

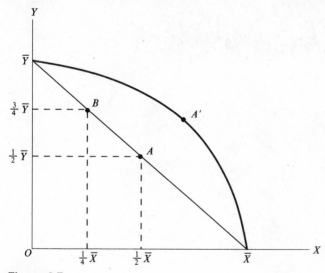

Figure 2.7

tion points outside the line $\overline{YX}$ yielding larger outputs of both commodities than those implied by points such as A and B. It is important to remember here that we have assumed different production functions for the two industries. Recall from Figure 2.6 that for a given wage-rental ratio, the capital-labor ratios in the two industries differ, and this suggests that simply dividing the two factors proportionally between the two industries will not result in the maximum amount of output. If the two outputs were guns and butter, it would not make much sense to allocate half of the farmland to the production of guns. Thus in Figure 2.7 a reallocation of factors between the two industries, and in particular, shifting more K to the production of Y and more L to the production of X, will result in a larger output of both commodities than that associated with points such as A on the line $\overline{YX}$. After the reallocation of factors, a production point such as A' could be possible. The same argument will apply to all points on the line $\overline{YX}$, with the obvious exception of the two points $\overline{Y}$ and $\overline{X}$, and the resulting production possibility locus would be $\overline{Y}A'\overline{X}$.

The preceding argument has presented an intuitive reason for believing that the production possibility curve lies everywhere above the equiproportions line $\overline{YX}$. Curves having this shape are said to be concave to the origin. A more rigorous demonstration of this fact is required, however; it will employ a construction known as the Edgeworth-Bowley box diagram. This construction, shown in Figure 2.8, gives a concise way of representing the information obtained in equations (2.5) to (2.8), and will demonstrate precisely what is meant by market efficiency.

In Figure 2.8 several representatives of the isoquants for the X industry have been plotted from origin O_x. The total available quantities of

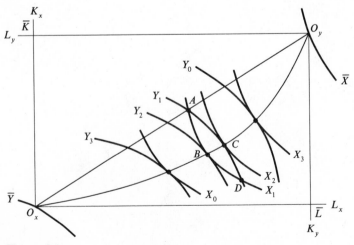

Figure 2.8

capital and labor, $\bar{K}$ and $\bar{L}$, are also shown in the diagram, and it is clear that the maximum amount of X that could be produced when all factors are allocated to the production of X is $\bar{X}$. This is the same $\bar{X}$ as shown in Figure 2.7. Exactly the same procedure is now employed for the Y industry, except that in this case the isoquant diagram is turned upside-down and plotted from O_y. Note that the output of Y increases as one moves from O_y toward O_x. From the point of view of the Y industry, O_x on isoquant $\bar{Y}$ represents the maximum possible amount of commodity Y that can be produced, for it represents the total allocation of $\bar{K}$ and $\bar{L}$ to the production of commodity Y. The isoquant $\bar{Y}$ thus gives the point $\bar{Y}$ of Figure 2.7.

All possible allocations of capital and labor between the two industries are represented by the points in the production box $O_x\bar{K}O_y\bar{L}$. Among these possible production points we seek a locus of points that is efficient in the sense that, for a given output of one commodity, the output of the other commodity is maximized. To take a specific example, suppose an output Y_1 of commodity Y is chosen, and that we seek to maximize X subject to this constraint. A possible allocation of factors between the two industries is now represented by all points along the isoquant Y_1 in Figure 2.8, and we want to find the particular point along this curve that maximizes the output of X. First, suppose that production were to take place at point A, halfway between O_x and O_y. Such a production point is clearly feasible, for it just exhausts the total available supply of capital and labor, and such an allocation results in the outputs of Y_1 and X_1 for industries Y and X, respectively. But while this production point is possible, it is clearly not efficient. Any movement along the isoquant Y_1 from A toward point C, although not reducing the output of Y, will clearly increase the output of X. Furthermore, moving beyond C along isoquant Y_1 toward D will begin to decrease the amount of X produced. Thus, given the constraint that Y_1 is to be produced, the allocation of capital and labor associated with point C results in the maximum possible output of commodity X. Point C is the tangency point for the two isoquants Y_1 and X_2, and thus, for a given quantity of Y, output of X is maximized at the point where the highest X isoquant is tangent to the appropriate Y isoquant.

There was, of course, no particular reason for choosing Y_1 as the quantity of commodity Y to be produced. Had Y_2 been chosen, then the efficient production point would have been B, implying an output of X_1 of commodity X. Indeed, any level of output of Y from 0 to $\bar{Y}$ could have been chosen and the output of X maximized subject to this constraint. Joining all these points would give the locus O_xBO_y, called the *efficiency locus*. Note that movements along this locus from O_x toward O_y imply increasing the amount of X produced and reducing the amount of Y produced. Indeed, all points on this locus have the characteristic that the output of one commodity cannot be increased without reducing the output of the other. It is precisely this criterion that describes the market efficiency referred to previously. It should also be noted that, if no restrictions are placed on the form of the production functions for X and Y, the efficiency locus can have any shape. Under the assumption that both production functions are homogeneous, however, the efficiency locus will be a smooth convex locus such as the one shown in Figure 2.8.

The production possibility curve can now be derived quite easily from the information given in Figure 2.8. With each point on the efficiency locus there is associated an output of X and an output of Y, and these points, when plotted in XY space, give a locus such as $\overline{X}A'\overline{Y}$ of Figure 2.7. Figure 2.8 allows a more rigorous demonstration of the fact that the production possibility curve has the shape shown in Figure 2.7. In the earlier discussion of the production possibility curve, the factors of production were arbitrarily allocated equally to the two industries, and this gave rise to the production point A in Figure 2.7. Note that, in terms of Figure 2.8, this allocation of factors between the two industries also gives rise to point A. Furthermore, because A is precisely in the center of the Edgeworth-Bowley box, and because of the assumption of constant returns to scale, output X_1, being halfway between O_x and O_y, must equal one-half $\overline{X}$. Similarly, Y_1 equals one-half $\overline{Y}$, and thus it is clear that in Figure 2.7 point A must lie midway between $\overline{Y}$ and $\overline{X}$. But it has already been shown that, in terms of Figure 2.8, the output associated with the allocation of factors at point A is not efficient. For example, moving from point A to point B increases the output of Y without reducing the output of X, or movement from point A to point C increases the output of X without reducing the output of Y. Thus the reallocation of capital and labor from a point such as A to points such as B or C will result in production points that lie outside the line $\overline{YX}$ of Figure 2.7. The allocation of factors along the line O_xAO_y in Figure 2.8 gives rise to the production points along the straight line $\overline{YX}$ of Figure 2.7, thus the same argument that is used for point A applies for any allocation of factors along the line O_xAO_y. Thus all points on the production possibility curve must lie outside the straight line $\overline{YX}$ in Figure 2.7.

It has been shown that the efficient allocation of resources requires that production take place at a point where an isoquant from one industry is tangent to an isoquant from the other. It has also been shown that, for the individual producer, the maximization of production subject to the cost constraint requires that the ratio of factor prices be equal to the slope of the isoquants. Since this condition is true for both industries, and since

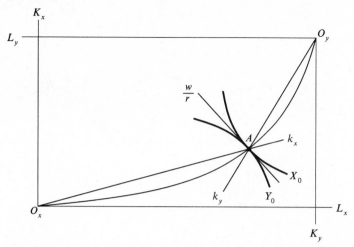

Figure 2.9

we have seen that market efficiency requires a tangency between the isoquants of the two industries, it is clear that production efficiency requires that both industries face the same wage-rental ratios. In Figure 2.9 the production of X_0 and Y_0 associated with the point A implies that the ratio of input prices will be w/r, the line that is jointly tangent to the two isoquants at point A. Note, also, that for production at point A, the capital-labor ratios in the two industries are k_x and k_y for industries X and Y, respectively. Thus this factor box diagram can be seen as an alternative way of plotting the information shown in Figure 2.6, but with the additional constraint of the fixed supply of the two factors of production. This additional constraint, which fixes the size of the factor box, increases the amount of information obtained. It can be seen from Figure 2.9, for example, that for any efficient output point, such as A, there is a unique wage-rental ratio. This, from Figure 2.7, implies that for every point on the production possibility curve there is associated a unique wage-rental ratio. This point will prove to be important in later chapters.

We are now in a position to illustrate the production equilibrium for our simple economy. First, we note that a condition for profit maximization for a competitive industry is that marginal costs equal price. Thus for our two industries we have $MC_x = p_x$ and $MC_y = p_y$. Dividing one by the other yields equation (2.9):

$$\frac{MC_x}{MC_y} = \frac{p_x}{p_y}. \tag{2.9}$$

In Figure 2.10 the slope of the production possibility curve at any point gives the rate at which one commodity can be converted into the

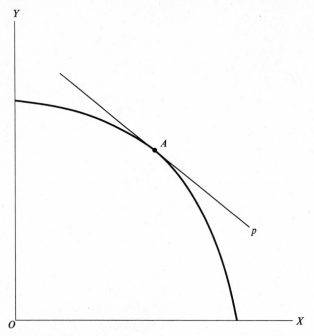

Figure 2.10

other through the reallocation of factors from one industry to the other. Thus the slope of the production possibility curve is the cost of one commodity in terms of the other, which is the ratio of marginal costs. Then since the slope of the production possibility curve is MC_x/MC_y, and given equation (2.9), the equilibrium for producers is given by point A in Figure 2.10 where the price ratio line is tangent to the production possibility curve.

6. NONCONSTANT RETURNS TO SCALE

To this point the discussion has assumed that both production functions were homogeneous of the first degree. The case in which production functions are homogeneous of degrees other than one is now considered. The question of particular interest is how homogeneity of different degrees will affect the shape of the production possibility curve. The discussion will employ the simple argument that was initially used to demonstrate the shape of the production possibility curve for the constant returns-to-scale case. Although a more rigorous demonstration could be provided, the geometry would become much more complex.

First, consider the case in which the production functions are assumed to be homogeneous of degree greater than one, so that increasing

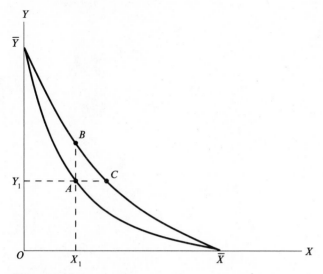

Figure 2.11

returns to scale exist. The production system can still be represented by equations (2.5) and (2.8), and the endpoints of the production possibility curve can be found by allocating the total amounts of capital and labor to industries X and Y, respectively. Thus, in Figure 2.11, the allocation of the entire capital and labor supply to the Y industry would yield point $\bar{Y}$, and the allocation of the entire stock of both factors to the X industry would yield point $\bar{X}$. Now suppose that half of both factors is allocated to each industry. Because of the assumption of increasing returns to scale, halving the inputs to the Y industry will more than halve output, so that we would get a point such as Y_1. Similarly, halving the inputs to the X industry would yield a point such as X_1, where X_1 is less than one-half $\bar{X}$. The resulting production point A of Figure 2.11 clearly lies below the straight line joining $\bar{Y}$ and $\bar{X}$. Other proportional allocations of the factors to the two industries would yield other production points, and the locus of all such points could be a line such as $\bar{Y}A\bar{X}$. Note that this is the equiproportions line for the increasing returns-to-scale case, and corresponds to the straight line $\bar{Y}A\bar{X}$ of Figure 2.7.

In Figure 2.11 we have relaxed the assumption of constant returns to scale, but have retained the assumption that the production functions for the two industries differ, and this implies that while A is a possible production point, it will not, in general, be efficient. Indeed, a figure exactly like Figure 2.8 could be used to illustrate the increasing returns-to-scale case, where again, point A of Figure 2.8 corresponds to point A of Figure 2.11. Just as in the constant returns-to-scale case, it can be shown that moving from point A to a point such as B or C will result in a larger

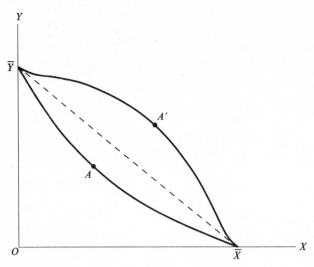

Figure 2.12

amount of one or the other of the two outputs, and would give rise to points such as B and C in Figure 2.11. Repeating this process for all points along the curve $\overline{Y}A\overline{X}$ would give rise to the production possibility curve $\overline{Y}BC\overline{X}$.

In Figure 2.11 the production possibility curve has been shown to be uniformly convex to the origin, but as Figure 2.12 illustrates, this need not necessarily be the case. With increasing returns to scale the equiproportions line must be below the straight line joining the endpoints $\overline{Y}$ and $\overline{X}$, but if the degree of homogeneity is not much larger than one, then the equiproportions line need not differ very much from a straight line, and we could get the line $\overline{Y}A\overline{X}$ of Figure 2.12. If at the same time the capital-labor ratios of the two industries differ widely, then a considerable increase in output could be generated by reallocating factors, resulting in the points such as A' lying outside the straight line $\overline{Y}\overline{X}$. Thus, even with increasing returns to scale, the production possibility curve can be concave to the origin throughout most of its length. For increasing returns to scale, two factors determine the position of the production possibility curve—the degree of homogeneity and the difference in factor intensities. The more the degree of homogeneity differs from one, the more we would expect the equiproportions line to be pushed toward the origin, and the greater the difference in the capital intensities of the two industries is, the more we would expect the production possibility curve to differ from the equipro-portions line. The exact position of the production possibility curve clearly depends on the relative strengths of these two forces.

In Figure 2.12 the production possibility curve has been shown to be

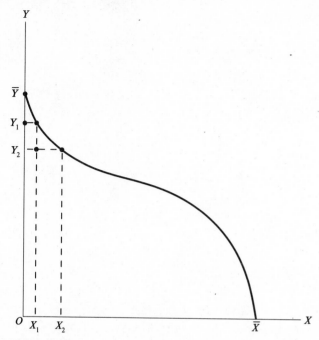

Figure 2.13

concave toward the origin throughout most of its length. However, it will be noticed that the curve becomes convex to the origin as either axis is approached. This will always be true as long as both industries exhibit increasing returns to scale, and although a formal demonstration of this fact is rather complex, an intuitive reason can be suggested.

To illustrate we consider, in Figure 2.13, an example where there are constant returns to scale in the Y industry but increasing returns to scale in the production of X. The endpoints $\overline{Y}$ and $\overline{X}$ of the production possibility curve can be found as before. Initially, suppose the economy is specialized in producing Y at $\overline{Y}$. Now suppose that one less unit of Y is produced, and that the bundle of factors released is transferred to the X industry. Output in the Y industry will be reduced from $\overline{Y}$ to Y_1, and the quantity of X equal to X_1 will be produced. Next, assume that almost the identical bundle of factors is again transferred from Y production to X production, resulting in an output of Y equal to Y_2 where $\overline{Y}Y_1$ is (almost exactly) equal to $Y_1 Y_2$. The question now is how will the output of X be affected. We recall that there are increasing returns to scale in the X industry. Thus the second bundle of factors will allow the additional production of more X than was produced with the first bundle, and $X_1 X_2$ must be larger than OX_1. This means that in the neighborhood of the Y axis the production possibility curve must be convex to the origin.

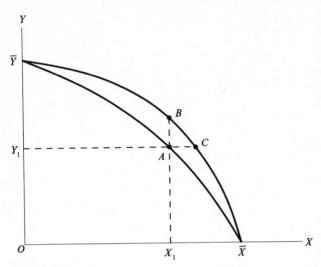

Figure 2.14

It is interesting that the convexity of the production possibility curve occurs next to the Y axis when the increasing returns to scale exist in the X industry. This has sometimes been a source of confusion in the literature. One final point is that while increasing returns in one industry and constant returns in the other can produce production possibility curves with the shape shown in Figure 2.13, this result is by no means necessary. The production possibility curve could also be convex throughout its entire length as shown in Figure 2.11.

The decreasing returns-to-scale case, or in other words, the case in which homogeneity is of degree less than one, can be handled in a similar fashion. In Figure 2.14 points $\bar{Y}$ and $\bar{X}$ again represent the maximum amounts of Y and X that could be produced by allocating the entire factor supplies to those two industries. Because of decreasing returns to scale, halving the inputs to both industries will less than halve output, resulting in points such as Y_1 and X_1 and production point A. Clearly, A will lie outside a straight line joining $\bar{Y}$ and $\bar{X}$. As before, while A is possible it is not efficient, and more of either or both output can be produced by a reallocation of factors. Such a reallocation would give rise to points such as B and C, and thus the production possibility curve would become $\bar{Y}BC\bar{X}$. In this case there are again two factors determining the position of the production possibility curve—the degree of homogeneity and differences in factor intensities. For decreasing returns to scale, the lower the degree of homogeneity, the more the equiproportions line, $\bar{Y}A\bar{X}$, will be pushed away from the origin, and the greater the difference in factor intensities, the more the production possibility line will differ from the equiproportions line. Since both factors act in the same direction, the production possibility curve will necessarily be concave to the origin throughout its length.

Economists differ in their views of the relevance of decreasing returns to scale, and some argue that decreasing returns would not be observed, particularly in general equilibrium situations of the kind we are concerned with here. The argument goes as follows: Suppose a firm is operating a production process at some level and that a higher rate of output is desired. With decreasing returns to scale present, the attempt to increase production will increase average cost and, with given prices, reduce profit. Another option is available, however. Rather than increasing the scale of the existing plant, a separate production facility could be constructed that would avoid the decreasing returns problem. As a specific example, when a firm is faced with the prospect of doubling output, rather than adding more inputs that would be subject to decreasing returns, a new identical plant could be constructed that would allow output to be doubled. Of course, the logical extension of this argument would require that all firms with potential decreasing returns operate at unit levels, for this would maximize output for given inputs.

Another argument is that the observation of decreasing returns is associated with missing factors of production. Suppose, for example, that one observed that in some agricultural process a doubling of the capital and labor inputs does not double output. Does this mean there are decreasing returns to scale? Probably not, for the role that land plays has not been considered, and one should ask how doubling the inputs of land, labor, and capital will affect output. If output doubles when all inputs are doubled, then there are constant returns to scale. While in this book we deal exclusively with the two-factor model, in practice, production often requires many inputs. And although it may not always be possible to increase all inputs, this does not mean that constant returns to scale would not be observed if we could. It may also be difficult to agree on a definition of what constitutes an input, so that there may well be uncertainty surrounding the issue of whether all inputs have been taken into account. But whatever their views about the existence and relevance of decreasing returns, most international trade theorists would agree that decreasing returns to scale is not of much importance for international trade theory. Thus for the remainder of this book we confine our attention to constant and to increasing returns to scale.

7. CONCLUDING REMARKS

The purpose of this chapter has been to describe the production functions that underlie the supply side of our model, and to demonstrate the derivation of the production possibility curve. Although increasing and decreasing returns to scale were considered, most of the analysis will be conducted under the assumption of constant returns to scale. The assumptions that will be made about the production function throughout most of the remainder of the book can thus be summarized as follows:

1. The production functions are concave increasing functions of all inputs.
2. Zero input of either factor implies zero output.
3. Production functions are assumed to be homogeneous of the first degree.
4. The production functions for the two industries are assumed to differ.

Throughout most of the subsequent analysis, the production possibility curve will be assumed to be concave to the origin, as shown in Figure 2.7. Underlying this production possibility curve will be the assumptions that:

1. Factors of production are in fixed supply.
2. The production functions differ between industries.
3. Both production functions exhibit constant returns to scale.

PROBLEMS

1. Suppose the production functions for commodities X and Y are identical. How will this affect the shape of the efficiency locus? What will the production possibility curve look like for the case of (a) constant returns to scale, (b) increasing returns to scale, (c) decreasing returns to scale? How will the efficiency loci differ for these three cases?
2. Suppose that in production functions (2.5) and (2.6) there is a single factor of production, say, labor. What will the production possibility curve look like for the cases of (a) constant returns to scale, (b) increasing returns to scale, (c) decreasing returns to scale?
3. Suppose that the total available quantity of labor increases and that the quantity of capital available decreases. How will this affect the shape and position of the production possibility curve?
4. Show that, for production functions homogeneous of any degree, the efficiency locus cannot cross the diagonal of the factor box.
5. In terms of Figure 2.8 show that the equilibrium wage-rental ratio increases as one moves from O_x to O_y along the efficiency locus.
*6. (a) What does the assumption of concavity of the production functions imply about the isoquants?
(b) The production function is said to be quasi-concave if, for an isoquant X_0, the set of all capital and labor combinations that yield at least as much output as X_0 is convex. Does quasi-concavity imply concavity?

*7. Suppose that in a figure such as Figure 2.9 the wage-rental ratios for the two industries differ. This could come about, for example, if one factor were taxed in one industry but not in the other. How would this affect the production possibility curve?

*8. Draw representative isoquants for the X industry and the Y industry such that, while k_x is less than k_y for some wage-rental ratios, k_x is greater than k_y for other wage-rental ratios.

NOTE

1. A set is said to be convex if, for any two points A and B in the set, all points on a line joining A and B are also in the set. Note that in Figure 2.2 the points on and above the isoquant X' (or any isoquant) satisfy this condition.

REFERENCES

Melvin, J. R. (1971). "On the Derivation of the Production Possibility Curve." *Economica* 39, 287–294.

Savosnick, K. M. (1958). "The Box Diagram and the Production Possibility Curve." *Swedish Economic Journal* 60, 183–197.

chapter *3*

Community Indifference
Curves

1. THE UTILITY FUNCTION

The previous chapter described the production or supply side of the traditional international trade model; in this chapter attention is focused on the demand side. Fundamental to the notion of a representable demand relationship is the assumption that consumers buy commodities because these commodities provide satisfaction, or *utility*. The relationship between the utility derived from such consumption and the quantities of the commodities consumed is summarized in a utility function of the form

$$U = U(X, Y).$$

This three-dimensional relationship has an obvious similarity to the production functions of Chapter 2, and, indeed, several of the characteristics of the production functions described in Chapter 2 will be assumed to hold for the utility function as well. One assumption that both production and utility functions have in common is that both are assumed to be increasing functions of both inputs. For the utility function this implies that a little more of either good always increases one's utility, or in other words, that one is never satiated with a particular commodity. Thus the utility function, like the production function, can be thought of as a three-dimensional hill, such that for any point on this hill a larger amount of either or both of the two inputs will yield higher utility.

There is, however, one important distinction between the production function and the utility function. For production functions there was no difficulty in attaching significance to the level of output of a particular commodity associated with a bundle of factor inputs. It was easy to imagine that for known technology a certain number of machines combined with the services of a known number of workers would produce a well-defined level of output. This output could easily be measured, and the relationships between the level of output and the levels of inputs could be easily determined. For utility functions, however, no such simple relationship exists between the inputs and the output. While the inputs to the utility function are easily measured, for these are just the amounts of the commodities consumed, the level of satisfaction or utility that this consumption generates is entirely subjective and inherently nonmeasurable. Not only are there no natural units of measurement for utility, there is also no obvious way of comparing different levels of utility. Although it is easy enough to conclude that eating two apples yields more utility than eating one apple, it would not make much sense to say that the level of utility from consuming two apples was twice as great as that achieved from consuming one. Utility or satisfaction is inherently an emotion, and it would make no more sense to say that utility was twice as high from consuming a certain bundle of commodities as opposed to some other bundle than it would to say that you are twice as angry today as you were yesterday, or that you are only half as much in love today as you were last year.

Because specific, comparable numbers cannot be attached to utility or satisfaction, geometric representations of utility as a function of either one or two inputs are not of much interest. Thus the geometric representations of utility that would correspond to Figures 2.1 or 2.3 for production functions will not be employed in the present analysis. But while meaningful numbers cannot be attached to various levels of utility, it is clear that utility levels associated with different commodity bundles can be compared. In general, individuals will be able to decide which of two bundles yields more satisfaction, or that two bundles yield the same satisfaction, leaving the individual "indifferent" between them. This kind of comparison is known as ordinal measurement, and it requires only that the various alternatives can be ordered or ranked. Thus although cardinal measurement, the kind of measurement assumed for production functions, requires not only that numbers be attached to each level of output, but also that a given numerical difference between levels of output always implies the same actual difference in output, for utility functions a much less precise form of measurement must be employed. Thus, even if a specific form of the utility function were assumed that gave numerical indices, say,

10, 20, and 30, for three different commodity bundles, such as (a), (b), and (c), no significance other than order could be attached to these three numbers. We know that (c) is preferred to (b) and (b) is preferred to (a), but it cannot be said that the increase in utility from (a) to (b) is the same as the increase from (b) to (c).

Although the ordinality of utility somewhat restricts the kinds of geometric representations that can be employed, there is one representation of the three-dimensional utility function that does not require that utility be measurable. If we think again of the three-dimensional utility hill, and imagine ourselves at some point on that hill, it is clear that the various points on the surface of the hill can be compared, even if we have no information about actual elevations above the ground level. Thus some points will be higher on the surface, some lower on the surface, and some at the same level. If points at the same level are traced out and projected on the YX plain, a locus such as I_0 of Figure 3.1 would be traced out. This is a contour line of the utility hill, and therefore represents the locus of all combinations of commodities X and Y that would yield a constant level of utility. Since the individual is assumed to be indifferent among all points on this locus, any such locus is referred to as an *indifference curve*. These indifference curves are obviously analogous to the isoquants of Chapter 2. Of course, since an indifference curve can be drawn for any level of utility, there are an infinite number of such indifference curves, only three of which are shown in Figure 3.1. In this figure, higher indifference curves represent higher levels of utility, since higher indifference curves represent contour lines that are farther up the utility surface. Note, however, that from a utility point of view, no significance can be attached to the distances between the various indifference curves.

While it has been convenient to describe the indifference curves in terms of the utility surface, it is worthwhile observing that indifference curves could be derived quite independently of the concept of the utility function. To illustrate, consider point A of Figure 3.1, containing 10 units of Y and 4 units of X. To construct a set of indifference curves for a certain individual, we could ask her to compare the utility received from other bundles of X and Y with the utility received from point A. It is first of all clear that, given the assumption that both goods yield positive utility, any point below and to the left of point A would yield less utility than A. Similarly, any point above and to the right of A would yield more utility and thus be preferred. A point such as B, however, contains more X but less Y, and thus no a priori judgment can be made on the relative merits of this point as compared to A. To find out whether or not B is preferred to A, the individual is asked whether she would be willing to give up A in exchange for B. If the answer is yes, then B must be preferred

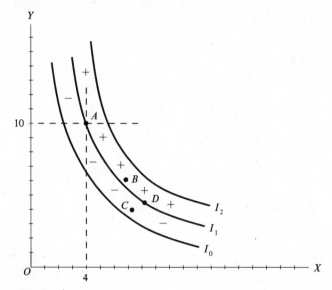

Figure 3.1

to A. For a point such as C she might respond negatively to the trade offer, indicating that A is preferred to C. If a positive sign is attached to a point where the individual answers yes, and a negative sign attached to every point at which the individual declines to exchange, and if the individual were asked to compare a large number of commodity bundles, a line separating all the pluses from the negatives could be drawn. This line would include all those points among which the individual is indifferent, and would produce an indifference curve such as I_1 in Figure 3.1.

2. CHARACTERISTICS OF INDIFFERENCE CURVES

The indifference curves for individuals have several characteristics of interest for the subsequent analysis. First, the indifference curves are assumed to be convex to the origin, as illustrated in Figure 3.1 or 3.2. As we will see later on, this characteristic is important in determining the equilibrium position for an individual consumer. The economic rationale for this assumption can be seen from considering points A, B, C, and D in Figure 3.2. Since these points are all on the indifference curve I_0, the individual is, by definition, completely indifferent as to which of these bundles of commodities she consumes. The four points have been chosen so that the movement from A to B and the movement from C to D both represent a reduction of two units of commodity Y. The increase in the amount of X that must be given to this individual to persuade her to give up these two units of Y varies significantly between these two sets of

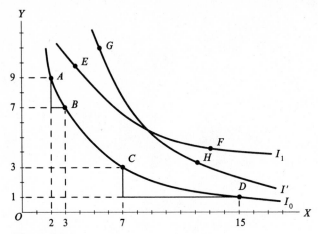

Figure 3.2

points, however. To persuade the individual to move from A to B, only one unit of X is required, while the movement from C to D requires an additional 8 units of X. The economic argument underlying this assumption is that, for commodity bundles with relatively large quantities of Y and small quantities of X, the reduction in the utility associated with giving up a unit of Y, the plentiful commodity, is much smaller than the increase in utility associated with receiving an extra unit of X, the scarce commodity. Thus, at A in Figure 3.2, the individual is prepared to give up 2 units of Y to obtain one additional unit of X. As the individual moves down the indifference curve, however, she receives more X and less Y, and as this movement takes place the extra utility associated with an additional unit of X will fall, relative to the reduction in utility associated with relinquishing a unit of Y. At point C the individual can be persuaded to give up 2 units of Y only by offering her 8 units of X. The slope of an indifference curve at any point is equal to the ratio of the marginal utilities of the two commodities, and is called the *marginal rate of substitution in consumption*. Indifference curves exhibiting the shape of those of Figure 3.2 are said to exhibit a diminishing marginal rate of substitution, referring to the fact that the utility associated with a unit of X falls relative to the utility associated with a unit of Y as one moves down the indifference curve from A to D.

The second important characteristic of indifference curves is that utility increases as the individual moves to higher and higher indifference curves. Consider, for example, the two indifference curves I_0 and I_1. (Ignore for the moment the indifference curve through points G and H.) Because we have assumed that additional amounts of either commodity increase utility, it is clear that point E on indifference curve I_1 is preferred to point A on indifference curve I_0. But how could points F and A be compared, where point F contains more X but less Y than point A? The answer to this follows directly from the definition of an indifference curve, for since E and F are both on the indifference curve I_1, they are equivalent from the individual consumer's point of view, and thus since E is preferred to A, F must be preferred to A as well. Thus all points on a higher indifference curve are preferred to all points on a lower indifference curve.

The final important characteristic of indifference curves is the fact that, for an individual, no two indifference curves can intersect. This fact is most easily demonstrated by supposing that two indifference curves do intersect and then showing that this is impossible by deriving a contradictory result. Thus in Figure 3.2 the indifference curve through points G and H has been drawn to intersect the indifference curve I_1. Now consider points G and E. Since G contains a larger quantity of both Y and X, it is clear that the individual would prefer point G to point E. Now points E and F are on the same indifference curve and thus the individual is indifferent between them. Similarly, the individual is indifferent between points G and H on the indifference curve I'. Thus since H is indifferent to G, since G is preferred to E, and since F is indifferent to E, it must follow that H is preferred to F. But this is impossible since F contains more of both X and Y than point H. Thus the intersection of the two indifference curves contradicts the basic assumption that more of both commodities is preferred, and it can, therefore, be concluded that indifference curves cannot intersect.

3. THE MAXIMIZATION OF UTILITY

So far the discussion of utility has been confined to the consideration of individual tastes, or relative preferences, for the various commodity bundles. The actual choice that the individual makes, however, will depend on the prices of the commodities and her income, as well as on her underlying taste patterns. Thus the level of utility that the individual can achieve will be constrained by the prices of the commodities and by her income. To illustrate how the actual consumption bundle is chosen, we assumed that the prices of the two commodities, p_x and p_y, and that income, M, are given. Assuming for the sake of simplicity that the individual spends her entire income on purchases of the two commodities, it is clear that the total expenditure on X plus the total expenditure on Y must exactly equal M. This gives the budget constraint that can be written as

$$M = p_x X + p_y Y. \tag{3.1}$$

To depict this budget constraint geometrically, or, in other words, to illustrate the set of possible consumption points, suppose that all income is spent on commodity Y. In terms of equation (3.1) this implies that $X = 0$, and solving for Y, we obtain $Y = M/p_y$. This point is shown in Figure 3.3 and represents the maximum amount of Y that could be purchased if all income were spent on this commodity. Similarly, if all income were spent on commodity X, consumption would take place at M/p_x in Figure 3.3. Furthermore, it follows that if income were divided equally between the two commodities, we would obtain, for Y, point $M/2p_y$, and for X, point $M/2p_x$. This gives the midpoint on the line joining M/p_y and M/p_x, and it is clear that any allocation of expenditure between the two commodities will give rise to some point on this straight line. Note that the slope of this budget constraint can be found by dividing M/p_y by M/p_x to obtain p_x/p_y.

An alternative method of plotting this budget constraint would be to note that equation (3.1) can be solved for Y to obtain

$$Y = \frac{M}{p_y} + \frac{p_x}{p_y}X. \tag{3.2}$$

This is a standard form of the equation of a straight line, where M/p_y is the intercept on the Y axis, and where p_x/p_y is the slope of the line.

The indifference curve map can now be combined with the budget constraint to illustrate how the equilibrium position is determined. In

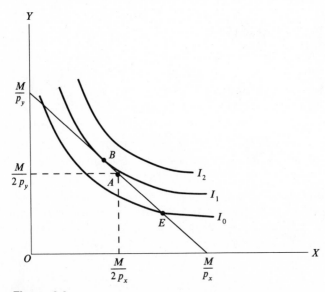

Figure 3.3

Figure 3.3 three representative indifference curves for the individual are shown. The individual consumer could choose a point such as E, since it is on her budget constraint, but will not do so since such an allocation of expenditure would not maximize her welfare. As she moves up the budget constraint to a point such as A, welfare is increased, since she crosses higher indifference curves, and at point B welfare is maximized, for she has now reached the highest level of utility consistent with the budget constraint. Since point B represents the tangency between the budget constraint and the highest indifference curve, utility is maximized by setting the marginal rate of substitution equal to the ratio of commodity prices.

Because international trade is concerned with general equilibrium questions, we are concerned not so much with the maximization of *individual* utility as with the conditions that characterize equilibrium for the *entire community*. To consider the simplest such case, suppose that the quantities of X and Y are fixed at $\bar{X}$ and $\bar{Y}$, respectively, and that the economy consists of two individuals. The locus of possible equilibrium points for this simple society is derived in exactly the same way as was the efficiency locus in Chapter 2. In the box diagram of Figure 3.4 we have plotted the indifference curves for the first individual from O_1, and the indifference curves for the second individual from O_2. Note that in terms of O_1, point O_2 represents the total available quantities of commodities X and Y. Superscripts have been used to distinguish the two sets of indifference curves.

One method of deriving the locus of equilibrium points for the two individuals is to consider the problem of maximizing the utility of one individual, subject to some fixed level of utility of the other individual, and to the constraint that the quantities of X and Y are fixed. Suppose, for example, we constrain the second individual to consume somewhere along his indifference curve I_1^2, and maximize the utility of the first individual subject to this constraint and to the constraint that $Y = \bar{Y}$ and $X = \bar{X}$. Would it be optimal for consumption to take place at a point such as B? The answer is clearly no, for movements from B toward point A, while leaving the second individual at the same utility level, would result in higher and higher levels of utility for the first individual. It can also be seen that at point A, the utility of the first individual is maximized subject to the constraints we have imposed. While points on higher indifference curves would be preferred, no such points can be achieved since they would require the total consumption of more commodities than exist in the economy. Thus although the first individual would clearly prefer to be at a point such as C, this could only be achieved by reducing the consumption of the second individual, moving him to a lower indifference curve. Thus point A is optimal in the sense that the utility of one individual cannot be increased without reducing the utility of the other individual. This is the *Pareto criterion of optimality* (named for the Italian economist, Vilfredo Pareto), and a point such as A is said to be Pareto optimal.

Of course, the choice of indifference curve I_1^2 was arbitrary, and the same argument would apply equally well for any other indifference curve. Suppose, for example, indifference curve I_0^2 had been chosen, and the utility of the first individual maximized subject to this constraint. In this case the Pareto optimal point is E, the point where I_0^2 is tangent to the highest indifference curve for the first individual. By choosing various other indifference curves for the second individual, and maximizing utility for the first subject to this constraint, the locus O_1AEO_2 would be traced out. This is the locus of all Pareto optimal consumption points, and is called the *contract curve*.

It is important to note that the criterion of Pareto optimality is entirely an efficiency condition and has nothing to do with equity. The movement from B to A, or from B to F, is desirable since such movements increase the utility of one individual without reducing the utility of the other. The Pareto criterion does not allow a comparison of points such as F and E, however, even though moving from F to E would substantially increase the utility of the first individual while reducing that of the second. Indeed, point O_2 on indifference curve I_3^1 is Pareto optimal, even though it implies that the first individual receives the entire available quantity of both X and Y while the second individual receives nothing.

From Figure 3.4 we see that the contract curve is the locus of tangency points between the indifference curves for the two individuals.

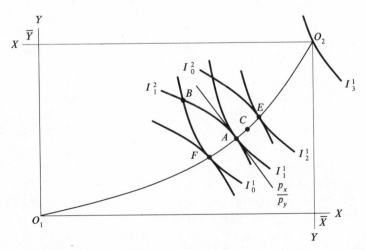

Figure 3.4

It was previously shown that the individual consumer is in equilibrium where the commodity price ratio line is tangent to her indifference curve. It therefore follows that, at any point on the contract curve, the equilibrium commodity price ratio line must be tangent to both indifference curves, such as is p_x/p_y at point A. A requirement for Pareto optimality is thus that both consumers face the same commodity price ratio.

4. AGGREGATING INDIVIDUAL PREFERENCES

As noted in the previous section, we will be concerned with preferences and demands by entire countries, and not just those of individuals. Unfortunately, it turns out that the preferences of individuals can only be aggregated together to get national or "community" indifference curves under special assumptions. This section provides a simplified discussion of the issues, while a more formal treatment is presented in the following section.

Suppose that individuals all have preferences of the type described in the preceding sections, which in turn gives rise to demand functions that depend on prices and income. Assume that there are only two goods and that the price ratio is denoted p. The income of individual I is denoted by M_i. If all individuals in the economy face the same price ratio but generally have different incomes, then the total demand for the good X can be written as the function D:

$$X = D(p, I_1, I_2, \ldots, I_n) \tag{3.3}$$

where it is assumed that there are n individuals in the country. The question of whether or not community indifference curves exist is essentially the same as the question of whether or not the demand function in equation (3.3) can be written as a function of aggregate income (the sum of the individuals' incomes); that is, whether or not the distribution of income affects total demand. The intuition here is that when we draw community indifference curves, we are saying that the country has preferences over aggregate bundles of goods that depend only on prices (the slope of the price line) and total income (the distance the price line is from the origin). Preferences and hence demands are independent of how that aggregate income is distributed.

Special assumptions are necessary for demand to be independent of the distribution of income. One problem that arises in aggregation is shown in Figure 3.5. Suppose that we have two consumers with identical but nonhomogeneous tastes. That is, at constant relative prices, the ratio of Y/X consumed is not independent of income. In Figure 3.5 consumers desire more X relative to Y as income increases at constant prices.

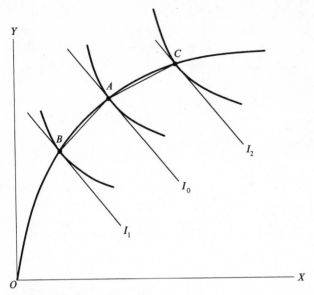

Figure 3.5

Now suppose that we have two consumers with identical (but non-homogeneous) tastes who are each at point A in Figure 3.5. Now we take some income away from consumer 1 and give it to consumer 2 so that they are now at points B and C, respectively, in Figure 3.5. The chord AB is steeper than the chord AC, and so the changes in the consumption of the two individuals do not balance. Even though we have not changed either prices or aggregate income, there will now be a higher aggregate demand for X and a lower aggregate demand for Y. Aggregate demand depends on the distribution of income, and hence community indifference curves do not exist in this situation.

Now consider homogeneous but nonidentical tastes. This situation is shown in Figure 3.6. Consumer 1, who has a relatively strong preference for Y, is initially at A_1, while consumer 2, who has a strong preference for X, is initially at A_2. Now take income away from consumer 1 and give it to consumer 2 holding prices constant. Consumer 1 moves to point B_1, while consumer 2 moves to point B_2 in Figure 3.6. Again, the changes in consumption do not cancel (more X and less Y will be demanded) even though prices and total income are constant. Community indifference curves do not exist when preferences differ.

This analysis suggests that community indifference curves will exist if all consumers have identical and homogeneous tastes (and, of course, face the same prices). We will show that this is indeed true in the next section. This is, however, a somewhat stronger assumption than we need, and a slightly weaker one is used at several points in later chapters. An

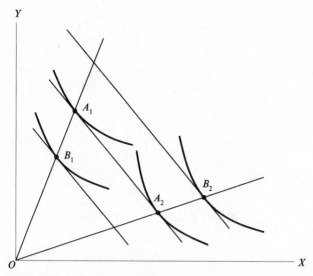

Figure 3.6

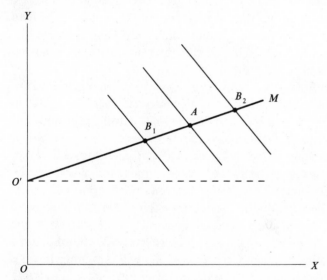

Figure 3.7

alternative condition is shown in Figure 3.7 where consumers are assumed to have identical but nonhomogeneous tastes. The income expansion path does not go through the origin, but it is linear and is shown as expansion path $O'M$ in Figure 3.7.

Assume that two consumers are both at point A in Figure 3.7 initially. Now take income away from consumer 1 and give it to consumer 2 so that they move to points B_1 and B_2, respectively. Note that the changes in their consumption levels cancel, so that there is no change in aggregate demand. This type of preference, sometimes called "quasihomotheticity," does imply the existence of community indifference curves. As we will see in later chapters these preferences are useful for dealing with differences in per capita income across countries. Note in Figure 3.7 that the ratio of Y/X consumed depends on income (per capita income for a country) at constant prices. In the case shown the share spent on X increases with income.

Throughout most of the book we will assume that preferences can be aggregated into community indifference curves. This permits an easy exposition of many points that do not rely on this assumption but that cannot be shown graphically without it.

*5. THE DERIVATION OF COMMUNITY INDIFFERENCE CURVES

The preceding section discussed, in relatively informal terms, the problem concerning the aggregation of the tastes of individual consumers into community indifference curves. We noted that strong assumptions are required in order that community indifference curves can be shown to exist and to possess the properties of individual indifference curves discussed earlier in this chapter. This section presents a more advanced discussion of this problem.

One simple example of a situation in which a well-defined community indifference curve does exist is the Robinson Crusoe economy, in which it is assumed that there is only one consumer. Utility maximization for this simple community would proceed in the same way as would maximization for a single individual, except that the constraints would differ. Under the assumption that the simple community possesses the capacity to produce commodities using different production functions, and assuming that these production functions exhibit constant returns to scale, then instead of the linear budget constraint of Figure 3.3, the individual would be faced with a production constraint of the kind derived in Chapter 2. Thus our Robinson Crusoe economy will maximize utilities subject to the transformation curve. In terms of Figure 3.8, where TAT' represents the production possibility curve, and where three representative indifference curves have been included, by an argument completely analogous to that used to demonstrate the condition necessary for the maximization of individual welfare, it can be shown that utility is maximized where the highest indifference curve is tangent to the production possibility curve. Thus in an economy in which no trade is allowed, the equilibrium production and consumption points will be point A in Figure 3.8.

This Robinson Crusoe economy is too simple to warrant further

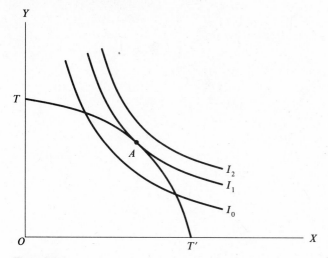

Figure 3.8

consideration. What we seek are conditions such that preferences for a group of individuals can still be represented by indifference curves such as those of Figure 3.8. To facilitate our understanding of what such conditions are, we will now construct a set of community indifference curves under quite general conditions, and compare the characteristics of these with the indifference curves for individual consumers. We begin with the case in which there are only two consumers, but it will become clear as we proceed that any number of consumers could be included.

An indifference curve for an individual consumer is defined as the locus of all those bundles of commodities for which utility is some constant. To be consistent with this definition, the aggregate indifference curves for two individuals must be the locus of all those bundles of commodities such that the levels of utility for both individuals are constant. We thus choose a specific indifference curve for each individual and seek a method of aggregating these two indifference curves. For the first individual we choose the indifference curve I_0^1 shown in Figure 3.9. We now choose some point on that indifference curve and call it O_2, the origin for the indifference curve map of the second individual. The indifference curve chosen for the second individual is I_0^2, as shown in the figure. To determine which point on the indifference curve for the second individual is the relevant one, we recall from the discussions surrounding Figure 3.4 that, in equilibrium, the indifference curves for the two individuals must have the same slope. We thus determine the slope of the indifference curve for the first individual at O_2, and then search along the indifference curve for the second individual until we find a point that has the same slope. Suppose this is point A in Figure 3.9. Point A, a bundle of commodities

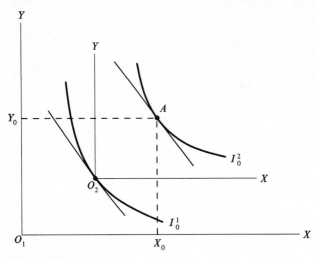

Figure 3.9

containing Y_0 of Y and X_0 of X, is clearly a point in outputs space that allows the individuals to have utilities associated with the indifference curves I_0^1 and I_0^2, and thus is a point on a community indifference curve for these two individuals. By placing O_2 at other points on the indifference curve I_0^1 of the first individual and repeating the same procedure, other points on the community indifference curve can be found. The locus of all such points could be considered as a type of community indifference curve for these two individuals. Note that point A is a point on the community indifference curve, and that the price ratio at this point is the same as that at O_2, suggesting that the slope of the community indifference curve will be the same as the slopes of the individual indifference curves from which that point was derived.

An alternative way of demonstrating the addition of the two indifference curves to arrive at the point A is to plot the indifference curves for the second individual not from O_2 but from A. This gives rise to a box diagram, Figure 3.10 (similar to that of Figure 3.4). Note that this figure gives precisely the same information as is contained in Figure 3.9, the only difference being that we are plotting the indifference curves for the second individual down from the aggregate commodity bundle, rather than up from point A, as in Figure 3.9. In this diagram the community indifference curve can be traced out by sliding the indifference curve for the second individual along that of the first and allowing the origin O_2 to trace out the community indifference curve. Thus the indifference curve for the first individual remains fixed, and we find other points along this curve where the indifference curve I_0^2 is tangent to it. Another such point would be B, and the origin for the second individual's indifference curve map will

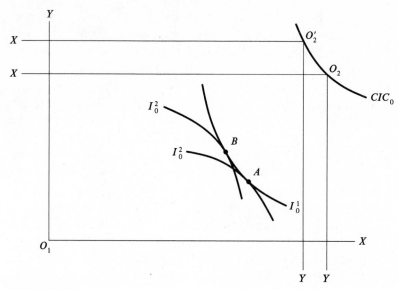

Figure 3.10

now be O_2'. The point O_2' is another point on the community indifference curve, and by repeating this procedure, we can find an entire locus of points such as CIC_0 of Figure 3.10. Note that for all points on CIC_0 the utility levels for the two individuals are constant.

Since curve CIC_0 in Figure 3.10 is a locus such that the levels of utilities for both individuals are constant, it thus must be a community indifference curve. But what properties does this community indifference curve have? In particular, does it have the same characteristics as did the indifference curves for individual consumers discussed in Section 2 of this chapter? Specifically, we wish to establish whether or not these community indifference curves could intersect, and whether higher community indifference curves necessarily imply higher levels of community welfare. To consider these questions, we have redrawn, in Figure 3.11, the initial situation of Figure 3.10 and have included the contract curve.

Another way of asking the question of whether community indifference curves such as CIC_0 intersect is to ask whether, through point O_2, there could possibly be another community indifference curve having a different slope. Two points are relevant to this question. First, as we previously observed, the slope of the community indifference curve at O_2 is equal to the slope of the two indifference curves at point A. Second, the choice of the two indifference curves tangent at A was entirely arbitrary, and any other pair of indifference curves could have been chosen. Suppose, for example, that instead of fixing the level of utilities for the two individuals equal to that associated with the indifference curves tangent at point

A, we had instead chosen the two indifference curves I_1^1 and I_1^2, tangent at point B. It is clear that exactly the same procedure described in Figure 3.10 for point A could now be carried out for point B, and a new community indifference curve could be constructed. The question now is whether this new indifference curve would be exactly the same as indifference curve CIC_0, the one derived from point A. That this need not be the case can easily be seen by observing that this new indifference curve must have the same slope at O_2 as the two individual indifference curves have at point B. But there is no reason that the slope of the indifference curves at point B need be the same as the slope of the indifference curves at point A. As the diagram has been drawn, the price line at point B is steeper than the price line at point A, and thus the community indifference curve associated with B must be steeper than that associated with A, and we would have a curve such as CIC_1. Furthermore, any point on the contract curve O_1AO_2 could have been chosen to derive a community indifference curve through point O_2, and in general, all such points would lead to a community indifference curve through point O_2, each with a slope different from that of CIC_0. There are, then, an infinite number of such community indifference curves through point O_2, all having different slopes.

Although it is certainly possible to define the curves such as CIC_0 and CIC_1 derived in Figure 3.11 as community indifference curves, they would not be very useful for illustrating the international trade propositions that we will subsequently derive. To give one simple example, suppose that in Figure 3.8 instead of the set of nonintersecting indifference

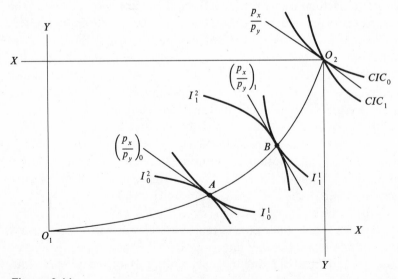

Figure 3.11

curves shown, we had a set of community indifference curves of the kind derived in Figure 3.11. In this case there would be a whole set of indifference curves through point A, all having different slopes, and there would be other indifference curves tangent to the transformation TAT' at points other than point A. In such a case it would not be at all obvious which of these particular tangency points would be the appropriate equilibrium position.

Our next question is whether there are conditions that could be imposed on the utility functions of the two individuals, such that the community indifference curves would not intersect. It is obvious from Figure 3.11 that only if the equilibrium price ratio line has the same slope at all points on the contract curve will there be a single community indifference curve through point O_2. Is there any reason to expect such a condition to hold? Certainly not in general, and as long as the utility functions for the two industries differ, we would expect the slopes of the equilibrium price lines along the contract curve to differ. This suggests that one criterion to be imposed is that the utility functions of the two individuals be the same.

But identical taste is not sufficient for the existence of nonintersecting community indifference curves, as can be seen from Figure 3.12. Identical taste will give rise to a linear contract curve such as that shown in Figure 3.12, but this in itself will not guarantee that the slopes of the price ratio lines at all points on this contract curve will be the same. Indeed, it is clear that only if the sets of indifference curves for the two individuals have the same slope along a ray from the origin will this condition necessarily be fulfilled. This condition is a familiar one, for it is precisely the characteristic that homogeneous production functions were found to have in Chapter

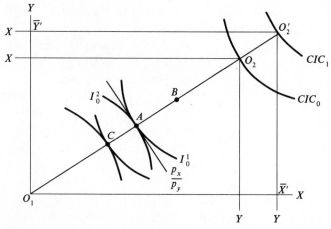

Figure 3.12

2. Thus the second condition that must be imposed on the utility functions of the two individuals is that they be homogeneous. Note that we are not concerned with the degree of homogeneity, for as was suggested earlier, because utility is an ordinal measure, no significance can be attached to the numbers associated with the various indifference curves.

With identical taste and homogeneity, the equilibrium price lines at all points on the linear contract curve of Figure 3.12 will have identical slopes. It then makes no difference which point on the contract curve is chosen to derive the community indifference curves, for in all cases the slope will be the same at point O_2. Furthermore, the same argument applies for different initial aggregate bundles of commodities X and Y. Suppose, for example, that $\bar{X}'$ and $\bar{Y}'$ were available for distribution between the two individuals. In Figure 3.12, O'_2 will be the origin for the indifference curve map of the second individual. The same procedure outlined earlier could be used to derive an indifference curve through O'_2, and again it is obvious that there will only be one such curve through this point, regardless of which initial point on the contract curve O'_1 is chosen. Thus a whole set of community indifference curves can be derived by choosing different aggregate bundles of commodities to be distributed between the two individuals. Note that the community indifference curve through O'_2 in Figure 3.9 will have the same slope as the community indifference curve through O_2; this demonstrates that the set of community indifference curves will also be homogeneous.

It has been shown that a set of nonintersecting community indifference curves will exist if, for the two individuals, the utility functions are (1) identical and (2) homogeneous. It has been shown that identical taste alone is not sufficient for the existence of nonintersecting community indifference curves. It is equally clear that homogeneity by itself is not sufficient, and indeed, the utility functions assumed in Figure 3.11, while not the same for the two individuals, could easily have been derived from homogeneous utility functions. A question that naturally occurs is whether there are any other sets of conditions that would give rise to nonintersecting indifference curves. To illustrate another possibility, we have in Figure 3.13 assumed that the utility functions for two individuals, while homogeneous, are not identical so that the contract curve would be O_1AO_2. The slope of the equilibrium price line will, in general, vary along the contract curve in Figure 3.13 just as it did in Figure 3.11. But suppose that in some way we are restricted in our choice of points along this contract curve. In particular, suppose that the initial endowment of X and Y received by the two individuals is represented by point E, the point at which both individuals receive equal quantities of the two commodities.

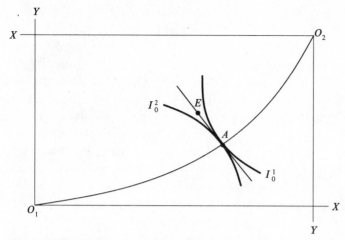

Figure 3.13

Because the two individuals have different tastes, E will not be an equilibrium point, and the two individuals will exchange with one another to reach point A. Indeed, it can be shown that for any endowment point there will be a unique equilibrium point on the contract curve, as long as the utility functions for the two individuals are homogeneous. Thus, with endowment point E, there is a single point on the contract curve that results in equilibrium for the two individuals, and thus only one community indifference curve can be constructed through point O_2. In this case, rather than insisting that the slope of the equilibrium price line be the same at all points on the contract curve, by specifying the initial endowment point, we have restricted the possible equilibrium positions to the single point A.

A second characteristic of the utility functions for individuals was that higher indifference curves represented higher levels of utility; we now want to consider whether community indifference curves have this same characteristic. Specifically, we wish to know whether being on a higher indifference curve results in an unambiguous improvement in community welfare, in the sense that both individuals will be better off. An examination of Figure 3.12 shows that without further restrictions this will not necessarily be the case. Suppose that the indifference curve CIC_0 had been derived from point A, and that the total endowment of the two commodities is increased such that the new origin for the isoquants of the second individual is O_2'. The new community indifference curve CIC_1 can now be constructed, and as we saw earlier this same curve will be derived regardless of which initial point on the contract curve is chosen. In particular, point C could be the equilibrium position for this new endowment, and although the utility for the second individual is much higher at point C than at point A, the level of utility enjoyed by the first individual is substantially lower. Of course, it is possible for both individuals to be better off with this new endowment, since the total available quantity of both X and Y has increased, and the allocation of some of this increase to both individuals will certainly make them both better off. The point is that without some restriction on how this increase in the output of the two commodities is allocated between the two individuals, they need not necessarily both be better off. While such an increase in output is potentially superior for both individuals, it will actually be superior only if some restrictions are imposed on the distribution of commodities between the two individuals. Thus, if community indifference curves are to be an index of community welfare, the distribution of commodities between the individuals must be restricted so that both receive some fixed share of total output.

6. CONCLUDING REMARKS

It has been shown that a set of nonintersecting community indifference curves can be assumed to exist if the utility functions for the individuals are homogeneous and if either (1) the utility functions are identical or (2) the distribution of income is fixed. For the case of identical and homogeneous utility functions, community indifference curves give unambiguous welfare comparisons only if the distribution of income is also fixed. While these conditions may seem somewhat severe, it should be noted that the conditions required for aggregation in any area of economics are very restrictive. Indeed, it can be shown that exactly the same conditions required for the existence of community indifference curves are required for the existence of aggregate consumption functions, so that from a theoretical point of view the aggregate consumption function used so widely in macroeconomics is as "unrealistic" as are the community indifference curves that will be employed in this analysis.

It should also be noted that, for the most part, community indifference curves will be used only for illustrative purposes, and that most of the conclusions we reach can be derived even if community indifference curves do not exist. Community indifference curves are thus employed mainly because of their heuristic value.

Although our discussion has been restricted to the two-individual case, our conclusions will be true for any number of individuals. Thus in the discussion of Figure 3.12 any number of individuals could have been assumed and the community indifference curve CIC_0 derived as long as *all* were identical with homogeneous preferences.

PROBLEMS

1. Show that, for an individual consumer maximizing utility subject to the budget constraint, the equilibrium position will not necessarily be unique unless the indifference curves are convex to the origin.
2. Show that if community indifference curves intersect, there could be many equilibrium positions in Figure 3.8.
3. In Figure 3.3 trace out a locus of consumption points as the price of X falls.
4. The construction of nonintersecting community indifference curves in Figure 3.12 was illustrated for two individuals. Show that the procedure applies equally well for three or more individuals.

REFERENCES

Chipman, J. S. (1965). "A Survey of the Theory of International Trade: Part 2, The Neo-Classical Theory." *Econometrica* 33, 685–760.
Melvin, J. R. (1975). "On the Equivalence of Community Indifference and the Aggregate Consumption Function." *Economica* 42, 442–445.
Samuelson, P. A. (1956). "Social Indifference Curves." *Quarterly Journal of Economics* 64, 264–289.
Scitovsky, T. (1942). "A Reconsideration of the Theory of Tariffs." *Review of Economic Studies* 9, 89–110.

chapter 4

The Offer Curve

1. THE AUTARKY EQUILIBRIUM

In Chapter 2 the production possibility curve, or the supply side of the model, was developed, and in Chapter 3 community indifference curves, one method of representing aggregate demand conditions, were derived. In this chapter these two constructs will be used to derive the *offer curve,* another geometric device that will prove useful in subsequent analysis. First of all, however, it is necessary to formalize the notion of equilibrium in this aggregate model. Initially, we assume a closed economy, or in other words, an economy in which no international trade takes place. This no-trade situation is commonly referred to as *autarky.*

In Figure 4.1 the production possibility curve TAT' has been drawn; three representative community indifference curves are also shown. It is clear that the potential welfare of the economy is maximized at point A, the point at which the highest community indifference curve is tangent to the production possibility curve. But we have not yet demonstrated that the market mechanism would lead to the establishment of this point as the equilibrium. To show that this will, in fact, be the case, suppose that initially the economy found itself at point B. It has already been established that for this to be an equilibrium for consumers, the commodity price ratio, p_x/p_y, must be tangent to the community indifference curve at this point. To simplify notation, we will define the ratio $p_x/p_y = p$

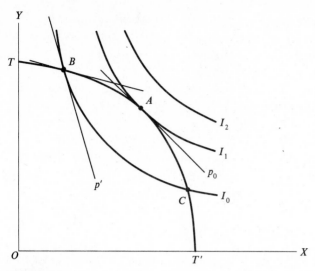

Figure 4.1

throughout the remainder of the book. Thus at point B the price ratio line p' must be tangent to the community indifference curve. The existence of this price ratio implies that consumers are prepared to exchange commodities X and Y at this ratio. Note, however, that the slope of the production possibility curve at B represents the rate at which one commodity can be transformed into the other. In other words, this slope shows the amount of Y that must be given up in order to get another unit of X through production. Of course, this transformation of Y into X does not mean that in some mysterious way one commodity is actually being converted into the other; it simply means that a reallocation of factors from one production function to the other would give rise to this kind of shift in aggregate production levels.

We have seen that the slope of the indifference curve at point B is the consumer price ratio, and that the slope of the transformation curve is the rate at which commodities can be transformed from one to the other through production. It is now easy to see that point B could not exist as an equilibrium position. At point B producers would note that consumers are apparently willing to exchange a relatively small quantity of X for a large quantity of Y. They would further note, from the rate of product transformation, that by foregoing the production of a small quantity of Y, they could produce a relatively large quantity of X. As profit-maximizing producers, they thus perceive that by producing more X at the cost to them of a relatively small amount of Y and by exchanging this X at the price ratio p', they could obtain a larger quantity of Y. Thus the production point will tend to move along the production possibility curve from B toward A. It is clear that this same argument could be made at all points between B and A, and that only at A will there no longer be an incentive to produce larger quantities of X. At point A the price at which consumers are prepared to exchange is exactly the same rate at which commodities can be transformed in production. It is also clear that had we begun at a point such as C, the story would have been precisely the same, except that in this case producers would have had an incentive to produce larger quantities of Y. Thus market forces will establish A as the autarky equilibrium position. The equilibrium price line associated with this point is the line p_0, the line jointly tangent to the production possibility curve and the community indifference curve.

2. THE OFFER CURVE: FIXED PRODUCTION

Point A of Figure 4.1 is the equilibrium position that would exist in a situation in which there was no possibility of international trade. The major concern of this book, however, is with situations in which this kind of exchange *does* take place, and we wish to examine the conditions under which such international trade would occur. It is clear from Figure 4.1 that even if the model were expanded to include other countries, no international trade would take place if the price ratio remained at p_0. This price ratio precisely equates the quantities of X and Y that the industries wish to produce and the quantities of X and Y that the consumers wish to consume. It is obvious, however, that international trade can take place if the world price ratio differs from p_0. We now turn to an examination of how domestic producers and consumers would behave when faced with price ratios that differ from the autarky price ratio of Figure 4.1.

The aim of this chapter is to illustrate the derivation of an offer curve for the most general case in which there is substitution in both consumption and production. As an initial step, however, it is instructive to begin with a simpler model in which production is fixed, such that the same aggregate production point is relevant for all price ratios. Thus in Figure 4.2 the point A with Y_0 and X_0 of commodities Y and X, respectively, is the only possible production point. There will be some price line, say, p_0, such that consumers demand quantities X_0 and Y_0. This is equivalent to the autarky position of Figure 4.1. (To avoid confusion, the indifference curve tangent to p_0 at A has not been included.)

We now suppose that producers and consumers in this country are faced with a new price line p_1, implying a relatively higher price for commodity Y. Both producers and consumers are assumed to maximize (output and utility, respectively) subject to this constraint, so that production remains at point A and consumption moves to point C_1. Note that

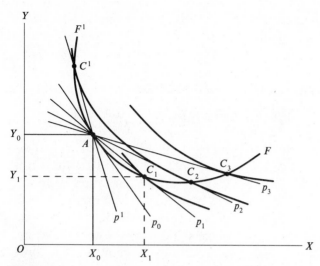

Figure 4.2

both A and C_1 must lie on the price line p_1, for while we are no longer insisting that the same quantities of the two goods be consumed as those that are produced, we do insist that the value of the consumption bundle be equal to the value of the production bundle. Consumption at C_1 would be possible if this country could find some other economy that was willing to accept the quantity of Y, $Y_0 - Y_1$, in exchange for the amount $X_1 - X_0$ of commodity X. For the moment, however, we are not concerned with the question of whether p_1 will be an equilibrium price line, but only with the question of how producers and consumers in this country would react when faced with a variety of different commodity price ratios.

Suppose the economy were faced with the price ratio line p_2. In this situation consumption would take place at point C_2 with production again at A, and for a price ratio line p_3, consumption would be at C_3. Note that in all these cases consumers maximize utility by moving to the point where this price line is tangent to the highest community indifference curve. If this procedure were carried out for a large number of such price lines, the equilibrium consumption points would trace out the line $AC_1C_2C_3F$. This is a type of *offer curve,* or *reciprocal demand curve.*

The points along the offer curve AF in Figure 4.2 were derived by considering the price ratio lines whose slopes became progressively less steep. It is clear, however, that exactly the same procedure could be used for price lines that are steeper than p_0. In Figure 4.2 only one such price line, p^1, implying production at A and consumption at C^1, has been included. If a variety of such price lines were used, then the curve AC_1F^1 could be traced out. It is important to note that if attention is restricted to those situations in which domestic consumers and producers face the same relative prices, the locus FAF^1 shows all possible equilibrium points that could exist for this economy.

3. THE OFFER CURVE: VARIABLE PRODUCTION

A similar procedure to that shown in Figure 4.2 can be used when production possibilities are represented by the locus TAT' of Figure 4.1. In this case, for every different price, producers as well as consumers will adjust quantities produced so as to remain in equilibrium. Such a situation is shown in Figure 4.3, where point A is the autarky point from Figure 4.1. Now for price line p_1, consumers will move to C_1 and producers will choose Q_1, where p_1 is tangent to TAT'. This would again require an exchange of $Y_0 - Y_1$ of Y for $X_1 - X_0$ of X if this is to be an equilibrium. In the same fashion, the production and consumption points for price lines p_2, p_3, and p^1 can be derived as in Figure 4.3. As before, the locus of equilibrium consumption points F^1AF can be constructed and will be a version of the offer curve or reciprocal demand curve.

In certain circumstances it is convenient to show the relationship depicted by FAF^1 of Figures 4.2 and 4.3 without specifically including the production possibility curve and the indifference curves. We have, in

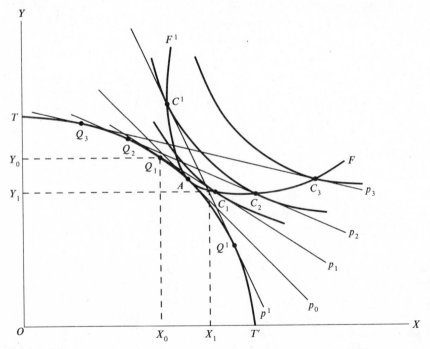

Figure 4.3

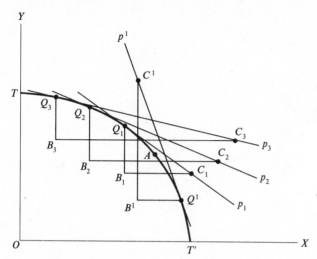

Figure 4.4

Figure 4.4, reproduced the relevant information from Figure 4.3 but have left out the indifference curves in order to avoid clutter. Initially we will consider only those price lines that are less steep than the autarky price line tangent at point A. For the three price lines illustrated we have drawn in the *trade triangles*. Thus, if price p_1 prevailed, the economy would wish to export $B_1 Q_1$ of commodity Y and import $B_1 C_1$ of commodity X. Similarly, $B_2 Q_2$ and $B_2 C_2$ would be the desired exports and imports of commodities Y and X, respectively, if the price were p_2. Note that these quantities of X and Y are just the excess demands and excess supplies that would prevail in the economy at these various price lines.

To illustrate more clearly the way in which the trade bundles vary as prices change, we have, in Figure 4.5, plotted only the exports and imports associated with the various price lines of Figure 4.4. We have, in other words, plotted the trade triangles from Figure 4.4 all from the common origin in Figure 4.5, such that $B_1 Q_1$ and $B_1 C_1$ of Figure 4.4 become OQ_1 and OC_1 of Figure 4.5, resulting in the point E_1. The trade triangles for p_2 and p_3 are plotted in exactly the same fashion, giving E_2 and E_3 in Figure 4.5. Had other price lines been considered, other points in Figure 4.5 could have been found, and these would have resulted in the locus OF. It is this locus that is commonly referred to as the *offer curve*.

In Figure 4.5, while the axes are the same as in Figure 4.4, the quantities being measured are not total production and total consumption, but are, rather, excess demands and excess supplies. In other words, we are plotting the desired exports and the desired imports for various possible commodity price lines. Note that in Figure 4.5, for any point E on the offer curve, the line from the origin to this point represents the commodity

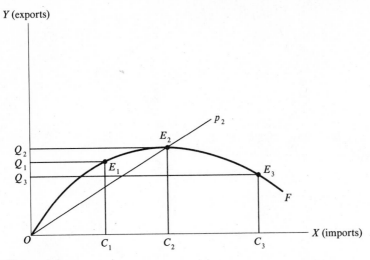

Figure 4.5

price line that generated that point. Thus for the point E_2 the price line p_2 is precisely the same as p_2 in Figure 4.4, except that as drawn it has the opposite slope. This is easily verified by noting that the triangle OC_2E_2 of Figure 4.5 is precisely the same as the triangle $C_2B_2Q_2$ of Figure 4.4.

In Figure 4.5 we considered only those price lines whose slopes are less steep than the autarky price line through point A of Figure 4.4. We now wish to consider price lines that are steeper than p_0. The first thing to be observed is that for any such price line, the excess demand and supply conditions will be the reverse of those of Figure 4.4. Thus, instead of exporting commodity Y and importing X, the economy will want to import commodity Y and export commodity X. One such trade triangle is shown in Figure 4.4, and it is clear that since consumers want to consume at C^1 and producers want to produce at point Q^1, there is an excess supply of commodity X equal to the amount B^1Q^1, and an excess demand for commodity Y equal to B^1C^1. These points can be included in Figure 4.6 by noting that negative exports of Y are imports of Y, and negative imports of X are exports of X. Thus the points C^1 and Q^1 can be plotted in the third quadrant of Figure 4.6, giving rise to point E^1. Other such points could be found in a similar fashion and the locus of all such points would give OF^1, the other branch of the offer curve. Note that the curve FOF^1 of Figure 4.6 gives exactly the same information about trade as does the curve FAF^1 of Figure 4.3. Of course, Figure 4.3 gives other information as well, for it shows us precisely where production and consumption take place for each of the equilibrium positions. Such information is not given in Figure 4.6.

From Figure 4.6 it can be seen that the offer curve is always concave

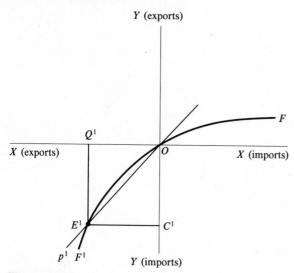

Figure 4.6

toward the import axis. The reason for this particular shape can be found by examining Figure 4.4, the diagram from which this information was obtained. We note first of all that at the price line p_0 (not shown in the diagram) excess demands and supplies for both commodities are zero, and this situation gives rise to the origin in Figure 4.5. It is also clear that as the price ratio declines, excess demands for X increase, as can be seen by comparing $B_1 C_1$, $B_2 C_2$, and $B_3 C_3$ in Figure 4.4. Thus we can say that the desired imports of X are an increasing function of the relative price of Y. Now consider the changes in the desired exports of commodity Y associated with these price ratios. At p_0 (not shown) excess supplies of Y are zero, and at p_1 excess supplies of Y are $B_1 Q_1$. As the price ratio continues to fall, the production of Y will continue to rise, but we note that at least after some point the consumption of Y will begin to rise as well. That this must be the case can be seen by noting that as the price line becomes closer and closer to the horizontal, excess supplies of Y must become closer and closer to zero. Thus as the price ratio falls, the excess supplies of Y will initially rise, will reach some maximum, and thereafter will decline. This gives an offer curve of the shape shown in Figure 4.6. It should be noted, however, that this argument depends crucially on the existence of homogeneous community indifference curves.

When we began the derivation of the offer curve we arbitrarily chose to consider price ratio lines that resulted in exports of Y and imports of X; that is, we chose price lines that were less steep than p_0. We could have started just as appropriately by increasing the slope of the price line and then considered prices like p^1 of Figure 4.4, which

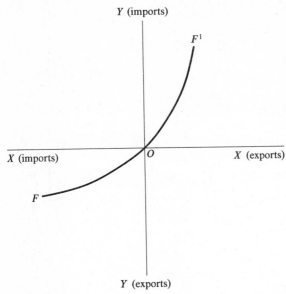

Figure 4.7

would imply imports of Y and exports of X. If the various excess demand and supply bundles for such price lines had been plotted in the first quadrant, then the offer curve would have been concave to the Y axis rather than to the X axis. This would have resulted in Figure 4.7. It should be noted that Figures 4.6 and 4.7 provide the same information and differ only in the initial choice of the commodity to be exported. All that is required to convert Figure 4.6 to Figure 4.7 is to interchange the first and third quadrants.

4. EQUILIBRIUM WITH TWO COUNTRIES

In the chapters that follow we will use offer curve diagrams to illustrate the determination of equilibrium prices in a variety of different circumstances and to show how prices change when various parameters of the model change. To anticipate this analysis, we will show in this section how the equilibrium terms of trade are established for a world in which there are two countries that trade exclusively with one another. To simplify the analysis, we assume that we know in advance which country will export which commodity. How the trade pattern is determined is, of course, a very important issue and this question will be considered in detail in subsequent chapters.

We assume that there are two countries, a home country that we designate as H and a foreign country that we designate as F. As before, we have two goods, X and Y, and we assume that in the final equilibrium country H imports X and therefore exports Y, and that country F exports X and therefore imports Y. Because country H is an importer of X, we need to consider only price lines such as p_1, p_2, and p_3 of Figure 4.4. These will produce an offer curve having the shape shown in Figure 4.5 and shown as OH in Figure 4.8. We note again that the offer curve is concave to the import axis. For country F which imports Y we will have an offer curve with the shape shown in quadrant I of Figure 4.7 and reproduced as OF in Figure 4.8. Again, the offer curve is concave to the import axis, which in this case is commodity Y.

As drawn, the two offer curves of Figure 4.8 intersect only once at point E. Through this point we have drawn price line p_1, and this will be the equilibrium free trade price line for this simple two-country model. To demonstrate that this is indeed an equilibrium, we need only consider how the offer curves were constructed. Recall that all points on the offer curve show the quantities of one good that the country is willing to exchange for a quantity of the other. Furthermore, we saw that the price line relevant to any point on the offer curve is a line from the origin through that point. Thus the offer curve OH of Figure 4.8 shows us that at price line p_1 the home country desires to import a quantity of X equal to X_1 and to export an amount of Y equal to Y_1. The offer curve OF indicates that the foreign country wishes to import an amount of Y equal to Y_1 and to export X_1 of commodity X. Clearly at price p_1 the exports of one country are exactly equal to the imports of the other, and thus the point E of Figure 4.8 is in equilibrium.

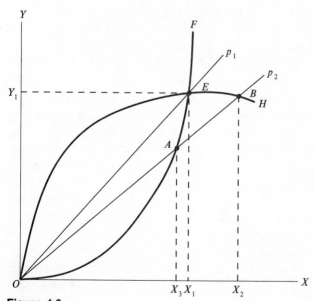

Figure 4.8

*5. STABILITY AND UNIQUENESS

We have seen that the intersection of the two offer curves OH and OF in Figure 4.8 produced an equilibrium at E with price line p_1. These two offer curves clearly intersect only once, and therefore this equilibrium is unique. It is easy, however, to construct situations in which more than one equilibrium exists, but before doing so, we will find it useful to examine the question of when an equilibrium such as E is stable.

An equilibrium is said to be stable if, after a slight displacement from the initial equilibrium position, there is a tendency for the original equilibrium to be reestablished. To investigate whether or not p_1 of Figure 4.8 is stable, we consider price line p_2, which is clearly not an equilibrium price line, and ask whether there are market forces that would tend to reestablish p_1. The price line p_2 intersects the home country's offer curve at point B and this means that at those prices country H wishes to import X_2 of commodity X. Price line p_2 intersects the foreign country's offer curve at point A, thus indicating that country F wishes to export X_3 of commodity X. Because country H wishes to import more than country F wants to export, there is clearly an excess demand for commodity X. Turning to commodity Y, we can similarly show that country H wishes to export more Y than country F wishes to import, and thus there is an excess supply of commodity Y. The excess demand for commodity X and the excess supply of commodity Y imply that the relative price of X will rise and the price line will rotate in a counterclockwise fashion through point O. Note that the excess demand for X and the excess supply of Y will continue to exist until the price line passes through E, the original equilibrium point. It can also be shown that for price lines steeper than p_1 there will be an excess demand for Y and an excess supply of X, and again, there will be a tendency for price line p_1 to be reestablished. Since there are market forces that tend to reestablish price line p_1 after any small perturbation of prices, equilibrium E is stable.

Now consider Figure 4.9 where the offer curves have been drawn to intersect three times so that we have a case of multiple equilibria. Points E_1, E_2, and E_3 are all equilibria and to each point there corresponds a commodity price line. We now wish to determine whether all three of these equilibria are stable. Beginning at equilibrium E_1 with price line p_1 we consider price line p' and ask whether market forces will tend to reestablish the equilibrium price p_1. The price line p' intersects the home country's offer curve at B, and thus quantity X_2 is the home country's desired imports of commodity X. Note that we have labeled Figure 4.9 to correspond to Figure 4.8. The intersection of price line p' with the foreign country's offer curve is at point A just as it was in Figure 4.8, and

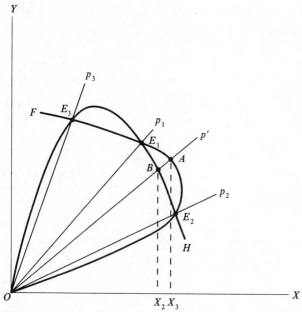

Figure 4.9

this leads to X_3 as the desired quantity of exports for country F. But while the desired imports of commodity X were greater than the desired exports of commodity X in Figure 4.8, the situation is reversed in Figure 4.9. X_3 is larger than X_2, and thus the foreign country wishes to export a larger quantity of commodity X than country H wants to import. It can similarly be shown that at price line p' in Figure 4.9 there is excess demand for commodity Y, and this combined with the excess supply of commodity X means that the relative price of Y will rise. An increase in the relative price of Y implies that the price line will rotate in a clockwise direction through O, and thus the price will move away from the equilibrium E_1. Indeed, the relative price of X will continue to fall until price p_2 is reached.

It can similarly be shown that a price line slightly steeper than p_1 will result in excess demand for X and excess supply of Y and result in prices moving toward p_3. Clearly, price p_1 is unstable, since any small perturbation of prices will move the equilibrium point away from E_1.

A consideration of points E_2 and E_3 would show that both these equilibria are stable. Indeed, a close examination of Figure 4.9 will show that E_2 and E_3 are both similar to equilibrium E of Figure 4.8 in terms of the excess demands and supplies that would exist at prices close to prices p_2 and p_3. Thus in Figure 4.9 the middle equilibrium E_1 is unstable, but stable equilibria exist on either side of E_1. This property can be shown to carry forward to other more complex situations. For cases where there are many equilibria, the equilibrium points will alternate between being stable and unstable, and all unstable equilibrium have a stable equilibrium on either side.

6. CONCLUDING REMARKS

As we have seen, the offer curve is a representation of the excess demands and supplies for the two commodities that will exist at various commodity price ratios. Given the offer curve and the equilibrium price line, the imports and exports can be immediately derived. The offer curve will thus be an important tool in the determination of equilibrium prices when more than one country is assumed.

The offer curves that have been derived in this chapter have assumed the existence of community indifference curves. It should be noted, however, that offer curves will exist whether or not community indifference curves exist, as long as, for any given price line, the equilibrium consumption bundles can be found. Thus in Figure 4.3 suppose that community indifference curves did not exist but that the consumption points C_1, C_2, and C_3 could, nevertheless, be found. It is obvious that in this case the offer curve of Figure 4.5 could be derived in precisely the same fashion. The only complication that arises if community indifference curves do not exist is that the consumption points of Figure 4.3 need not necessarily lie along the smooth line AF. If they do not, then the offer curve of Figure 4.5 will not necessarily have the shape shown. As will be seen in subsequent chapters, variations from this shape can complicate the analysis; thus, for the most part, smooth offer curves concave to the import axis will be assumed. The important point, however, is that this is largely a matter of convenience; offer curves can generally be assumed to exist, regardless of whether or not community indifference curves do.

PROBLEMS

1. With a single factor of production, the production possibility curve will be linear. Using the techniques of Figures 4.3 and 4.4, show how the offer curve can be constructed in this case.
2. Show that if the offer curves of Figures 4.6 and 4.7 were superimposed on one another they would be tangent at the origin.
3. Suppose that in Figure 4.3 the maximum producible quantity of Y were larger and the maximum producible quantity of X were smaller. Show how this would change the position of the offer curve.
4. Show how changes in taste could affect the position of the offer curve.
5. Show that E_2 of Figure 4.9 is stable.

6. Draw a pair of smooth, concave offer curves that intersect five times. Which equilibria are stable?

*7. Derive the offer curve for the case in which increasing returns to scale result in a production possibility curve that is convex to the origin.

REFERENCES

Chipman, J. S. (1965). "A Survey of the Theory of International Trade: Part 2, The Neo-Classical Theory." *Econometrica* 33, 685–760.

Johnson, H. G. (1959). "International Trade, Income Distribution and the Offer Curve." *Manchester School* 27, 241–260.

Lerner, A. P. (1953). *Essays in Economic Analysis.* London: Macmillan.

Meade, J. E. (1952). *A Geometry of International Trade.* London: Allen & Unwin.

Melvin, J. R. (1985). "Domestic Taste Differences, Transportation Costs and International Trade." *Journal of International Economics* 18, 65–82.

chapter 5

The Gains from Trade

1. THE CLOSED (AUTARKY) ECONOMY EQUILIBRIUM

We are now in a position to address one of the most fundamental issues in the study of international trade—the gains from trade. We will be able to show that under certain circumstances a country's overall welfare is in some sense improved by international trade, which should thus be viewed as desirable. Yet the popular press often seems to assert that imports and trade are not beneficial for the national economy. A correct understanding of the gains from trade is thus important not only from an academic point of view, but also because of the practical need to evaluate various antitrade arguments put forward by business, labor, and even government groups.

A closed or autarky equilibrium, in which a country does not trade, is shown again in Figure 5.1 by point A. Three conditions determine this equilibrium. First, the consumers' marginal rate of substitution (the slope of the indifference curve) must be equal to the price ratio. If this is not the case, then the consumers would not be maximizing their utility, as we saw earlier. Second, the producers' marginal rate of transformation (the slope of the production possibility curve) must be equal to the price ratio if producers are competitive and maximizing their profits. Third, the amount of each good produced must be equal to the amount consumed. These three conditions together imply that production and consumption take place at point A in Figure 5.1, where a community indifference curve

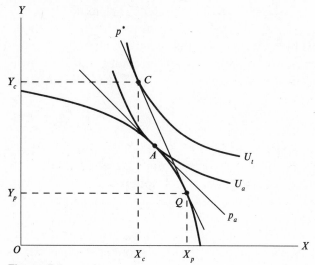

Figure 5.1

and the production possibility curve are tangent to one another and to the autarky price ratio, denoted p_a.

2. THE OPEN (TRADING) ECONOMY EQUILIBRIUM

What is the relevance of the three closed-economy equilibrium conditions to an economy that engages in international trade? The first two really have nothing to do with whether or not the economy engages in trade. Consumers will still equate their *MRS* (marginal rate of substitution) to the price ratio, and producers will choose outputs such that the *MRT* (marginal rate of transformation) equals the price ratio. The only difference is that the relevant price ratio is now determined by the larger world market (we will call it the "world price ratio") rather than simply by domestic demand and supply.

It is, in fact, the third condition that changes with the introduction of international trade. With trade, the domestic demand and supply (consumption and production) of any particular good need not be equal. The United States produces more wheat than it consumes and consumes more bananas than it produces. The excess production of wheat is, of course, exported and exchanged for imports such as bananas. International trade thus in a sense removes the binding constraint that we can only consume what we ourselves are able to produce.

Since the quantities produced and consumed of a good are not equal when there is trade, we will need a notation that distinguishes between the two. Let X_p and X_c denote the quantities of X produced and consumed, respectively. Y_p and Y_c can be similarly interpreted. The closed economy must of course have $X_p = X_c$ and $Y_p = Y_c$. In the open economy these restrictions are replaced by the restriction that what the country buys on world markets (imports) must be equal to what the country sells. We will refer to this as the "balance-of-payments constraint." It is written algebraically as follows:

$$p_x^*(X_c - X_p) + p_y^*(Y_c - Y_p) = 0 \qquad (5.1)$$

where p_x^* and p_y^* denote the world prices of X and Y. In equation (5.1), $(X_c - X_p)$ and $(Y_c - Y_p)$ are referred to as the "excess demands" for X and Y, respectively (i.e., the excess of consumption demand, X_c, over production, X_p). Excess demand is positive for an imported good and negative for an exported good. Equation (5.1) requires that the values (price times quantity) of the excess demand equal zero. Alternatively, this balance-of-payments constraint requires that the value of imports equal the value of exports. What we buy from the world markets must be equal to what we sell.

Suppose, for example, that we export X and import Y. Then $(X_c - X_p) < 0$ is the quantity of exports and $p_x^* (X_c - X_p)$ is the value of exports. $(Y_c - Y_p) > 0$ gives the quantity of imports and $p_y^* (Y_c - Y_p)$ gives the value of imports. Figure 5.1 shows a trading equilibrium with prices $p^* = p_x^*/p_y^*$. Production takes place at Q where $MRT = p^*$, and consumption takes place at C where $MRS = p^*$. The horizontal distance $(X_p - X_c)$ gives exports and the vertical distance $(Y_c - Y_p)$ gives imports. The ratio $(Y_c - Y_p)/(X_p - X_c)$ is equal to the world price ratio or to the slope of the price line connecting C and Q in Figure 5.1. Indeed, it is in this manner that we can check that the situation shown in Figure 5.1 satisfies the balance-of-payments constraint. Equation (5.1) can be rewritten as equation (5.2):

$$p^* = \frac{p_x^*}{p_y^*} = \frac{(Y_c - Y_p)}{(X_p - X_c)}. \qquad (5.2)$$

The ratio of quantities exchanged must equal the price ratio. Equation (5.2) is, of course, satisfied in Figure 5.1 since $p^* = (Y_c - Y_p)/(X_p - X_c)$, as just noted.

Before dealing explicitly with the gains from trade, we should make one final point about the balance-of-payments constraint. Note that equation (5.1) or (5.2) can also be rewritten as

$$p_x^* X_p + p_y^* Y_p = p_x^* X_c + p_y^* Y_c. \qquad (5.3)$$

The left-hand side of (5.3) gives the value of production, while the right-hand side gives the value of consumption for the domestic economy. Thus, if the value of exports equals the value of imports, it must also be true that the value of production equals the value of consumption. A deficit in the balance of payments refers to a situation in which the value of imports exceeds the value of exports, and would therefore correspond to the case in which equation (5.1) is positive in value. It can then be shown that in this case the right-hand side of equation (5.3) exceeds the left-hand side. A deficit in the balance of payments is thus a situation in which the country is consuming more than it is producing. Although this is in a sense very desirable, such a deficit must, of course, be paid for by either borrowing from foreigners or running down the nation's financial assets such as gold or foreign currencies. It is in this sense that deficits are viewed as bad: A country in a deficit situation is overspending its income and will eventually run out of assets or incur large debts (just as any individual would in such a situation) if the trend is not reversed.

Now let us return to the issue of the gains from trade. Figure 5.1 shows that the country attains a higher level of utility at the free-trade equilibrium (U_t) than at the autarky equilibrium (U_a). The country thus gains from trade. Is this just because of the way we have drawn the diagram, or is it in fact a very general result? It can be shown, using somewhat more advanced techniques, that the gains-from-trade result is indeed very general. Provided that the world price ratio differs from the domestic autarky price ratio, gains will be realized from trade. As later sections and chapters will show, any difference in these price ratios allows a country to gain by selling to the foreigners goods that can be produced relatively cheaply at home, and by importing from the foreigners goods that are expensive to produce at home.

Figure 5.2 illustrates the fact that any divergence between the world and domestic price ratios is sufficient for gains. p_a gives the prices that would prevail in autarky, while p_1^* and p_2^* give two different possible world price ratios. p_1^* is greater than p_a, indicating that the world price of X is higher and the world price of Y lower than the respective domestic autarky prices. Thus the country can realize welfare gains as shown by exporting X (the good that is relatively cheaper to produce at home) in exchange for imports of Y (the good that is relatively expensive at home). p_2^* gives the opposite case. In this instance p_2^* is less than p_a, indicating that the world price of X is lower and the world price of Y higher than the respective domestic autarky prices. The country now has an opportunity to gain by exporting Y and importing X. The country will in this case produce at Q_2 and consume at C_2, whereas at prices p_1^* it produces at Q_1 and consumes at C_1.

The point of Figure 5.2 is simple. Gains from trade can be realized provided only that p^* differs from p_a. Whether p^* exceeds p_a or vice versa

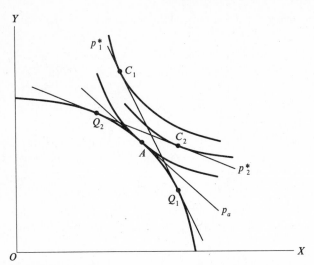

Figure 5.2

will determine the direction of trade (which good is exported) but gains
will be realized in either case. Trade always gives a country the potential
of consuming more of both goods.

It can also be shown that community indifference curves are not
necessary for this last proposition (see Samuelson [1939, 1962]). This
gains-from-trade result does not rely on any assumptions about demand
and is therefore considered to be a strong result.

3. THE GAINS FROM EXCHANGE

It turns out that the gains from trade can be conveniently broken down
into gains from two distinct sources—gains from exchange and gains from
specialization. The gains from exchange refer to the fact that if individuals
or countries are endowed with different amounts of goods or have different
preferences, they can each gain by trading with one another.

Suppose that we have two individuals, Frido and Liz, and that Frido
has six bottles of beer and no bags of peanuts, while Liz has five bags of
peanuts but no beers. As shown in Figure 5.3, Liz and Frido will each
attain utility level U_a in their respective diagrams. But various possibilities
exist for mutual gains. Liz could, for example, give Frido three bags of
peanuts for two beers. They would then move to point C in their respective
diagrams, each attaining a utility level of U_t. An implicit trading price is
established, insofar as three bags of peanuts are deemed to be equal in
value to two beers. Beer is relatively more valuable; the price of beer in
terms of peanuts is $3/2 = 1.5$.

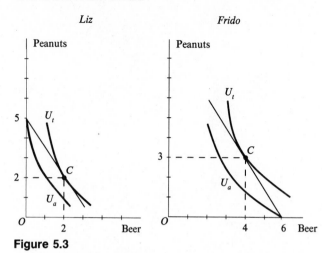

Figure 5.3

Other trades could have been arranged, such as two bags of peanuts for two beers, establishing a price ratio of 1. Obviously, Liz would prefer this trade, while Frido would prefer the one mentioned in the previous paragraph. Thus different trades affect the distribution of gains between the traders, and stronger or smarter traders will tend to move the terms of trade to their advantage. This will be important in later chapters. The important point here is that both individuals will gain something from voluntary trade (otherwise they would not trade); that is, voluntary trade is beneficial. This is in fact an extremely important point in economics, insofar as many popular opinions about trade seem to assume or argue that any gain by one country must be another's loss. It is not true that a consumption gain by Japan or the United States in trading with Canada must mean an equivalent loss for someone in Canada. Trade results in mutual gains, as we have just shown.

This result can be demonstrated more formally with the aid of a box diagram as in Figure 5.4 (similar to the box diagrams in Chapter 3). The two goods are again X and Y and the two individuals are 1 and 2. The initial endowment point is point E. The welfare levels of 1 and 2 at this endowment point are given by U_{1a} and U_{2a}, respectively. You should be able to convince yourself that moving from E to any point in the interior of the "lens" formed by U_{1a} and U_{2a} will make both individuals better off. But not all of the possible moves are Pareto optimal—that is, moves after which we could not make one individual better off without making the other one worse off. Beginning at E in Figure 5.4, the set of Pareto optimal trades is given by the segment of the contract curve between A and A' where indifference curves are tangent. Point T illustrates one possible Pareto optimal trading equilibrium between A and A' at which

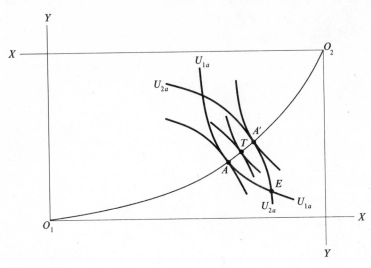

Figure 5.4

gains are shared fairly equally. As discussed earlier, other trades between
A and A' shift the gains more toward one trader or the other, but both
definitely do gain.

4. THE GAINS FROM SPECIALIZATION

The previous section assumed that the total quantities of all goods were
fixed. In fact, individuals or countries can generally increase total production and realize additional gains by specializing in the goods they produce
most efficiently. This proposition is usually fairly obvious in the case of
individuals. However, in modern society no one is self-sufficient, and
indeed, most people engage in an extremely narrow range of work activities in order to earn income to buy a wide range of goods and services.
Everyone seems to grasp the idea that we would have a much lower
standard of living if people all tried to grow their own food, make their
own clothes, build their own houses, and so forth. Specialization in a
narrow range of activities is efficient.

The same principle holds true for countries, although for some reason people seem to lose sight of this fact. One frequently hears arguments
in the United States to the effect that we should be producing such and
such a good here, rather than importing it from abroad. Consider a simple
example in which we have two countries, the U.S. and Japan, which
produce two goods, wheat and steel. Suppose that the number of tons of
wheat or steel that one man can produce per year in each country is given

in Table 5.1. One man-year of labor devoted to wheat production in the U.S. thus results in 30 tons of wheat, and so forth. The U.S. appears to be relatively more productive in wheat and Japan relatively more productive in steel. Suppose we now move one worker in the U.S. out of steel and into wheat production. Similarly, we move one Japanese worker out of wheat production and into steel production. Changes in outputs following this reallocation are given in Table 5.2. This shows that simply moving workers in each country into the industry in which the country has the advantage results in an increase in the world outputs of *both* goods. The countries may then engage in trade such that both are made better off.

Suppose that Japan were more productive in both goods. Would the two countries still have an incentive to trade? The answer is a definite yes, as was first pointed out by the nineteenth century British economist David Ricardo. Let us double the productivities of Japanese workers shown in Table 5.1. We will now have the situation in Table 5.3. In this example Japan is said to have an "absolute advantage" in both goods, whereas in Table 5.1 the U.S. had an absolute advantage in wheat and Japan an absolute advantage in steel. But in both cases the U.S. is said to have a "comparative advantage" in wheat, meaning that the American economy is relatively more productive in wheat; the U.S. can produce 3 tons of wheat from the same resources used to produce 1 ton of steel, whereas in Japan the ratio is 1 to 1. Ricardo noted that as long as some pattern of comparative advantage exists, there will be gains from trade, regardless of the fact that one country may have an absolute advantage in all goods. To see this, suppose we now reallocate two workers in the U.S. from steel to wheat, and one worker in Japan from wheat to steel. The changes in outputs are now given in Table 5.4. Once again, we see that the total outputs of both goods can be increased if the two countries each specialize according to their pattern of comparative advantage. Gains from special-

Table 5.1   ONE MAN-YEAR OF PRODUCTION

	U.S.	Japan
Wheat	30	20
Steel	10	20

Table 5.2   CHANGES IN OUTPUTS DUE TO REALLOCATION

	U.S.	Japan	Total
Wheat	$+30$	-20	$+10$
Steel	-10	$+20$	$+10$

Table 5.3   ONE MAN-YEAR OF PRODUCTION

	U.S.	Japan
Wheat	30	40
Steel	10	40

Table 5.4   CHANGES IN OUTPUTS DUE TO REALLOCATION

	U.S.	Japan	Total
Wheat	$+60$	-40	$+20$
Steel	-20	$+40$	$+20$

ization will always exist if countries have different production ratios (i.e., if there exists some pattern of comparative advantage).

Figure 5.5 summarizes our discussion by showing how the total gains from trade can be decomposed into gains from exchange and gains from specialization. Point A gives the autarky production/consumption point and U_a gives the autarky utility level. Suppose the economy can now trade at prices p^*, and suppose that the economy cannot change its output levels (production is fixed at A). Gains from exchange can still be realized by trading to point E. The movement from A to E and the increase in utility from U_a to U_e illustrate the gains from exchange. But further gains can be realized if we move the production point to Q, showing relatively more specialization in good X. The movement from E to C and the increase in

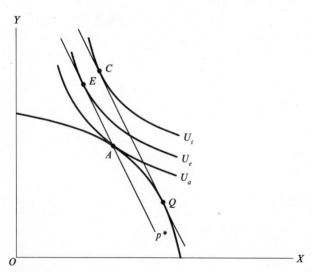

Figure 5.5

utility from U_e to U_t in Figure 5.5 thus illustrate the gains from specialization.

5. THE DISTRIBUTION OF GAINS WITH HETEROGENEOUS TASTES[1]

The preceding sections have shown that a country will gain from international trade in the sense that the country can potentially consume more of both goods. The gains were illustrated with the use of community indifference curves, although we noted that such indifference curves are not necessary for the main argument. But while trade may result in aggregate consumption gains, it is important in understanding certain trade policy questions to emphasize that the gains from trade are not necessarily distributed evenly among members of a society. Indeed, it is possible that certain groups will actually be worse off in a situation of free trade than in an autarky or a restricted trade situation.

One possibility occurs when individuals in a society have very different tastes. Suppose that the world price ratio exceeds the price ratio that would prevail in autarky ($p^* > p_a$) so that the country exports X and imports Y, as in Figure 5.1. Consider now two individuals with the same income but different tastes. Let AA' be the autarky budget line for each of these two individuals in Figure 5.6. Individual 1 has a high preference for Y and so chooses his autarky consumption bundle A_1. Individual 2 has a high preference for X and therefore chooses bundle A_2. Their utility levels are given by U_{1a} and U_{2a}, respectively.

As shown in Figure 5.1, trade has the effect of raising the relative price of X, which we illustrate in Figure 5.6 by rotating the budget line to TT'. Individual 1 increases his consumption from A_1 to T_1 and experiences an increase in welfare from U_{1a} to U_{1t}. But the increased price for X has affected individual 2 so adversely that his consumption falls from A_2 to T_2 and his welfare from U_{2a} to U_{2t}. Thus when individuals have heterogeneous tastes, the gains from trade will be distributed unevenly and some groups may indeed become worse off.

One illustration of this problem was the entry of Great Britain into the European Economic Community (EEC) in the early 1970s. Prior to entering, Great Britain had imported inexpensive food from countries such as New Zealand and Australia. After entering, the British were forced to pay much higher European prices for many foods, especially meat. In exchange for this, the British were able to purchase a wider range of manufactured goods at cheaper prices. The net benefit to a household would surely depend on the household's income, number of children, and

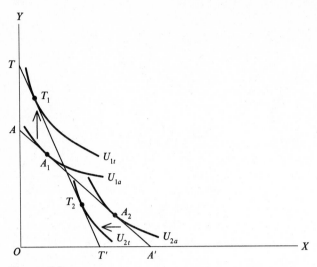

Figure 5.6

so on. It is likely that some large families with low incomes that were spending a large fraction of family income on food were made worse off by entering the EEC.

6. THE DISTRIBUTION OF GAINS WITH HETEROGENEOUS ENDOWMENTS

A second example of uneven distribution of gains from trade occurs when individuals differ widely in their factor endowments. Suppose there really are two distinct groups in society called capitalists and laborers, and assume that laborers own no capital and that capitalists perform no labor. Assume also that X is labor-intensive and that Y is capital-intensive.

Budget lines for laborers and capitalists are shown in Figure 5.7, with each group's initial autarky income constraint given by AA' and initial welfare level by U_a. Now assume that trade raises the price of X as in Figure 5.1. The economy responds to this change by shifting resources out of Y production and into X production. The outputs of the economy move from point A in Figure 5.1 to point Q.

In a later chapter, we will show that this increase in the output of X, the labor-intensive good, leads to an increase in the demand for and price of labor. Similarly, the decrease in the production of Y, the capital-intensive good, leads to an overall decrease in the demand for and price of capital. The commodity price changes caused by trade thus in turn cause factor price changes. In these circumstances the budget line of laborers will shift out everywhere as in Figure 5.7. Laborers will be better

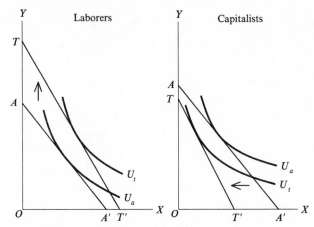

Figure 5.7

off even if they wish only to consume X, the good whose price has risen with trade. Conversely, the budget line of capitalists may shift in everywhere, due to the decrease in the price of capital and therefore to the decrease in capitalists' income. Capitalists thus lose from the income redistribution caused by trade.

A good example of income redistribution caused by international price changes occurred in the U.S. during the 1970s. The redistribution was between states and between economic groups and was due to the oil price increases that occurred during that decade. The energy-producing states realized huge gains from the price changes, while the energy-consuming states were certainly much worse off.

7. CONCLUDING REMARKS

In Sections 2, 3, and 4 of this chapter we showed that a country will gain from trade in an overall sense. We used community indifference curves to illustrate this gain, but in fact, they are not needed for the result. More advanced treatments will show that the gains-from-trade result is one of the most powerful and robust in all of international economics.

In Sections 5 and 6, however, we noted that the gains may be unevenly distributed among individuals in a country and that some individuals may, in fact, lose due to trade. This possibility is more likely, the greater the differences are among individuals' preferences and factor endowments. It is, therefore, not at all surprising to find certain groups in society opposing freer trade or asking for restrictions on imports.

Are these latter results consistent with the result concerning overall gains? The answer is clearly yes. What can be shown using more advanced techniques is that there will exist aggregate gains from trade such that, even if some individuals lose from trade, the gainers could always compensate the losers such that everyone is better off with free trade than with autarky. In terms of Figure 5.6, for example, it can be proved that the people who prefer Y are sufficiently better off that they could bribe or compensate the individuals who prefer X to accept free trade, so that everyone is better off. Similarly, in terms of Figure 5.7, it can be proved that the gains to the laborers exceed the losses to the capitalists, so that income could be redistributed in such a way that everyone is made better off with trade. It is only when such redistribution actually takes place that community indifference curves (if they exist) can be given a welfare interpretation, as noted in Chapter 3.

Much more will be said about this issue later in the book, and thus we will not dwell on the policy implications at great length here. Perhaps we can simply state in summary that although trade may make some individuals worse off, it can potentially make everyone better off. Thus, instead of restricting trade, it may be better for governments to search for a set of policies that, when combined with free trade, will ensure that the gains are widely distributed throughout society.

PROBLEMS

1. Show how equations (5.2) and (5.3) can be derived from equation (5.1).

2. Show that if the left-hand side of equation (5.1) is positive (there is a balance-of-payments deficit), then the right-hand side of equation (5.3) must be greater than the left-hand side.

3. With respect to Figure 5.2, show that if $p_a = p^*$, then there are no possibilities of gains from trade.

4. In the Liz and Frido example of Figure 5.3, convince yourself that if three bags of peanuts trade for two beers, the price of beer in terms of peanuts is 3/2 = 1.5, not 2/3 = .67.

5. With reference to Section 4, show that if there is no pattern of comparative advantage (production patterns are the same in the two countries), then no gains from specialization exist.

6. Redraw Figure 5.5 for the case in which the world price ratio is less than the autarky price ratio. (If you can't do this, you don't really understand the diagrams.)

7. Suppose we know that with trade the total amounts of both goods consumed exceed the amounts consumed in autarky. With reference to either Section 5 or 6, can you prove that the group that is better off with trade could compensate the losers, such that both groups end up better off relative to autarky?

NOTE

1. A more advanced analysis of the distribution of gains among individuals is given by Chacholiades (1978), Chapter 12.

REFERENCES

Chacholiades, M. (1978). *International Trade Theory and Policy.* New York: McGraw-Hill.

Kemp, M. C. (1969). *The Pure Theory of International Trade and Investment.* Englewood Cliffs, N.J.: Prentice-Hall.

Samuelson, P. A. (1939). "The Gains from International Trade." *Canadian Journal of Economics and Political Science* 5, 195–205.

———. (1962). "The Gains from International Trade Once Again." *Economic Journal* 72, 820–829.

two

CAUSES AND CONSEQUENCES OF TRADE

chapter **6**

The Causes of International Trade

1. THE NO-TRADE MODEL

Chapter 1 emphasized the fact that trade takes place between any economic units ultimately because of price differences. In terms of a simple partial equilibrium demand and supply analysis, it was argued that price differences could be due either to differences in demand or differences in supply. In Part One the aggregate counterparts of the partial equilibrium demand and supply curves were derived, and it was shown that, in a perfectly competitive system, the general-equilibrium commodity price ratio was determined by the interaction of the aggregate supply and aggregate demand relationships. The determination of equilibrium prices was illustrated by assuming conditions sufficient for the existence of community indifference curves and then showing that equilibrium would exist where the highest such commodity indifference curve was tangent to the production possibility curve. It is clear that if trade is to exist between nations, the autarky price ratios must differ, and that such price differences ultimately depend on the underlying supply and demand relationships. The focus of this section is the question of why trade takes place; thus we will concentrate on those factors that could give rise to differences in the demand and supply relations between countries.

A convenient method of examining the causes of trade is to begin by imagining a world in which there is no trade. In terms of our simple model, this would mean that all autarky price ratios were identical. While there are many configurations of demand and supply among countries that would give rise to this result, the simplest method of achieving identical autarky prices is to assume that identical demand and supply conditions prevail in all countries. Thus we begin by imagining a situation in which all countries have identical production possibility curves, and where the same set of community indifference curves prevails in all countries. We are thus assuming that all countries can be represented by the situation of Figure 6.1.

What assumptions are necessary in order that the demand and supply situations in all countries be identical? This question is easily answered by recalling from Chapters 2 and 3 the underlying assumptions that were made in deriving the production possibility curve and the community indifference curves. On the demand side it is sufficient to assume that identical and homogeneous tastes exist throughout the world. On the production side it was found that three things determine the position and shape of the production possibility curve—the degree of homogeneity, factor endowments, and the production functions. Thus to achieve identical production possibility curves in all countries, it is clearly sufficient to assume that all countries have the same linear homo-

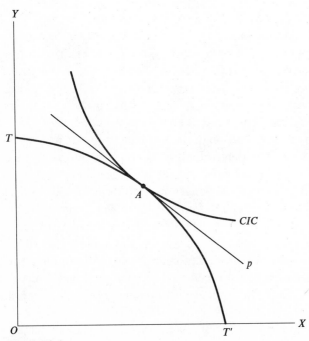

Figure 6.1

geneous production functions and that all countries have the same factor endowments. These assumptions will give the same aggregate demand and supply relationships in all countries, but there is one further restriction that we must impose. We are seeking conditions such that commodity price ratios will be the same in all countries, and this will only be the case if commodity prices are determined by aggregate demand and supply. We must, in other words, ensure that equilibrium prices are determined by the tangency between the highest community indifference curve and the production possibility curve as shown in Figure 6.1, and to ensure this we assume that there are no distortions in the model. We can thus write down a set of five conditions that will guarantee the no-trade situation. These are:

1. Identical production functions among countries
2. The same relative endowments in all countries
3. Constant returns to scale
4. Identical and homogeneous tastes in all countries
5. No distortions

While these five conditions clearly imply that there will be no trade, there are obviously many other models that could be invented in which autarky prices would be identical so that no trade would take place. In other words, while these assumptions are sufficient for no trade, they are by no means necessary. This is illustrated in Figure 6.2, where subscripts h and f refer to the home and foreign country, respectively. Production conditions are clearly different in the two countries, with H producing relatively more Y and F relatively more X at any common price ratio. Demand conditions also differ, however, and in the situation shown the differences in demand just offset the production conditions, leaving autarky prices identical.

These five conditions are important not simply because they describe a world in which there will be no trade, for such a situation is clearly not of much interest, but because they summarize the various things that can *cause* trade. If we have been efficient in deriving this set of no-trade conditions, in other words, if none of these five conditions could be dispensed with, then it is clear that the relaxation of any one of them will give rise to a situation in which trade will be possible. These five conditions can thus be thought of as the five broadly defined determinants of trade. Indeed, the next seven chapters will be a careful investigation of how the relaxation of these five assumptions can give rise to international trade, and the implications of the models so derived.

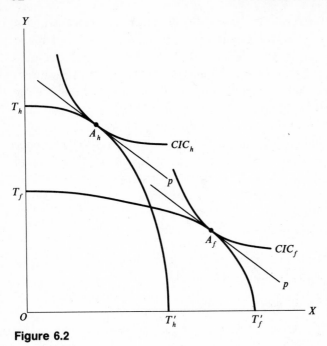

Figure 6.2

2. SOME METHODOLOGICAL CONSIDERATIONS

In the last section it was argued that the relaxation of any one of the five assumptions listed could give rise to a situation in which international trade could take place. The approach that will be employed will be to relax each of the assumptions in turn, maintaining all four of the others, and to examine the implications for international trade. For example, to examine the implications of taste differences, it will be assumed that while tastes differ among countries, all countries have the same production functions, that these production functions exhibit constant returns to scale, that endowments are proportional in all countries, and that there are no distortions in the model. The other four models will be treated in a similar fashion. This approach is sometimes criticized as being unrealistic, in the sense that the models so generated do not accurately describe the real world. To assess the relevance of this criticism, we must understand precisely why this approach is being employed, and what kind of conclusions we expect to be able to draw from the analysis.

At this stage of our discussion, our purpose is to isolate the various determinants of trade, and to examine the implications for the other variables in the model. It has been claimed that the relaxation of any one of the assumptions of Section 1 could give rise to international trade, and, this being the case, it is clear that no conclusions about a specific cause of trade could be derived unless we can be sure that no other things are causing trade at the same time. Thus one could not identify the effects of demand differences in a model in which endowments were also different, for in general, it would be impossible to separate the effects of these two variables. This is the situation of Figure 6.2, where the two conditions are offsetting and result in identical autarky prices. Our analysis can therefore be thought of as a kind of theoretical experiment, where, in order to study the effects of one variable, all other variables are neutralized. This kind of theoretical experiment is not unlike the notions in physics of balls falling in vacuums or objects sliding down frictionless planes. At this stage of the analysis, then, the question of whether the model is "realistic" is not a relevant one, for no claim has been made about its predictive powers. In each of the models considered the strict assumptions made are necessary in order to isolate the effects of the particular determinant being examined. The assumptions of no distortions, of identical production functions, and so on, are made, not as descriptions of the real world, but simply as a methodological device to allow individual determinants to be considered in isolation.

While the question of realism is not relevant for the kind of theoretical experiments that we have just described, if one is interested in empirical tests of trade models, one will be faced with the question of what assumptions are appropriate for a model used to explain real-world trade flows. If the implications of the various determinants of trade models are different, then ideally we would wish to include any variable which could cause trade. In practice, of course, some simplification will be necessary, and it will be very much up to the investigator to decide which of the variables he thinks are important and which are not, and how the model is to be constructed. These issues will be discussed in more detail in Chapter 13.

chapter 7

The Classical Model

1. A SIMPLE MODEL OF PRODUCTION FUNCTION DIFFERENCES

The determinants-of-trade question will be analyzed in the next five chapters of this part by relaxing, in turn, each of the five assumptions from Chapter 6 and examining the implications for international trade. The first model we consider is one in which production functions differ; an early example of such a model is the one developed by David Ricardo. The Ricardian model, however, does not conform precisely to the general approach outlined in the last chapter. The major difference is due to Ricardo's assumption that all commodities ultimately derive their value from the amount of labor input necessary for their production. Thus, while Ricardo recognized that capital was necessary for production, he argued that, because capital was produced, it was not a primary factor of production but simply reflected earlier uses of labor in production. Ricardo also recognized the existence of resources, but his approach was either to treat them as being included in the form of the production function or to assume that they did not impose a constraint on the production process. In Ricardo's model, then, the only effective constraint on production is labor, and the model developed from the use of this assumption has become known as the *labor theory of value.* In terms of the production functions of Chapter 2 this means that there is a single input to the production process of both commodities, and this in turn implies that the production possibility curve will be linear. As we will see later, this assumption significantly simplifies the analysis, and in particular, it will allow us to relax the restrictions we imposed on demand conditions.

2. THE LAWS OF ABSOLUTE AND COMPARATIVE ADVANTAGE

The Ricardian model, then, assumes that labor is the only constraint on the production process. Thus, assuming that two goods, X and Y, are produced, the production functions and the labor constraint can be written as

$$X = F_x(L_x) \tag{7.1}$$
$$Y = F_y(L_y) \tag{7.2}$$
$$\bar{L} = L_x + L_y. \tag{7.3}$$

Implicit in the Ricardian model is the assumption that production functions are homogeneous of the first degree, and this implies that equations (7.1) and (7.2) take the simple form

$$X = \alpha L_x \tag{7.4}$$
$$Y = \beta L_y \tag{7.5}$$

where α and β are some positive constants. The assumption that production functions differ between countries implies that the values of α and β will be different in the two countries. At this stage of the analysis no particular assumptions are required about the demand side of the model or about relative factor endowments, and the set of assumptions for the model is completed by assuming the absence of distortions and that labor, while perfectly mobile domestically, is completely immobile internationally.

The Ricardian approach was to argue not in terms of output per unit of input, but in terms of the input cost of a specified quantity of output. In terms of production functions (7.4) and (7.5) this means that we solve for L_x and L_y rather than for X and Y, and this gives equations (7.6) and (7.7):

$$L_x = 1/\alpha X \tag{7.6}$$
$$L_y = 1/\beta Y. \tag{7.7}$$

The Ricardian approach is illustrated in Table 7.1, where we show the labor cost of production of two commodities, X and Y, in two countries, H and F. It is assumed that in country H, 20 units of labor are required

Table 7.1   LABOR COST OF PRODUCTION

	X	Y
H	20	20
F	10	30

to produce some quantity of commodity X, whereas the same amount of X can be produced in country F with 10 units of labor. Commodity Y, on the other hand, requires 20 units of labor in country H and 30 units of labor in country F. Thus for country H we have $1/\alpha = 20$ ($\alpha = .05$) and $1/\beta = 20$ ($\beta = .05$), and for country F we have $1/\alpha = 10$ ($\alpha = .1$) and $1/\beta = 30$ ($\beta = .033$).

It can be shown that in this situation, profitable exchange is possible for both countries. Country F has a clear advantage in the production of X, while country H has an advantage in the production of commodity Y, and we can imagine a situation in which country F specializes in X and country H specializes in Y and in which consumers in both countries maximize their utility through international trade. In Table 7.1 country F is said to have an *absolute advantage* in the production of X and country H to have an *absolute advantage* in the production of Y.

Now consider Table 7.2, where again we show the labor costs of production for the two commodities in the two countries, but where we have changed the labor costs of production of both X and Y in country H to 5 units of labor rather than 20. Now country H is more efficient in the production of both commodities, and country H is said to have an absolute advantage in the production of both X and Y. The question that now arises is whether in this situation profitable trade is still possible. A little thought will convince us that it is, for we observe that while country F has an absolute disadvantage in the production of both commodities, there is a *comparative advantage* for F in the production of commodity X. In country F it takes 30 units of labor to produce a unit of Y and only 10 units of labor to produce a unit of X, which means that it costs the economy three times as much to produce a unit of Y as it does to produce a unit of X. Looking at it the other way around, a unit of X can be produced for a third of the cost of the production of a unit of Y. In country H, on the other hand, the labor costs of production of X and Y are identical.

These relative efficiency differences suggest the possibility of profitable exchange between these two countries. Suppose, for example, that world prices imply that two units of X exchange for one unit of Y, so that $P_X/P_Y = 1/2$. Country H will find it profitable to exchange at this ratio, for through exchange she can obtain two units of X for one unit of Y, while in

Table 7.2   LABOR COST OF PRODUCTION

	X	Y
H	5	5
F	10	30

production only one unit of X can be obtained by foregoing the production of one unit of Y. Country F will also find exchange profitable at this price ratio, for whereas in domestic production it costs three times as much to produce a unit of Y as to produce a unit of X, through international trade it costs only twice as much. Thus at the rate of exchange of $2X$ for $1Y$, country H will want to specialize in the production of Y and country F will want to specialize in the production of X. Of course, there is no reason to expect that this price ratio will result in an equilibrium, which would require that the amount of Y that country H wants to export is exactly equal to the amount of Y that country F wants to import, and that the excess demands and supplies of X balance. At this stage we do not have enough information to determine what the equilibrium price will actually be, for as of yet no assumptions have been made about demand. The rate of exchange of $2X$ for $1Y$ is just one of an infinite number of price ratios we could have chosen, all of which are equally likely at this stage of the analysis. From Table 7.2 we note that the domestic price ratio that would prevail in country H, that is, the autarky price ratio for country H, would be $1X$ for $1Y$. In country F the autarky price ratio would be $3X$ for $1Y$, so that the price of X in terms of Y is equal to one-third. We thus have $p_h = 1$ and $p_f = 1/3$, where p_h and p_f are the autarky price ratios in countries H and F, respectively. Recall that $p = p_x/p_y$. It is clear that any price ratio that falls between the autarky price ratios of the two countries is a candidate for the world equilibrium terms of trade. Writing the world terms of trade as p_w, we have

$$p_h \geq p_w \geq p_f. \tag{7.8}$$

Thus the world terms of trade must lie somewhere between the autarky price ratios of the two countries. Note that at any price ratio outside this range, both countries would want to specialize in the production of the same commodity, and this could not possibly lead to an equilibrium situation.

Table 7.2 and inequality (7.8) illustrate an interesting contrast between the determination of domestic autarky prices and the world equilibrium terms of trade. We have argued that the autarky price ratios will be determined by the relative efficiency of labor in the domestic economy, or in other words, will be determined entirely by domestic cost conditions.

The domestic cost conditions for the two countries define a range within which the world terms of trade must fall, but, without information on the demand side, the equilibrium world price ratio cannot be determined. Thus although domestic prices are determined entirely by cost, world prices are determined by demand, constrained by equation (7.8).

We have seen that absolute efficiency in production is not required in order that profitable trade take place. From Table 7.2 we saw that although country H had an absolute advantage in the production of both goods, it was, nevertheless, profitable for this country to specialize in commodity Y and import commodity X. Similarly, it was advantageous for country F to specialize in the production of X and import commodity Y. Although country F does not have an absolute advantage in the production of either of the two commodities, she has a comparative advantage in the production of X, in the sense that X can be produced relatively less expensively than it can in country H. Country F thus has a comparative advantage in the production of X, while country H has a comparative advantage in the production of Y. The observation that profitable international trade depends only on comparative advantage and not on absolute advantage was one of the major contributions made by Ricardo.

It has been argued that while domestic prices are determined by cost conditions, equilibrium world prices depend on demand conditions. To understand precisely why this is the case, suppose that in Table 7.2 we had compared two cities in the same country, rather than two countries. Assume, for example, that H and F were Chicago and Detroit, respectively. Would the same argument still apply? Would it still be profitable for Detroit to specialize in the production of X even though Chicago was absolutely more efficient in the production of this commodity? The answer is no, for if such efficient production processes for both X and Y existed in Chicago, we would expect that the entire production of both commodities would take place in this city. In other words, labor would never be used to produce X in Detroit when the same units of labor in Chicago could produce twice as much. Thus all labor would move to Chicago, and Detroit would cease to exist. Why does this same argument not apply for two countries? The answer is that different assumptions have been made about the mobility of labor in these two cases, and this turns out to be the crucial factor. Domestically, labor is assumed to be perfectly mobile and thus moves to the point where the most efficient production process exists. Internationally, on the other hand, labor is assumed to be completely immobile, and thus must make do with the production processes at hand. If, in the previous example, the assumption of the international immobility of labor had been relaxed, then the entire population of country F would have moved to country H to take advantage of the more efficient production techniques in that country. Thus in the domestic economy labor will move in order to ensure that the quantities of the two commodities that are produced are exactly equal to the quantities demanded. If in the domestic economy demand shifts from one commodity to another, labor will move from one industry to the other until production again exactly equals demand. In the international economy this kind of adjustment process is not possible, and equality between aggregate demands and supplies must be equated through changes in commodity prices.

3. THE PRODUCTION POSSIBILITY CURVE

Because the Ricardian analysis focused on the contributions of labor, the production processes were described in terms of labor inputs per unit of output. To facilitate the construction of the production possibility curves, we now invert this relationship and think in terms of output per unit of input. In order to construct the production possibility curve, we need the maximum possible levels of output for the two commodities, and to derive these we obviously need information on the total available supply. We will arbitrarily assume that the quantity of labor available for country H is 50 units, whereas the quantity of labor in country F is 150 units. These endowments of labor, along with the information of Table 7.2, give rise to Table 7.3, which shows the maximum producible quantities of the two commodities in the two countries. The entries in Table 7.3 are found by dividing the total labor supply by the labor costs of production of each commodity in each country. For country H this information is depicted diagrammatically in Figure 7.1. Note that because of constant returns to scale, the allocation of one-half the total labor supply to each industry would result in 5 units of Y and 5 units of X, and thus the production possibility curve is linear.

On the assumption that a set of community indifference curves exists, the equilibrium autarky position will be A, where the highest community indifference curve is tangent to the production possibility curve. The autarky equilibrium price ratio is tangent to the community indifference curve and the production possibility curve at point A, and thus lies along the production possibility curve. Note that the point of tangency between

Table 7.3 MAXIMUM PRODUCIBLE QUANTITIES

	X	Y
H	10	10
F	15	5

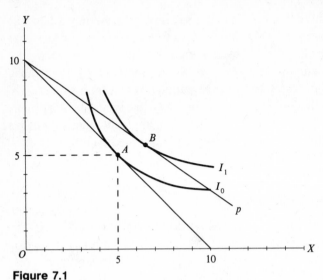

Figure 7.1

the community indifference curve and the production possibility curve is irrelevant for the determination of autarky prices, for wherever the tangency occurs autarky prices will be equal to the slope of the production possibility curve. This is a further illustration of the point made earlier that, in autarky, domestic prices are determined by cost conditions and are invariant with respect to demand. If the economy were allowed to trade at a price ratio such as p, producers would specialize in the production of Y and consumers would maximize utility by moving to a point such as B, the tangency between the price ratio p and the highest indifference curve. For price ratio lines less steep than the slope of the production possibility curve, specialization will always take place at Y, for specialization in X would result in a consumption point lying inside the production possibility curve, and this would result in a lower level of welfare than would be possible at autarky. Note that in Figure 7.1 point B is clearly to be preferred to point A, for it contains more of both commodities, and thus there is the potential to make every individual better off by a movement from A to B. Of course, as was shown in Chapter 5, gains from trade will exist even if B does not contain more of both commodities.

In Figure 7.2 the production possibility curves for both countries have been plotted in the same diagram. Note that for all price ratio lines such as p, flatter than the slope of the production possibility curve for country F, both countries would want to specialize in the production of Y. For price ratio lines steeper than the slope of the transformation curve for country H, both countries would wish to specialize in commodity X. Since the world equilibrium must imply production of both commodities,

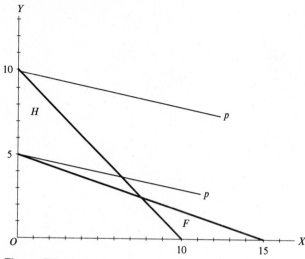

Figure 7.2

it is clear that the equilibrium terms of trade must lie between the slopes of the production possibility curves for the two countries.

4. THE INTERNATIONAL EQUILIBRIUM

Figure 7.2 illustrates the range in which the equilibrium world price ratio must fall; we now want to illustrate how this equilibrium price line can be found. The approach will be similar to that used to derive the offer curves in Chapter 4, and will begin by considering a variety of possible world price ratios and deriving, for each of them, the excess demands and supplies that would prevail. In Figure 7.3 the production possibility curve for country H has been redrawn, and the price lines p_1 and p_2 have been included. With these price lines, and indeed for any price line with slope less than 1, country H will be specialized in the production of commodity Y. The consumption points for price lines p_1 and p_2 will be C_1 and C_2 respectively, and the locus of all such points will be $AC_1C_2F_h$. The other branch of the offer curve could be constructed by considering price lines with slope greater than 1, implying production at T'. However, from the information of Figure 7.2 we know that equilibrium could never occur at price lines steeper than TT', for such price lines would result in specialization by both countries in commodity X. Thus the other branch of the offer curve is irrelevant for our present purposes.

In Figure 7.4, O_f is the origin for the production possibility curve of the foreign country, and the offer curve A_fF_f has been constructed in the manner described in Figure 7.3, except that this time price lines

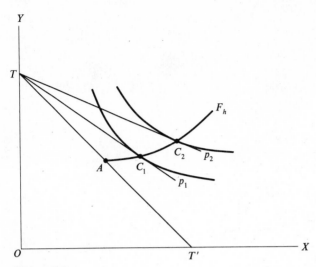

Figure 7.3

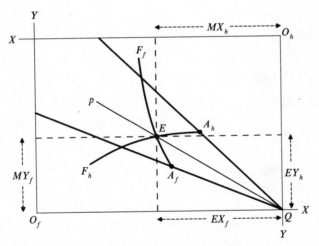

Figure 7.4

steeper than the production possibility curve have been assumed. Again, from Figure 7.2, we know that only price lines steeper than the production possibility curve of country F need be considered, for all other price lines would lead to the specialization of both countries of commodity Y. We now have the offer curve for both countries, and thus have information about the excess demands and supplies that would exist for all possible equilibrium price ratios. The next task is to combine this information in order to establish what the actual equilibrium price line will be. One such method is illustrated in Figure 7.4. Under the assumption that the foreign country will specialize in the production of commodity X and that the home country will specialize in the production of Y, the world production point can be found by inverting the diagram for country H and superimposing the two production points. Thus, from the point of view of the origin point O_f, the point O_h represents the world's supply of the two commodities, for O_fQ is the world production of X, while QO_h is the world production of Y. Now consider the price line from Q through point E, the intersection of the two offer curves. The offer curves, by definition, give the desired imports and exports of the two commodities for the two countries. Thus from price line p and offer curve A_fF_f we see that country F wants to export the quantity EX_f of commodity X and wants to import the quantity MY_f of commodity Y. For price line p and from the offer curve A_hF_h we see that the home country wishes to export the quantity EY_h of commodity Y and wishes to import the quantity MX_h of commodity X. It is clear that EX_f equals MX_h, and that EY_h equals MY_f, and thus world excess demands and supplies for both commodities are zero. Price line p is thus the equilibrium world terms of trade.

Although the method used here to derive the offer curves for the two countries may seem somewhat different from the one employed in Chapter 4, it is easy to show that the methods are, in fact, completely equivalent. In Figure 7.5 we have plotted the offer curves for the two countries from the origin rather than from the common production point Q as in Figure 7.4. Note that Figures 7.4 and 7.5 are identical except for the location of the origin, and the fact that in Figure 7.5 the production possibility curves for the two countries have not been included. These offer curves now more closely resemble the offer curves of Chapter 4, except for the linear portions OA_h and OA_f. The reason for the linear sections of the two offer curves can be seen from examining Figure 7.3. Although production and consumption points are unique for price ratio lines such as p_1 and p_2, if the price line is equal to the slope of the production possibility curve, then while the consumption point will be at A the production point could be anywhere along the curve TAT'. In other words, if the world terms of trade is TT' then domestic producers will be completely indifferent as to where along the curve TT' they choose to produce, and the corresponding trade triangles could be the origin, where there would be no trade, or the trade triangle OA_hB of Figure 7.5, or any other similar triangle between these two. For all such trade triangles the world terms of trade is equal to TT', and this gives rise to the linear section OA_h of the offer curve of Figure 7.5.

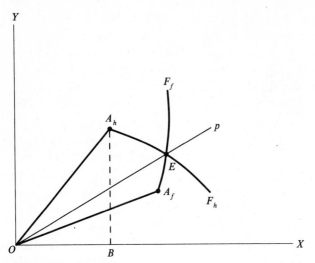

Figure 7.5

5. THE DETERMINANTS OF THE EQUILIBRIUM PRICE

We have seen how price is determined, and now want to investigate the determinants of what this price will actually be. The basic answer to this question is obvious; the price must ultimately depend on the demand and supply conditions in the two countries. To illustrate the effects of demand, suppose, in Figure 7.3, that there was a shift in the preferences of the residents of country H toward commodity X. This could be illustrated by shifting the entire set of indifference curves toward the X axis, and the result would be that the offer curve would also be shifted toward the X axis and would start at some point between A and T'. The effect of such a shift on the world equilibrium price ratio can be seen from Figure 7.6, which reproduces 7.5 and shows the original offer curve for the home country and the original equilibrium price with broken lines. With the shift in demand we have described, the new offer curve for the home country could be $OA'F'_h$, and this would result in a new equilibrium price line p'. Thus the increase in demand for commodity X in country H has resulted in an increase in the world equilibrium price of commodity X. This is what we would expect, and simply reflects the fact that at every price ratio line the world demand for commodity X is larger than it formerly was.

Country H exports commodity Y, and it is clear from Figure 7.6 that the relative price of Y has fallen. Such a reduction in the relative price of the export commodity is referred to as a deterioration in the terms of trade. It is obvious from Figure 7.6 that if demand continued to shift toward commodity X, this deterioration in the terms of trade for country

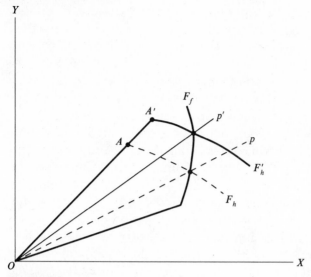

Figure 7.6

H would continue, and if the shift in demand were large enough, it is possible that the world equilibrium price ratio could become coincident with the production possibility curve for country H. This implies that even though trade is taking place, country H is consuming at the autarky point, which means that country H receives no benefit from international trade. In general, shifts in demand toward the import commodity will tend to deteriorate the terms of trade and reduce the gains from trade.

On the production side, one of the things that will influence the equilibrium terms of trade will be the size of the countries. Given the production functions and the fact that there is a single factor of production, the determinant of the size of the country will be the labor force. Suppose, in terms of Figure 7.3, that the labor force for country H increases. This would result in an outward and parallel shift of the production possibility curve, and because of the assumed homogeneity of preferences, the new situation will simply be a scaled-up version of Figure 7.3. The new equilibrium can also be illustrated in Figure 7.6. Because country H has increased in size, the autarky demands for both X and Y will have increased, and this means that the distance OA' must be longer than OA. The effect of this change in the size of country H has been to reduce the relative price of Y, and thus the change has again resulted in a deterioration in the terms of trade for country H. This is the expected result, for an increase in the size of country H has increased the demand for both commodities, and in particular has increased the demand for X, the good that country H imports. Any such increase in the demand for the imported commodity would be expected to increase its price, or in other words, would be expected to reduce the price of the export commodity, thus deteriorating the terms of trade. We can thus conclude that an increase in the labor force in one country relative to the other would be expected to deteriorate its terms of trade. Note, however, that although there has been a deterioration in the terms of trade, this does not necessarily imply that the aggregate consumption bundle for country H is smaller than it was formerly. World production has increased, and thus it is quite possible that both countries will be consuming larger quantities than they did in the original situation. On the other hand, it is clear that per capita consumption in country H will have fallen, for in terms of the original population the terms of trade have deteriorated, and this will imply consumption on a lower community indifference curve. In Figure 7.3 this would imply, for the original inhabitants, a consumption shift such as implied by the shift from p_2 to p_1. Thus, under the assumption that the additions to the labor force have the same preferences as the original consumers, it is obvious that this increase in the size of the country has resulted in a per capita reduction in consumption and a reduction in welfare for all consumers.

The other major determinant of equilibrium prices on the production side will be the forms of the production functions, and in general, changes would be expected to change the slope of the production possibility curves. In particular, an improvement in technology in country H, in terms of Figure 7.3, would increase the maximum amount of Y that could be produced, thus moving T farther from the origin and increasing the slope of TT'. Similarly, an improvement in the technology in the X industry would shift point T' farther from the origin and would result in a reduction in the slope of the production possibility curve. Note, in Figure 7.4, that small improvements in technology in the X industry will have no immediate effect on the equilibrium terms of trade. The reason for this is quite simple; because country H does not produce any X, changes in the technology of this industry are clearly irrelevant. On the other hand, changes in the technology of industry Y, the export industry, clearly will have an effect on the equilibrium price ratio. The effect will be similar to an increase in population, in that it implies a shift out in the production possibility curve, but combined with that shift there will be a change in the slope of the production possibility curve. The final result will be a deterioration in the terms of trade, but this again will be combined with an increase in world output, and it is quite possible that both countries will consume more in the new equilibrium situation. Note that in this case if aggregate consumption for country H increases, this implies an improvement in the welfare of all consumers, for the labor force has not increased.

The models that have so far been described have shown the equilib-

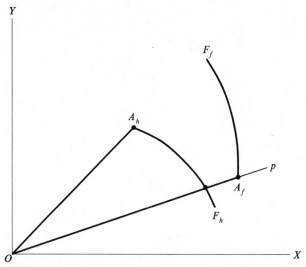

Figure 7.7

rium world price line lying strictly between the cost ratios for the two
countries. It is clear from both the discussion of the effects of differences in
taste and from the analysis of changes in production conditions that the
equilibrium world terms of trade might become equal to the ratio of
domestic cost in either of the two countries. Figure 7.7 shows a case in
which country H is small relative to country F, so that the intersection of
the offer curves for the two countries does not result in a price ratio line
lying strictly between the ratios of their domestic costs. In Figure 7.7 the
offer curve for country F is OA_fF_f, while the offer curve for country H is
OA_hF_h. This implies that the equilibrium world terms of trade will be p, the
domestic cost ratio for country F. Equilibrium price ratios lying strictly
between the cost ratios of the two countries are only possible if both
countries have the capability of producing a large enough quantity of one of
the goods to satisfy total world demand. When one country is small relative
to the other, as in Figure 7.7, this is no longer possible. Total world demand
for commodity Y is larger than the amount that the small country can
produce. The large country must therefore produce some of both commodities, and the only price line that would lead to this result is the price line
tangent to the production possibility curve of the large country.

PROBLEMS

1. Can the notion of comparative advantage apply to trade among individuals?
Suppose a lawyer is a better typist than her secretary. Who should do the
typing? Why?

2. For Table 7.1 suppose that both countries have 120 units of labor. Draw the production possibility sets for both and find the possible range of equilibrium commodity prices.

3. Assume that the total available supply of labor in H and F is 50 units and 150 units, respectively. Using equations (7.4) and (7.5) show that Table 7.3 can be derived from Table 7.2.

4. Suppose, for Table 7.3, that the quantity of labor available in both H and F is doubled. How will this affect Figure 7.2 and Figure 7.4? Will the equilibrium price be affected?

5. Show that the answer to problem 4 depends on whether tastes are homogeneous.

6. (a) Use the technique developed in Chapter 4, Section 5, to show that the equilibrium E in Figure 7.5 is stable.
   (b) Construct an offer curve diagram that has an unstable equilibrium.
   (c) Does the existence of an unstable equilibrium imply that stable equilibria also exist?

7. Show that even if one country is small, as in Figure 7.7, for certain demand conditions both countries could gain from trade.

REFERENCES

Chipman, J. S. (1965). "A Survey of the Theory of International Trade: Part 1, The Classical Theory." *Econometrica* 33, 477–519.

Graham, F. D. (1948). *The Theory of International Value.* Princeton: Princeton University Press.

Melvin, J. R. (1969). "On a Demand Assumption Made by Graham." *Southern Economic Journal* 36, 36–43.

———. (1969). "Mill's Law of International Value." *Southern Economic Journal* 36, 107–16.

Ricardo, D. (1817). *On the Principles of Political Economy and Taxation.* London: John Murray.

chapter *8*

The Endowment Model

1. THE EFFECTS OF ENDOWMENT DIFFERENCES

In Chapter 6 a set of assumptions was presented that resulted in a no-trade situation, and in Chapter 7 it was shown that the relaxation of one of these assumptions, namely, the assumption that production functions were the same between countries, could result in international trade. In this chapter the assumption that endowments are the same will be relaxed, and the implications for international trade will be examined. It is important to note that the other four assumptions are being retained; in particular, it will be assumed that production functions are the same among countries but differ among goods, that there are constant returns to scale, that tastes are homogeneous and identical among countries, and that there are no distortions. Other assumptions will be introduced as required.

It should be emphasized that we are concerned with *relative* endowments and that the absolute size of countries is not important. We are thus concerned with the capital-labor ratios in the two countries, and in particular, we assume that the capital-labor ratio in country H is greater than it is in country F. This gives equation (8.1):

$$(K/L)_h > (K/L)_f. \tag{8.1}$$

To illustrate the effect of endowment differences we begin by considering the case where endowments are the same for two countries, H and

F. This endowment point is represented by point E of Figure 8.1, and for this point the maximum producible quantities of X and Y are $\bar{X}$ and $\bar{Y}$. These two maximum output points are shown in Figure 8.2; the corresponding production possibility curve could be $\bar{Y}\bar{X}$. We now consider the effect of changing the endowment point for one of the two countries; specifically, we will assume that the endowment point for the home country is E_h. Note that E_h and $E = E_f$ satisfy equation (8.1), for we have increased the capital endowment and reduced the labor endowment for

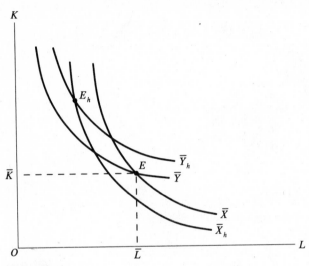

Figure 8.1

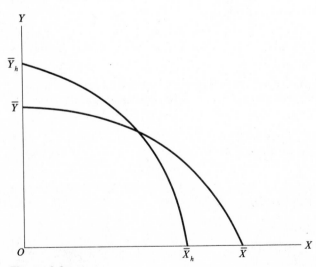

Figure 8.2

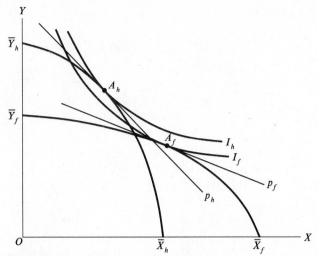

Figure 8.3

country H. There will be an isoquant for both industries passing through point E_h, and these will give the new maximum levels of output of the two commodities. It is clear from the diagram that the isoquant through E_h for commodity Y will lie above Y, whereas the isoquant for commodity X will lie below $\bar{X}$. These two isoquants are represented by $\bar{Y}_h$ and $\bar{X}_h$, respectively, and produce the two points $\bar{Y}_h$ and $\bar{X}_h$ of Figure 8.2. We note that the increase in the endowment of capital and the reduction in the endowment of labor has resulted in a rise in the maximum output of Y, the capital-intensive commodity, and a reduction in the maximum output of X, the labor-intensive commodity.

In Figure 8.3 we have reproduced the production possibility curves for the two countries and have added the two indifference curves that show the autarky equilibrium points. For the foreign country, the highest community indifference curve is tangent at A_f, while A_h is the autarky equilibrium point for the home country. Because of our assumption that tastes are identical and homogeneous for both countries, which implies that the slopes of the indifference curves are the same along any ray from the origin, in autarky the equilibrium price ratio line will be steeper in country H than in country F. These autarky price ratios, the price ratio line tangent jointly to the production possibility curve and the highest community indifference curve at the autarky point, are p_f and p_h for countries F and H, respectively. Thus in autarky we have

$$p_h > p_f. \tag{8.2}$$

Recall that p is defined to be p_x/p_y.

2. THE HECKSCHER-OHLIN MODEL[1]

Figure 8.3 shows the autarky equilibrium point for the two countries of our model. We now want to examine the implications of opening up the model to allow international trade. From equation (8.2) we see that in autarky the relative price of X is higher in country H than it is in country F. When international trade is permitted, the domestics of country H will observe that the price of commodity X is cheaper in the foreign country than it is at home, and the domestics of country F will observe that the price of Y is relatively cheap in the home country. Thus there will be an incentive for residents of country H to shift some of their purchases of commodity X to the foreign country, and an incentive for residents of country F to purchase commodity Y in the home country. Indeed, as long as the price of a commodity is lower in one country than it is in another, consumers will continue to shift from purchasing goods in the high-priced market to purchasing them in the market where prices are lower. Of course, this shift in demand also implies a shift in production. In country H, because consumers in the foreign country are now bidding for some of the domestic output of commodity Y, and because some domestics in H are purchasing X in the foreign country, the production point in country H will shift toward the Y axis. Furthermore, because the slope of the production possibility curve becomes flatter as we move toward the Y axis, this shift in production implies that in the home country the price ratio will fall. An exactly analogous argument can be made for country F. Because there is an overall increase in the demand for commodity X, and an overall decrease in the demand for commodity Y, the production point in country F will shift toward the X axis. Because such movements imply an increase in the slope of the production possibility curve, the result will be an increase in the slope of the price ratio line.

Under the assumption that there are no impediments to international trade, this process will continue until the excess demands and supplies for both commodities in both countries have been satisfied. Production will continue to change until trade has equalized price ratios in the two countries. Thus the first important point to be observed is that, under the assumption that there are no impediments to trade, trade will result in the equalization of commodity prices in the two countries. But the equality of prices in the two countries does not, by itself, imply that a new equilibrium position has been reached. We must impose the further condition that world excess demands and supplies of the two countries be zero, or in other words, that the amount that one country wants to export will be exactly equal to the amount the other country wants to import. Such a

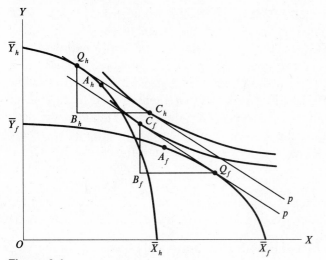

Figure 8.4

situation is illustrated in Figure 8.4, where the price ratio line p is tangent to the production possibility curve for country H at point Q_h and tangent to the production possibility curve for country F at Q_f. Note that these two price lines, while not coincident, have the same slope, and therefore represent the same relative prices in the two countries. These two price lines are tangent to community indifference curves at C_h and C_f for countries H and F, respectively. In country H the production of commodity Y is greater than the desired consumption by the distance $Q_h B_h$, while in country F desired consumption is greater than production by the distance $B_f C_f$. Similarly, in the home country the consumption of X is higher than the production of X by the distance $B_h C_h$, while in the foreign country production of X is higher than consumption by $B_f Q_f$. Since $Q_h B_h = C_f B_f$ and $B_h C_h = B_f Q_f$, the trade triangles for the two countries are identical, so that world demands and supplies for both commodities are equal, and the situation shown in Figure 8.4 represents a world trade equilibrium. Note that because of our assumptions of the homogeneity of tastes and constant returns to scale production functions, the equilibrium position will be expected to be both unique and stable. The reader could easily verify that a reduction in the slope of the price ratio line in both countries would result in an excess demand for commodity X and an excess supply of commodity Y. This would result in an increase in the price of commodity X and a reduction in the price of commodity Y, and the original equilibrium position, as shown in Figure 8.4, would be reestablished. If the price ratio line were more steep than the one shown in Figure 8.4, there would be an excess demand for commodity Y and an excess supply of commodity X; the price of Y would rise, the price of X would fall, and equilibrium would again be reestablished.

We have shown that, for a trade equilibrium, two conditions are necessary; prices in the two countries must be identical, and trade must be balanced. Figure 8.4 also shows what the pattern of trade will be. We note that country H, which is relatively well endowed with capital, is exporting Y, the commodity that uses K intensively. Similarly, country F, which is relatively well endowed with labor, is exporting X, the commodity that is labor-intensive. We thus can state the Heckscher-Ohlin theorem.

The Heckscher-Ohlin Theorem

Given the assumptions of the model, a country will export the commodity that uses its abundant factor most intensively.

The reader will have noted that some assumptions have been added to the original list of five given in Chapter 6. First, we have assumed that there are no impediments to trade. This implies that there are no tariffs or quotas, which is an assumption about what kind of economic policies the two countries pursue. The no-impediments assumption, however, also implies that there are no transportation costs between the two countries, and this is clearly at variance with what we observe in the real world. It is thus important to note that the assumption of no transportation costs is not crucial for the statement of the Heckscher-Ohlin theorem. The introduction of transportation costs would mean that prices in the two countries would not become equal, but rather, would differ by the amount of the transportation cost. This would result in smaller trade triangles in Figure 8.4 but would not affect the basic conclusions about the patterns of trade. However, although the assumption of no transportation costs is not crucial for the Heckscher-Ohlin theorem, we will see in later sections that certain theorems derived from this model do depend on this assumption.

Another assumption implicitly made but not yet discussed is that there is no factor mobility between the two countries. As we will show in the following section, in the autarky positions where commodity price ratios differ and where production functions are identical between countries, factor prices will also differ. This could result in movements of factors from one country to another in order to take advantage of higher returns. Any such movements will result in changes in the basic shape of the production possibility curves in the two countries, and would thus make the analysis considerably more complex. Such factor movements, however, would not invalidate the Heckscher-Ohlin theorem, although they could result in the complete elimination of international trade. The effect of factor mobility is examined in detail in Chapter 19. A final assumption that has been implicitly included is the assumption that there are no factor intensity reversals. The importance of this assumption will be fully considered in Section 7.

We have seen that the Heckscher-Ohlin theorem, when the appropriate assumptions are made about tastes and technology, permits an unambiguous statement of how trade flows depend on relative factor endowments. This model involves much more than just trade flows and endowments, however. As has already been seen from Figure 8.4, in equilibrium a unique set of commodity prices is determined. These commodity prices, in turn, can be shown in certain circumstances to determine relative factor prices, and relationships between changes in commodity prices and real factor rewards can also be derived. In circumstances where commodity prices are fixed, a relationship between changes in factor endowments and output changes can also be derived. The remaining sections of this chapter will investigate these effects.

3. THE FACTOR-PRICE-EQUALIZATION THEOREM

The factor-price-equalization theorem states that, given a certain set of assumptions, the equalization of commodity prices through trade will result in the equalization of relative factor returns. In other words, given the appropriate assumptions, if the ratio of commodity prices is equal in two countries, then the wage-rental ratio will be equal as well. Indeed, the factor-price-equalization theorem is essentially a demonstration of the fact that the wage-rental ratio can be written as a single-valued function of the commodity price ratio, or in other words,

$$w/r = G(p_x/p_y). \tag{8.3}$$

Here G is a function that depends on the production functions for the two commodities, and with production functions identical between countries, G would be identical as well. Thus, given the fact that trade equalizes the commodity price ratio between countries, the wage-rental ratio will also be equalized.

The factor-price-equalization theorem is most easily illustrated by introducing the concept of the *unit-value isoquant.* In Figure 8.5 we have chosen an isoquant for each industry such that the value of output for the two industries is exactly the same. Thus the output of X times the price of X equals the output of Y times the price of Y, and with prices p_x and p_y we have

$$X_0 p_x = Y_0 p_y. \tag{8.4}$$

Thus, given a set of commodity prices, we simply choose the levels of output for X and Y such that equation (8.4) is satisfied. Note that because of the assumption of homogeneity of the first degree, it makes no difference what levels of output are chosen, as long as equation (8.4) is satisfied.

In Figure 8.5 we have also included the isocost lines for an arbitrarily chosen pair of factor prices. Given factor prices, the slopes of the isocost lines are determined, and the condition for cost minimization is that the isocost lines be tangent to the isoquants. It is clear, however, that the situation shown in Figure 8.5 cannot be an equilibrium at which both commodities are produced. Because the cost line tangent to X_0 is farther from the origin than the cost line tangent to Y_0, and since isocost lines represent lines of equal cost, it must be true that the cost associated with the production of X_0 is higher than the cost associated with the production of Y_0. However, by the definition of the unit-value isoquants, we know that the values of X_0 and Y_0 are identical. In this model with constant returns to scale and perfect competition, total cost must equal total revenue, and for Figure 8.5 this condition cannot hold for both X_0 and Y_0. If it holds for Y_0, then it must be true that the cost of producing X_0 is greater than the revenue that could be received from selling this quantity of output, and thus X_0 would never be produced. If total revenue is equal to total cost for industry X, then in industry Y profits are being made and this cannot be an equilibrium situation. It can thus be seen that an equilib-

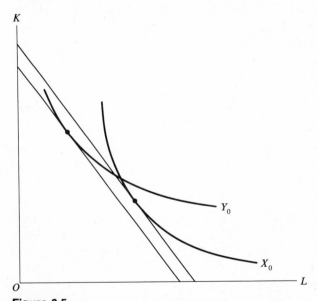

Figure 8.5

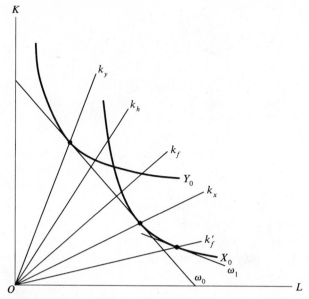

Figure 8.6

rium in which both commodities are being produced, and such that total revenue is just equal to total cost in both industries, requires that the same isocost line be tangent to both unit-value isoquants. Such a situation is shown in Figure 8.6. The points of tangency between the two unit-value isoquants and the isocost line give the capital-labor ratios for the two industries.

The capital-labor ratios shown in Figure 8.6 are the same capital-labor ratios shown in the factor box diagram of Figure 2.9, and they give the ratios in which capital and labor are used in the production processes for commodities Y and X. The area between the two capital-labor ratios is referred to as the *cone of diversification*. If both commodities are produced it will be true that the *average* capital-labor ratio for the two commodities must lie between k_y and k_x. Furthermore, this average capital-labor ratio must be just the endowment ratio for the economy as a whole. Thus, if both goods are produced, the economywide capital-labor ratio must lie between k_y and k_x. Putting this the other way around, if the overall endowment ratio lies between k_y and k_x, then the economy will produce some of both X and Y. Furthermore, given the prices assumed when the unit value isoquants of Figure 8.6 were defined, the wage-rental ratio will be w_0, the line tangent to both X_0 and Y_0 in Figure 8.6.

Figure 8.6 illustrates one of the conditions required in order that the equalization of commodity prices results in the equalization of wage-rental ratios. Under the assumptions of the Heckscher-Ohlin model, production functions among countries are identical, so that if trade equalizes commodity prices, then unit-value isoquants for all countries must also be identical. Thus in our two-country model, isoquants Y_0 and X_0 represent the unit-value isoquants for both country H and country F. Now suppose k_h is the overall capital-labor ratio for country H, and that k_f is the capital-labor ratio for country F. Because both overall endowment ratios are within the cone of diversification, both countries face the same wage-rental ratio, namely, ω_0. Thus, with the same production functions, if trade equalizes commodity prices and if both countries are in the same cone of diversification, then wage-rental ratios will be equalized as well. This is the essence of the factor-price-equalization theorem. Note that if the endowment of one country lies outside the cone of diversification, and is k_f' for example, although commodity prices might well be equalized by trade, wage-rental ratios would not, for it is clear that $\omega_0 > \omega_1$. The relationships among endowments, commodity outputs, and factor prices will be discussed in more detail in Section 6.

In the example of Figure 8.6 the statement that the endowments of both countries lie in the same cone of diversification is equivalent to the statement that both countries produce both goods. This equivalence, while true in the situation shown, need not be true in general. It is shown in Section 7 that if factor intensity reversals exist, there may be two or more cones of diversification. If the two countries are in different cones, then both may produce both goods but factor prices will not be the same. Of course, even if there are two cones of diversification, if the endowment ratios for both countries fell in the same cone, then the situation would be analogous to Figure 8.6 and factor prices would be equalized. Thus the presence of factor intensity reversals does not preclude the possibility that trade will equalize factor prices; it simply means that the theorem is not true in general. From the preceding discussion we can now state the factor-price-equalization theorem.

The Factor-Price-Equalization Theorem

If

1. production functions are the same between countries,
2. production functions are homogeneous of the first degree,
3. there are no distortions,
4. there are no impediments to trade such as tariffs, quotas, or transportation costs,
5. both commodities are produced in both countries in equilibrium, and
6. there are no factor intensity reversals,

then free trade, through the equalization of relative commodity prices, will equalize relative factor prices.

4. THE RYBCZYNSKI THEOREM

The Rybczynski theorem is concerned with the relationship between changes in endowments and changes in the outputs of the two commodities, when commodity prices are assumed to be given. The theorem essentially states that, given relative commodity prices and assuming that both commodities continue to be produced, an increase in the endowment of one factor will increase the output of the commodity that uses that factor most intensively and will reduce the output of the other commodity. The theorem is most easily demonstrated through the use of the factor box diagram of Figure 8.7. It has origins O_x and O_y and reproduces Figure 2.9, except that the efficiency locus has been omitted. It will be recalled that point A represents the common tangency between an isoquant from each of the two industries. The ratios k_y and k_x represent the capital-labor ratios for industries Y and X, respectively, and are the same capital-labor ratios shown in Figures 8.6.

We now assume that the endowment of labor is increased by the amount ΔL, and we have represented this by shifting the origin for commodity Y from O_y to O'_y. We are interested in how this change in endowments will affect the outputs of the two commodities. The first point to be noted is that because commodity prices are not changed, the capital-labor ratios in the two industries are also unchanged. This can be seen from Figure 8.6. There, as we previously observed, the unit-value isoquants, and therefore the wage-rental ratio, will be unchanged as long as commodity prices do not change. In terms of Figure 8.7 this implies that, even though the endowment of labor has increased, k_x does not change

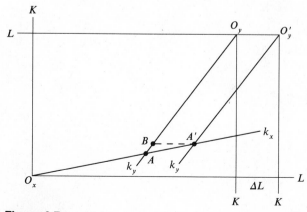

Figure 8.7

and k_y shifts in a parallel fashion as the origin O_y shifts to O'_y. Thus AO_y is parallel to $A'O'_y$. Note that A' is the new equilibrium position, and that there will be a new efficiency locus $O_x A'O'_y$ (not shown).

The effects of the increase in the labor supply can easily be seen from Figure 8.7. Since A' is farther from O_x than A, it is obvious that the output of commodity X has increased. That the output of commodity Y has decreased can be seen by drawing, from A', a line $A'B$ parallel to the L axis. Since BO_y is equal to $A'O'_y$ we see that $AO_y > A'O'_y$, implying that A' is on a lower Y isoquant than A so that the output of Y has decreased. We can thus state the Rybczynski theorem.

The Rybczynski Theorem

Given that production functions are homogeneous of the first degree, if commodity prices are given, and if both commodities continue to be produced, then an increase in the supply of a factor will lead to an increase in the output of the commodity using that factor intensively and a decrease in the output of the other commodity.

The Rybczynski theorem can be illustrated by the production possibility diagram of Figure 8.8. An increase in the endowment of labor will shift out the production possibility curve from $\overline{Y}\overline{X}$ to $\overline{Y'}\overline{X'}$, and since X is the labor-intensive commodity, we would expect that the maximum producible quantity of X would increase more than the maximum producible quantity of Y. The equilibrium production point in the initial situation is A, the point where the price line p is tangent to the production

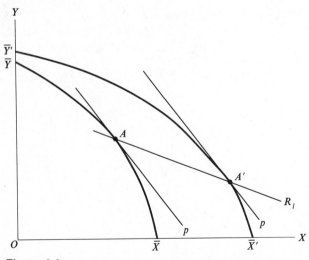

Figure 8.8

possibility curve. After the increase in the labor supply, and for the same price ratio p, the new equilibrium position will be A'. We note that A' implies a larger output of X but a smaller output of Y, and this is consistent with the conclusion reached from Figure 8.7.

The line R_l through A and A' is called the Rybczynski line and shows how output changes as one factor changes with given commodity prices. A similar line for increases in K could be constructed that would show increases in Y and reductions in X. The Rybczynski lines will be linear if constant returns to scale are assumed for both industries.

Note that the Rybczynski theorem does not really say anything about international trade, for nowhere have trade flows been considered. At the same time, one of the assumptions of the model is that commodity prices do not change, and this would not be expected to be the case unless international markets were determining the price ratio faced by this particular country.

5. THE STOLPER-SAMUELSON THEOREM

In the discussion of the factor-price-equalization theorem it was shown that under certain circumstances a given configuration of commodity prices would uniquely determine relative factor rewards. The principal thrust of the Stolper-Samuelson theorem is to show the relationship between changes in commodity prices and changes in factor rewards. It will come as no surprise to the thoughtful student to learn that there is a unique relationship between changes in relative commodity prices and relative factor returns, and that this relationship depends on technology; what is somewhat more surprising is that this determinate relationship applies to real factor rewards as well as to relative factor rewards.

The relationship between relative commodity prices, p, and relative factor returns, ω, is easily established in Figures 8.9 and 8.10. In Figure 8.9, p_a is the initial equilibrium commodity price ratio giving rise to production at point A with Y_a and X_a the quantities of Y and X, respectively. In the factor box diagram of Figure 8.10, the corresponding production point is again A, which, of course, is the point of tangency between the X_a and Y_a isoquants. The slope of the common tangent at point A is ω_a, the equilibrium wage-rental ratio. Note that given the endowments, technology, and the assumption of constant returns to scale, there is a unique ω for each p for which some of both goods are produced.

Now suppose there is a relative increase in the price of commodity X to p_b leading to production at point B. The outputs of X will rise and of Y will fall, and in the factor box diagram the corresponding point will be B. The question now is how will the ω at B compare to ω_a? The answer

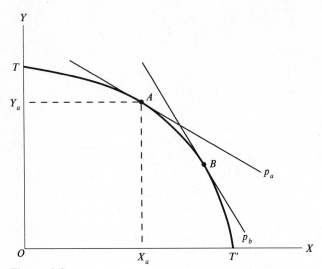

Figure 8.9

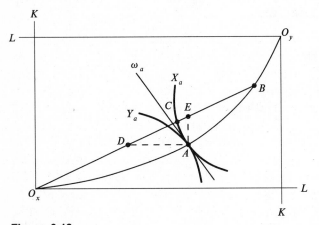

Figure 8.10

is straightforward when one remembers that, for constant-returns-to-scale production functions, all isoquants have a constant slope along any ray from the origin. Thus the slope of ω_b must be the same as the slope of X_a at C, and thus $\omega_b > \omega_a$.

In the situation represented in Figure 8.10, it has been assumed that commodity X is labor-intensive. Recalling that $\omega = w/r$, we thus see that an increase in the relative price of a commodity (in this case, X) will increase the relative reward of the factor used intensively in that industry (in this case, labor).

While this relationship between commodity prices and relative factor rewards is interesting, a much stronger result can also be derived. In particular, it can be shown that, with a relative increase in the price of X, the wage rate, measured in terms of the price of either X or Y, will rise, whereas the return on capital, measured in terms of either commodity price, will fall. Thus we wish to show that both w/p_x and w/p_y increase and that both r/p_x and r/p_y decrease when p_x/p_y increases.

A condition for profit maximization embedded in the optimization procedure assumed throughout is that firms will pay each factor the value of their marginal product. Thus for labor and capital in the X industry we must have, respectively, that $MP_l \cdot p_x = w$ and $MP_k \cdot p_x = r$. These can alternatively be written as

$$MP_l = \frac{w}{p_x} \tag{8.5}$$

$$MP_k = \frac{r}{p_x}. \tag{8.6}$$

A similar pair of conditions hold for the Y industry. Since these equations must hold in equilibrium, it is clear that showing that both w/p_x and w/p_y increase is equivalent to showing that the MP_l increases in both industries. Similarly, r/p_x and r/p_y will both decrease if, and only if, the MP_k falls in both industries. The final piece of information needed to establish our proposition is the result, from Chapter 2, that for constant returns-to-scale production functions, the slopes of the isoquant, and thus the marginal products, are constant along any ray from the origin.

Now again consider the movement from A to B in Figure 8.10. We wish to establish, first, how the marginal product of labor will have been affected by such a change. Since the marginal products of both capital and labor are constant along the line $O_x CB$, any point on this line can be used to establish our result. Thus consider point D where the line AD is parallel to the L axis. A movement from A to D thus involves a reduction in the amount of L used in the production of X, with no change in the input of K. Recall from Chapter 2 that the law of diminishing returns applies to such movements, and that a movement from A to D is a movement down the total product curve for labor. In Figure 8.11 a typical total product curve for L is shown, with points A and D corresponding to those of Figure 8.10. The slope of the total product curve is, of course, the marginal product, and thus we see that the MP_l at D is higher than the MP_l at A. Recall that the movement from A to D is equivalent, from the point of view of the marginal products, to a movement from A to B. We thus have established the result that the relative increase in the price of X (A to B in Figure 8.9) has increased the MP_l and, from equation (8.5), has increased w/p_x.

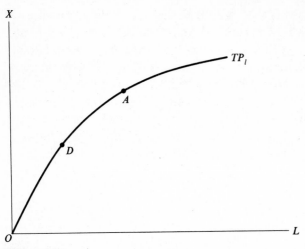

Figure 8.11

Now consider the movement from A to E in Figure 8.10, recalling again that anything true about the marginal products at E is equally true at B. The movement from A to E represents an increase in the use of K in industry X with an unchanged labor input. This movement to the right along the total-product-of-capital curve of Figure 8.12 implies, by the law of diminishing returns, a reduction in the MP_k. This in turn implies from equation (8.6) that r/p_x falls. Thus we have the desired results for both factors in the X industry.

Now consider factors in the Y industry. An identical argument could be constructed, but fortunately, a shortcut is possible. Note that the movement from A to B in Figure 8.10 (or to any other point on $O_x B$) was

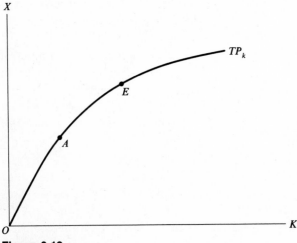

Figure 8.12

a movement from a point on the k_x ratio O_xA to a point on the k_x ratio O_xB. Thus the results we have derived depend on the fact that the capital-labor ratio has increased in the X industry. Indeed it can be shown that *any* increase in the capital-labor ratio must reduce the real return to capital and increase the real return to labor. But now consider the Y industry. The movement from A to B also involves an increase in the capital-labor ratio, and thus the effects on the marginal products and therefore on the real return to the factors is exactly the same as for the X industry. We have thus established the Stolper-Samuelson theorem.

The Stolper-Samuelson Theorem

Given the assumptions of constant returns to scale and no distortions, a relative increase in the price of a commodity will increase the real return to the factor used intensively in that industry and will reduce the real return of the other factor.

It should be noted that this statement of the theorem is not exactly that of the original presentation. Stolper and Samuelson were concerned with the effects of tariffs on real factor rewards. Tariffs, of course, would generally be expected to affect directly relative commodity prices, and when the direction of the price change has been determined, the argument follows as before. This topic will be taken up again in the discussion of tariffs.

One final observation: The Stolper-Samuelson theorem as presented here is not really a theorem about international trade, for no mention has been made of trade flows nor of the existence of trade partners. Although, as has just been argued, the results could be due to tariff changes, they could just as well be due to internal changes in a closed economy. Changes in commodity taxes or fundamental shifts in consumer preferences, for example, could have been the reason for the commodity price change. And because this is essentially a single-country, production-side result, several of the assumptions found necessary for the Heckscher-Ohlin theorem are not required here. Thus neither tastes nor production functions need be the same between countries, and no assumptions about factor intensity reversals are required. Indeed the only assumptions needed are constant returns to scale and the absence of distortions.

*6. ENDOWMENTS, OUTPUTS, AND PRICES

This section continues the discussion of the relationship among factor endowments, commodity outputs, factor prices, and commodity prices,

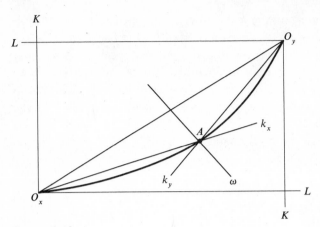

Figure 8.13

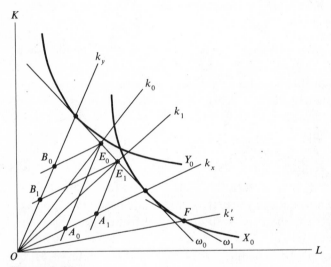

Figure 8.14

and expands on the results of Sections 3, 4, and 5. We make use of the unit-value isoquant diagram and the factor box diagram, and we begin by showing that these two figures do not provide different information but are really just different versions of the same basic figure. We can show, for example, that one can be derived from the other. This can be illustrated by reference to Figures 8.13 and 8.14, where in Figure 8.13 we have constructed the factor box diagram that would correspond to Figure 8.14. The basic difference between the two diagrams is that, in Figure 8.14, rather than plotting the two sets of isoquants from different corners of the factor box, they have both been plotted from the same origin. The overall endowment *ratio,* that is, the line O_xO_y from Figure 8.13, is shown as the overall endowment ray k_0 in Figure 8.14. The tangency between the two isoquants (not shown) at the point A of Figure 8.13 gives the same wage-rental ratio ω_0 as shown in Figure 8.14.

To illustrate further the relationship between Figures 8.13 and 8.14, we have assumed that in Figure 8.14 the overall endowment point is point E_0, so that point E_0 in Figure 8.14 corresponds to point O_y of Figure 8.13. The overall endowment E_0 is, of course, just the sum of the amounts of capital and labor used to produce the equilibrium quantities of X and Y. Furthermore, we know that commodity Y must be produced by using capital and labor according to the ratio k_y, and that X is produced by using capital and labor in the ratio k_x. Thus OE_0, the overall endowment vector, is some weighted sum of the two vectors k_y and k_x. To find the lengths of the two vectors k_y and k_x that sum to the vector OE_0, we can draw, from E_0, a line A_0E_0 with slope equal to that of k_y intersecting the vector k_x at point A_0. The X isoquant through A_0 gives the amount of X that would be produced given the capital-labor ratios of the two industries and the overall endowment E_0. Note that the point A_0 of Figure 8.14 corresponds exactly to point A of Figure 8.13, and that the triangle OE_0A_0 of Figure 8.14 is similar to the triangle O_xO_yA of Figure 8.13. The efficiency locus OA_0E_0 could be drawn in Figure 8.14, and thus we have constructed Figure 8.13 from Figure 8.14.

An alternative approach would have been to draw, from E_0, a line parallel to k_x intersecting k_y at point B_0. The Y isoquant through B_0 would give the output of commodity Y measured from the origin O. The distance E_0A_0 is equal in length to the distance OB_0 since $OB_0E_0A_0$ is a parallelogram. Points A_0 and B_0 of Figure 8.14 give the amounts of capital and labor used in the two industries, and the two vectors OB_0 and OA_0 sum to OE_0.

Figure 8.14 also shows how a change in the overall capital-labor ratio will affect the output of the two commodities. For the overall capital-labor ratio k_0 the output of Y is B_0 and the output of X is A_0. For a lower overall capital-labor ratio, as illustrated by k_1, the output of Y is B_1 whereas the output of X is A_1. It can be seen that $B_1 > B_0$ and that $A_0 > A_1$, and thus a reduction in the overall capital-labor ratio leads to a reduction in the output of Y and an increase in the output of X. It is important to note that the preceding comparison has been made under the assumption that commodity prices have not changed, which in turn implies that the unit-value isoquants have not changed. The Rybczynski theorem is just a special case of this proposition where a reduction in the capital-labor ratio is accomplished by increasing the quantity of labor without changing the amount of capital.

A continuation of this argument demonstrates the fact that as we consider lower and lower overall capital-labor ratios, we will find that the output of Y, the capital-intensive commodity, will continue to fall, whereas the output of X, the labor-intensive commodity, will continue to rise. Indeed, when the overall capital-labor ratio becomes equal to k_x, the output of Y will become zero and all resources will be used in the production of commodity X. Similarly, an increase in the capital-labor ratio will result in an increase in the output of Y and a reduction in the output of X, and when the overall capital-labor ratio becomes equal to k_y, the output of X will be zero and all factors will be used in the production of Y. Note that for all capital-labor ratios between k_y and k_x the wage-rental ratio, ω_0 from Figure 8.14, is a constant. This assumes that commodity prices are unchanged, which in turn implies that the unit-value isoquants are unchanged.

Now suppose we continue to reduce the capital-labor ratio beyond the point where specialization in commodity X has taken place. In particular, assume that the overall capital-labor ratio becomes k'_x. There will be specialization in X, and for cost minimization the wage-rental ratio must be tangent to the isoquant at F, the point where the wage-rental ratio ω_1 is tangent to the isoquant X_0. Note that for this wage-rental ratio it will not be profitable to produce commodity Y, for the tangency between Y_0 and an isocost line with slope ω_1 would imply a much higher cost than is associated with the isocost line through point F.

A similar argument would demonstrate that for overall capital-labor ratios higher than k_y there will be specialization in commodity Y, and the wage-rental ratio will be equal to the slope of the isoquant Y_0 at the relevant production point. Thus in the area between the K axis and k_y we will have specialization in commodity Y, with the wage-rental ratio being equal to the slope of the isoquant Y_0. Throughout the range k_y to k_x both commodities will be produced and the wage-rental ratio will be equal to ω_0. Between the ray k_x and the L axis we have specialization in X and the wage-rental ratio equal to the slope of X_0. The cone formed by k_y and k_x is referred to as the *cone of diversification*, because, if the overall capital-labor ratio lies within this cone, production is diversified in the sense that some of both commodities are produced. Outside this cone of diversification, that is, between the capital axis and k_y, or between k_x and the L axis, variations in the overall capital-labor ratio result in changes in the wage-rental ratio. Inside the cone of diversification, variations in the overall capital-labor ratio leave the wage-rental ratio unchanged, but result in a change in the levels of output of the two commodities.

*7. THE FACTOR-INTENSITY-REVERSAL CASE

In Sections 2 and 3 it was argued that the proofs of both the Heckscher-Ohlin and factor-price-equalization theorems required the assumption that no factor intensity reversals be present. In this section it will be shown why such reversals can result in the failure of these two theorems. We begin by defining "factor intensity reversals."

Factor intensity reversal refers to the situation where, at one set of relative factor prices, commodity X is capital-intensive relative to commodity Y, and where at another set of factor prices, commodity X is labor-intensive relative to commodity Y. This phenomenon is illustrated in Figure 8.15, where X_0 and Y_0 are representative isoquants for the two commodities. We see that at wage-rental ratios such as ω_0 we have $k_x > k_y$, whereas at factor price ratios such as ω' we have $k_y > k_x$. It can thus be seen that since for some factor price ratios $k_x > k_y$, and for other factor price ratios $k_y > k_x$, there must be some wage-rental ratio that results in the same capital-labor ratios in both industries. This is represented by k_r in Figure 8.15, and is referred to as the *factor-intensity-reversal ray*.

Now imagine a situation where, for one of the countries, the endowment point lies on the factor-intensity-reversal ray. If the factor box diagram were now constructed, it would be found that the efficiency locus would be the diagonal of the box, and this in turn will imply that the production possibility curve would be linear. Of course, it would be very

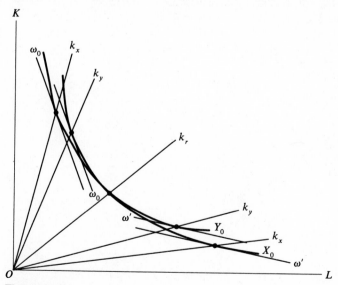

Figure 8.15

unusual if the endowment point for any country were precisely on the factor-intensity-reversal ray, and the important conclusion to be drawn from this special case is that for capital-labor ratios close to the factor-intensity-reversal ray, the production possibility curve will be almost linear. For capital-labor ratios that differ significantly from the factor-intensity-reversal ray, the production possibility curve will have the usual bowed-out shape. We thus could have the situation shown in Figure 8.16, where the production possibility curve for country H is almost linear, and the production possibility curve for country F is more bowed out. This could result in a situation where the production possibility curves for the two countries intersect more than once, and then trade patterns would depend crucially on the nature of demand conditions. This can be illustrated by supposing that, in autarky, the highest community indifference curve for country F is tangent at A_f, whereas the autarky point for country H is A_h. If we now ignore all of the diagram below Y_0 we see that the situation is quite similar to that represented in Figure 8.4. In particular, when trade is allowed, country H would export commodity Y and country F would export commodity X.

But suppose that, instead of the tastes represented by indifference curve I_0, we had assumed that preferences in both countries were much more biased toward commodity X, resulting in indifference curves such as I'. This indifference curve is tangent to the production possibility curve for country F at A_f', and an indifference curve from this family would be tangent to the production possibility curve for country H at A_h'. Now, ignoring all of the diagram to the left of X_0, it is clear that the pattern

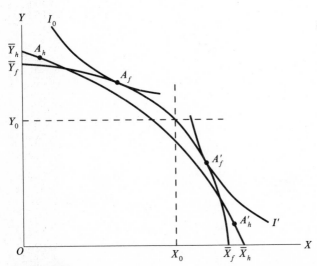

Figure 8.16

of trade which would result is exactly opposite to what it was for the initial tangency at A_f. Here country F exports Y while country H exports X, and thus the pattern of trade is reversed. It is thus obvious that if the Heckscher-Ohlin theorem holds for one of these situations, it cannot hold for the other so that, in general, the Heckscher-Ohlin theorem cannot be proved unless factor intensity reversals are excluded.

In the discussion of the factor-price-equalization theorem, it was argued that a factor intensity reversal could result in more than one cone of diversification. This can be seen from Figure 8.17, which is essentially the same as Figure 8.15, except that in Figure 8.17, rather than drawing the two isoquants tangent, the Y isoquant has been shifted toward the origin so that the two isoquants intersect twice. In Figure 8.17 there are two cones of diversification, or in other words, there are two isocost lines tangent to both isoquants that allow the production of both commodities. If the overall capital endowment ratio for country H is k_h in the cone defined by k_x and k_y, then the wage-rental ratio in country H will be ω_h. If the capital-labor ratio for country F is k_f in the cone of diversification defined by k'_y and k'_x, then the wage-rental ratio in F will be ω_f. In this example both countries produce both commodities, but since production takes place in different cones of diversification, the wage-rental ratios are not the same, and thus factor prices are not equalized. We have thus confirmed the statement in Section 3 that a rigorous proof of the factor price equalization theorem must preclude the possibility of factor intensity reversals.

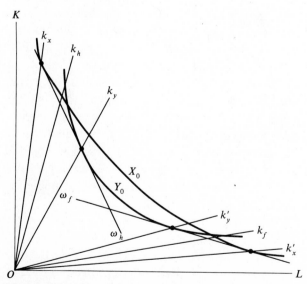

Figure 8.17

Figure 8.17 also illustrates why the Heckscher-Ohlin theorem need not hold when there are factor intensity reversals. Recall from the discussion of Figure 8.14 that the production of two commodities for each country depends on the location of the overall endowment ratio within the cone of diversification. Thus if k_h were close to k_x, country H would be producing a relatively large quantity of commodity X. Similarly, if k_f were close to k'_y, country F would be producing a relatively large amount of commodity Y. With identical tastes in the two countries, this implies that H exports X and F exports Y. But we could just as easily have assumed that k_h was close to k_y and k_f close to k'_x, in which case the opposite trade pattern would be observed. Note that in both cases country H is relatively well endowed with K, since $k_h > k_f$. Thus predictions of trade patterns cannot be made from knowledge about relative endowments if factor intensity reversals are present.

*8.   A COMMENT ON DIMENSIONALITY

Throughout our analysis it is assumed that there are only two goods and two factors, and the question naturally arises as to what extent the model can be generalized to higher dimensions. One generalization would assume that the X and Y of our analysis are not individual commodities, but rather, groups of products, such as all manufactures, or all agricultural products. If it is then assumed that relative commodity prices within the two groups are unchanged, then all the preceding conclusions will hold.

Generalizing to allow more than two distinct commodities does produce difficulties, even with only two factors of production, for the simple ratios earlier employed need no longer produce unique results. Thus suppose a third good, Z, is added and one finds that $K_y/L_y > K_x/L_x > K_z/L_z$. What would the pattern of trade in a two-country world be? While one might think that the country well endowed with capital would export Y and the country well endowed with labor would export Z, with some indeterminacy about good X, this need not be true. Indeed, it is possible for either country to export *both* Y and Z and import X. What can be shown is that the bundle of commodities exported by the capital-intensive country will be capital-intensive, but could be made up of some of both Y and Z, the two extreme goods.

With more than two factors, additional problems arise, for it is no longer clear what is meant by factor intensities. With a third factor R, resources, one could have $K_x/L_x > K_y/L_y$ but $K_x/R_x < K_y/L_y$. In such a case, which good is capital-intensive? It obviously depends on how the comparison is made. Bilateral comparisons do not have much meaning in a world with more than two factors. Results such as the Stolper-Samuelson theorem and the Rybczynski theorem, which make use of such comparisons, therefore, do not easily generalize to higher dimensions. A theorem that *does* generalize is the factor-price-equalization theorem, and it can be shown to be true for any number of factors and goods as long as the number of goods is equal to the number of factors. It can also be shown to hold for three commodities and two factors, but it is not known whether further generalizations are possible.

9. CONCLUDING REMARKS

This chapter has considered a model in which the only difference between countries is in relative endowments. It was shown that a country will export the commodity that uses the well-endowed factor most intensively; this gave the Heckscher-Ohlin theorem. An important implication of this model is that if there are no impediments to trade, and if factor intensity reversals are absent, the equalization of commodity prices will equalize factor prices. The relationship between commodity prices and factor prices and the implications of changing factor supplies were also investigated, although these latter two questions have broader application in that they will hold for any economy, as long as there are constant returns to scale and no distortions.

PROBLEMS

1. Show that, in a two-country model, increasing the size of one country (increasing both K and L in the same proportions) will change commodity prices, factor prices, outputs, and the volume of trade in both countries, but cannot change the pattern of trade.

2. How will the production possibility curves of Figure 8.2 differ if in Figure 8.1 country H has more K but the same amount of L as country F?

3. In Figure 8.4 show that with different demand conditions one of the two countries may be completely specialized after trade.

4. Illustrate a case in which, with trade, both countries specialize completely.

*5. The factor-price-equalization theorem makes no assumption about demand. Nevertheless, demand conditions may well determine whether or not factor prices are equalized. Explain this seemingly paradoxical result.

6. Show that factor prices will be unequal if the technologies in the two countries differ for industry X (or Y).

*7. Suppose in Figure 8.11 that the indifference curves intersect three times rather than twice. How will this affect the production possibility curves?

8. Show that, for a small country, an increase in the labor supply could either increase or decrease the volume of trade.

*9. For an increase in the supply of labor, how will the terms of trade be affected in the two-country model (recall Problem 8)?

NOTE

1. Professor P. A. Samuelson has made so many contributions to this model that it is often called the Heckscher-Ohlin-Samuelson model. We have chosen to stay with the more traditional title.

REFERENCES

Chipman, J. S. (1966). "A Survey of the Theory of International Trade: Part 3, The Modern Theory." *Econometrica* 34, 18–76.

Johnson, H. G. (1961). "Factor Endowments, International Trade and Factor Prices." In H. G. Johnson *International Trade and Economic Growth,* pp. 17–30. Cambridge, Mass.: Harvard University Press.

Jones, R. W. (1956–57). "Factor Proportions and the Heckscher-Ohlin Theorem." *Review of Economic Studies* 24, 1–10.

Melvin J. R. (1968). "Production and Trade with Two Factors and Three Goods." *American Economic Review* 63, 1249–1268.

Metzler, L. A. (1949). "Tariff, the Terms of Trade and the Distribution of National Income." *Journal of Political Economy* 57, 1–29.

Rybczynski, T. N. (1955). "Factor Endowments and Relative Commodity Prices." *Economica* 22, 336–341.

Samuelson, P. A. (1948). "International Trade and the Equalization of Factor Prices." *Economic Journal* 58, 163–184.

―――. (1949). "International Factor Price Equalization Once Again." *Economic Journal* 59, 181–197.

―――. (1953). "Price of Factors and Goods in General Equilibrium." *Review of Economic Studies* 21, 1–20.

Stolper, W. F., and P. A. Samuelson (1941). "Protection and Real Wages." *Review of Economic Studies* 9, 58–73.

chapter *9*

The Specific Factor Model

1. INTRODUCTION

Chapter 8 considered the endowment model where two factors of production, capital and labor, were used to produce two outputs, and where both factors were perfectly mobile between the two industries. This endowment model, or the Heckscher-Ohlin model as it has come to be called, has formed the central structure for most of the theoretical international trade literature that has developed in the last four decades. Recently, however, international trade economists have begun to be interested in models that go beyond the assumptions of this endowment model, and indeed, the remaining chapters in this section will consider a variety of models that relax assumptions that are central to the Heckscher-Ohlin framework. In the present chapter we relax the assumption that both factors are perfectly mobile between the two industries.

The Heckscher-Ohlin model, because of its assumption that both factors can move freely between the two industries, is clearly long run in nature. The assumption of perfect mobility of capital implies that we are considering a time period long enough to allow industries to convert one kind of capital into another, and in many circumstances this may take a considerable period of time. The capital used to produce automobiles is much different from the capital required for wheat or textiles, and capital mobility between such diverse industries will require time for physical capital to depreciate in some uses and for new investment to take place in others.

Although the long run is clearly important and deserving of analysis, many changes may also have important short-run consequences. Thus we may be interested in the effects of tariffs or in changes in the terms of trade in time periods that are shorter than would allow for the complete mobility of capital between industries. We may also be interested in whether the short-run effects of such changes are the same as the long-run consequences discussed in Chapter 8. For example, will we expect factor prices to be equalized in the short run if the conditions for equalization described in Chapter 8 are maintained? Will the Rybczynski theorem and the Stolper-Samuelson theorem derived for the long-run conditions of the endowment model also apply in the short run? Of even more importance is the issue of whether the basic Heckscher-Ohlin theorem that allows prediction of trade flows from a knowledge of factor endowments holds in a short-run version of this model. It is with these questions that we will be concerned in this chapter.

The model employed here is similar to the Heckscher-Ohlin model except that one factor, namely capital, is assumed to be useful only for the production of one commodity. Thus automobiles require one kind of capital and textiles require another, and in the short run the amount of capital allocated to each of the two industries is fixed and no substitution between industries can take place. Capital is therefore specific to a particular industry, and the model we describe has become known as the specific factor model. Although this model has a long history in the economic literature, recent interest in this model dates from the work of Jones (1971) and Samuelson (1971). It should also be noted that although we are considering the specific factor model as a short-run version of the Heckscher-Ohlin model, the specific factor model has other interpretations. In particular, we can consider the specific factors to be quite distinct kinds of inputs, such as different resources, and thus the analysis could be used to produce a model in which natural resources form the basis for international trade. Other uses of the specific factor model will be mentioned in the concluding section.

2. THE SPECIFIC FACTOR MODEL

In many respects the specific factor model is similar to the model used for the Heckscher-Ohlin analysis of Chapter 8. We assume two commodities produced with production functions that exhibit constant returns to scale. It is further assumed that two factors of production are required for both production functions. Tastes are assumed to be homogeneous and identical for all consumers so that preferences can be represented by a set of community indifference curves.

The basic difference between the specific factor model and the endowment model is that while both production functions require two inputs, only one input is common to the two production functions. Thus instead of the two production functions (2.5) and (2.6) of Chapter 2, we have the production functions shown in equations (9.1) and (9.2):

$$X = F_x(R_x, L_x) \tag{9.1}$$

$$Y = F_y(T_y, L_y). \tag{9.2}$$

Here R_x and T_y represent types of capital that are specific to industries X and Y, respectively. Corresponding to the factor constraints of equations (2.7) and (2.8) of Chapter 2, we have equations (9.3), (9.4), and (9.5):

$$\bar{R} = R_x \tag{9.3}$$

$$\bar{T} = T_y \tag{9.4}$$

$$\bar{L} = L_x + L_y. \tag{9.5}$$

Equations (9.3) and (9.4) simply show that the entire available stock of factor R is used to produce commodity X and the entire endowment of factor T is used to produce commodity Y. Note that again we are assuming that all factors of production are fully employed. The return to labor (the wage rate) is defined to be w, and the returns to R and T will be defined to be r and s, respectively.

The fact that both production functions use the entire available endowment of the specific factor makes the construction of the production possibility curve somewhat easier than was the case for the endowment model of Chapter 8. Recall from Chapter 2 that one of the representations of a production function such as (9.1) is the total product curve that fixes the input of one of the factors and shows total output as a function of varying quantities of the other factor. This was illustrated in Figure 2.3, where K was assumed fixed and L variable. In the present model, with T_y fixed at $\bar{T}$ for industry Y, the total product curve provides a complete description of production conditions in the Y industry. Such a total product curve is shown in quadrant II of Figure 9.1 where the vertical axis measures the output of Y and the horizontal axis measures the input of L_y, where L_y is measured leftward from the origin. The total available supply of labor is shown by $\bar{L}$ on the L_y axis, and the use of $\bar{L}$ by the Y industry would result in an output of $\bar{Y}$. The total product curve for industry X is shown as F_x in quadrant IV, and $\bar{X}$ is the maximum amount of X that could be produced by using the entire endowment of L in the X industry.

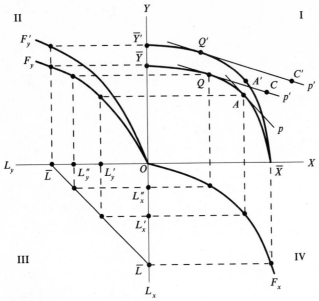

Figure 9.1

The 45° line $\overline{LL}$ in quadrant III provides a convenient method of illustrating all possible ways that the total endowment of labor can be divided between the two industries. Thus, if L'_y of labor is used in the Y industry, then L'_x is available for use in industry X. This allocation of labor would result in the output of X and Y shown by point A in quadrant I. Other allocations of labor between the two industries would give other points on $\overline{LL}$, and these would produce other points on the production possibility curve. Thus the production possibility curve will be $\overline{Y}A\overline{X}$ as shown in quadrant I.

It is now easy to see how changes in the endowments of either the specific factors or labor would change the production possibility curve. First, consider an increase in the amount of $\overline{T}$ used in industry Y. With more T available for all allocations of labor to the Y industry, the total product curve would shift to F'_y in quadrant II. Now the entire allocation of labor to the Y industry produces point $\overline{Y}'$, and the allocation of labor between the two industries that originally produced point A now gives point A'. We note that the production possibility curve $\overline{Y}'A'\overline{X}$ is entirely above the original production possibility curve except at the end point $\overline{X}$. For an increase in the endowment of R the argument is exactly similar. The total product curve F_x would shift out and the production possibility curve would shift out everywhere except at point $\overline{Y}$. An increase in the available endowment of labor could be illustrated by shifting the $\overline{LL}$ 45° line in quadrant III farther away from the origin. This would increase the maximum producible quantities of both Y and X, and therefore would result in the production possibility curve shifting outward over its entire length. Of course this expansion of output need not be uniform along the production possibility curve, for the outward shift will depend on the shapes of the total product curves for the two industries.

The production possibility curves of Figure 9.1 can now be used to illustrate trading equilibrium in exactly the same way as was shown for the endowment model of Chapter 8. Thus suppose A is the initial autarky equilibrium and that p is the domestic price ratio. Assume for the moment that the world price ratio is fixed at p'. When trade is allowed production will move from A to Q and consumption from A to point C, where C represents a tangency between a community indifference curve (not shown) and the price line p'. In this situation Y is exported and X is imported. If we now assume an increase in the amount of the specific factor T, the production possibility curve will shift out to $\overline{Y}A'\overline{X}$, and the new production and consumption points will be Q' and C'.

In Chapter 8 we were able to derive relationships between factor prices and commodity prices and between endowment changes and output changes, and we now turn to an examination of these issues in terms of the specific factor model. Such a discussion is most easily carried out in terms of Figure 9.2, which presents a slightly different feature of the specific factor model. Quadrant III in Figure 9.2 is exactly the same as quadrant III in Figure 9.1, and shows the total quantity of labor available to the two industries. In quadrants II and IV, however, we now show the marginal product curves rather than the total product curves shown in Figure 9.1. The marginal product curve is simply the slope of the total product curve, and since both F_y and F_x are concave to the labor axes (exhibit diminishing returns), the marginal product curves are both downward sloping. In Figure 9.2 the curve MP_y in quadrant II corresponds to F_y of quadrant II of Figure 9.1, and at all points on the labor axis such as L'_y the curve MP_y is a measure of the slope of F_y at that same labor allocation to the Y industry. Note that while the axes of quadrant I in Figure 9.2 are in units of X and Y just as they are in Figure 9.2, the scales are quite different. Figure 9.1 shows the total output of X and Y, while Figure 9.2 shows the payments to labor measured in terms of X and Y.

In a perfectly competitive industry in a profit-maximizing equilibrium factor owners receive their marginal product in payment for their services, and thus in the Y industry we have $MP_y = w/p_y$. Thus in Figure 9.2 point M gives the real return to labor for workers in the Y industry. Similarly MP_x is the marginal product or the real return to labor in the X industry. Note also that since $MP_y = w/p_y$ and $MP_x = w/p_x$, then

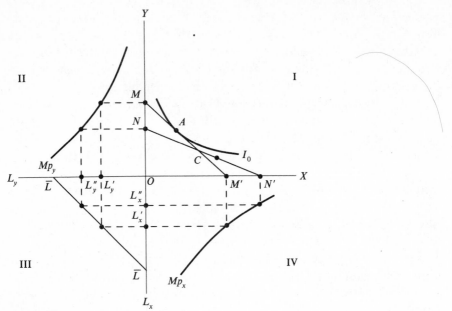

Figure 9.2

the slope of MM' in Figure 9.2 is $p_x/p_y = p$, which is the price ratio associated with point A of Figure 9.1. Note also that since M is the return to labor for workers in the Y industry and M' is the return to labor for workers in the X industry, the line MM' is simply the budget constraint for a representative worker. Thus point A, the tangency between an indifference curve and the budget constraint, represents the equilibrium consumption point for a representative worker. Note that because all consumers in the economy have identical and homogeneous preferences, point A in Figure 9.2 represents the same Y/X consumption ratio as does point A of Figure 9.1. Of course, point A in Figure 9.1 represents aggregate consumption, while point A in Figure 9.2 represents the individual worker's consumption point.

Figure 9.2 can be used to show the relationships between changes in commodity prices and factor prices and to illustrate how outputs change when endowments change, but before doing so, we will find it useful to review some of the properties of production functions that exhibit constant returns to scale. In Chapter 2 we noted that for production functions that are homogeneous of the first degree (i.e., where we assume constant returns to scale) the marginal products are constant along any capital-labor ratio. Thus in Figure 9.3 the marginal products of both L and R are constant along the capital-labor ratio k_x. This property was used in the proof of the Stolper-Samuelson theorem in Chapter 8, where it was shown that the change in the marginal products of both inputs depends

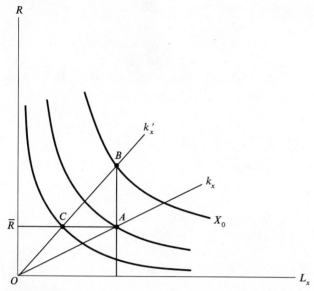

Figure 9.3

only on the change in the capital-labor ratios. Thus, if the capital-labor ratio in Figure 9.3 changes from k_x to k_x', the direction of change in the marginal product for R can be found by comparing points A and B, while the direction of change in the marginal product for L can be found by comparing points A and C. The movement from A to C, for example, keeps R fixed at $\bar{R}$ and reduces the input of L and this is equivalent to moving along the curve F_x toward the origin in Figure 9.1. As we move toward the origin, the slope of F_x increases, or in other words, the marginal product increases. Thus the marginal product of L is an increasing function of the capital-labor ratio. In exactly the same way we can show that the marginal product of R is a decreasing function of the capital-labor ratio.

We have seen that the marginal products, or in other words, the real returns to the factors, depend on the capital-labor ratios, and thus changes in the real returns to factors are known as soon as changes in capital-labor ratios are found. Of even more importance for our present discussion is the fact that since the marginal products are functions *only* of the capital-labor ratios, if we know how one marginal product changes we immediately know that the other marginal product has changed in the opposite direction. Thus an increase in the marginal product of labor implies a decrease in the marginal product of capital, or in other words, if we find that w/p_x falls, we know that r/p_x must necessarily increase. Note that these relationships hold regardless of what is happening to output or to endowments.

3. COMMODITY PRICES AND FACTOR PRICES

We are now in a position to consider how price changes will affect factor payments. In Figure 9.1 it was assumed that point A was the autarky equilibrium and that with trade, production moved to Q and consumption to C on price line p'. This change resulted in a movement of labor out of the X industry and into the Y industry, and the new labor allocation is given by points L_y'' and L_x''. This same allocation of labor is shown in Figure 9.2 and we have the new budget constraint for labor shown by the line NN'. Note that NN' is the price line p' from Figure 9.1.

How have the factors of production been affected by this price change? We note that the marginal product of labor has fallen from M to N in the Y industry and risen from M' to N' in the X industry, and thus the welfare of a representative worker will depend on consumption patterns. In the situation shown in Figure 9.2 the new budget line NN' is below the indifference curve I_0 through point A, and thus labor has been made worse off by the relative increase in the price of Y. But note that this result depends on the position of the indifference curve. Had preferences been biased toward commodity X it would be perfectly possible for labor to have benefited by this price change. In general, then, the effect of a price change on the welfare of labor is uncertain, for workers may be made better off or worse off depending on their preferences for the two commodities. This result has become known as the neoclassical ambiguity. Note that this conclusion is in sharp contrast to the findings of Chapter 8 where it was shown that commodity price increases have unambiguous effects on factor prices; specifically, it was shown that the factor used intensively in the industry whose price has risen will benefit.

How have the returns of the specific factors been affected by the relative increase in the price of Y? We have noted that the marginal product of labor has fallen from M to N in the Y industry, which implies, from our previous discussion, that the marginal product of T has necessarily increased. Then since $MP_T = s/p_y$, where s is the return to T, it is clear that the return to T has increased. In the X industry the marginal product of labor has risen from M' to N', and therefore the marginal product of R has fallen, and so r/p_x, the real return to owners of factor R, has been reduced. Thus a relative increase in the price of commodity Y is a benefit to the specific factor used to produce Y but reduces the income of the specific factor used in industry X. We thus have the following proposition.

Commodity Price and Factor Prices

A relative price increase is beneficial to the specific factor used in that industry, will reduce the income of the other specific factor, and will have an ambiguous effect on labor.

Again note the contrast of these results with the results of the Stolper-Samuelson theorem from Chapter 8.

4. ENDOWMENT CHANGES AND FACTOR PRICE EQUALIZATION

The effects of endowment changes are shown in Figure 9.4, which takes as the initial situation the trading equilibrium of Figure 9.2 with consumption at point C on budget constraint NN'. We now consider the increase in T that resulted in the shift of the total product curve from F_y to F'_y in Figure 9.1. Because of the assumption of constant returns to scale, the total product curves of Figure 9.1 all have the same slope along any ray from the origin. Thus the upward shift in the total product curve results in an upward shift of the marginal product curve as shown in quadrant II. For a small open economy with fixed p the increase in the endowment of T shifts out the production possibility curve in Figure 9.1 to $\overline{Y}'Q'\overline{X}$, and the production point shifts from Q to Q'. With commodity prices unchanged the new budget constraint for workers will have the same slope as NN' and is shown as VV' in Figure 9.4.

The effects of an increase in the endowment of T are now clear from Figure 9.4. The marginal product of labor has increased from N to V in industry Y and from N' to V' in industry X. Consumption is now at point C', which lies on a higher indifference curve than C, and thus labor is unambiguously better off. Since the marginal product of labor has increased in Y the marginal product of T in the Y industry has necessarily fallen and therefore owners of T have been made worse off by the increase in the endowment of T. Similarly, because the marginal product of labor has increased in the X industry, the returns to R, the factor specific to the X industry, have also fallen. Thus an increase in the endowment of T reduces the return to both specific factors and increases labor's real income. It is easily seen that exactly the same result will hold for an increase in the supply of R, for it is clear that the effects of increases in the specific factors are symmetrical. Thus an increase in R will lower the return to both specific factors and increase the return to labor. In general, then, any increase in the endowment of a specific factor at constant commodity prices will lower the real return to both specific factors and increase the

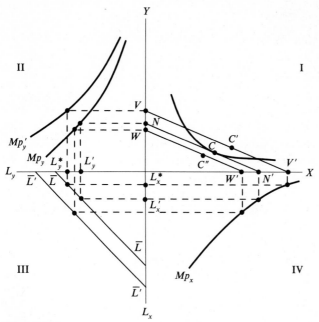

Figure 9.4

return to labor. These results are in sharp contrast to the results derived in Chapter 8, where it was shown that endowment changes with given commodity prices would not affect factor prices if both commodities continued to be produced.

Now, with the marginal product curve MP_y, consider an increase in the endowment of labor. This will shift the labor endowment curve in quadrant III to $\bar{L}'\bar{L}'$, and with the same commodity prices this generates the new budget constraint WW' with consumption at point C''. The increase in the endowment of labor has lowered the marginal product of labor in both industries and unambiguously makes labor worse off. At the same time, because both marginal products of labor have fallen, the marginal products of both the specific factors have increased, and consequently, the returns to both specific factors have risen. Thus an increase in the endowment of labor is beneficial to both specific factors and harmful to workers. Thus we have the following proposition.

Endowment Changes and Factor Prices

At constant factor prices any increase in the endowment of a specific factor will increase the return to labor and lower the return to both specific factors. An increase in the endowment of labor will reduce the return to labor and increase the return to both specific factors.

The output effects of changes in endowments can also be seen from Figure 9.4. First consider the increase in T that resulted in the upward shift of the total product curve for commodity Y shown in Figure 9.1. From Figure 9.4 the shift in the budget line from NN' to VV' was accomplished by a reduction in the labor force in industry X from L'_x to L_x^*. With a reduction in the labor input, and because the input of R is fixed, output of commodity X must necessarily have been reduced. In industry Y we note that labor has increased from L'_y to L_y^*, and since the input of T has also increased, it is clear that the output of Y has increased. Thus the increase in T results in a production shift from Q to Q' in Figure 9.1 resulting in more Y and less X at the new equilibrium. Similar results will be found for industry X, and thus we have demonstrated that an increase in the specific factor will increase the output of the commodity that uses that factor and reduce the output of the other commodity.

An increase in the endowment of L will, at fixed commodity prices, result in the allocation of more labor to both industries as is shown in Figure 9.4. Thus an increase in the endowment of labor will shift out the production possibility curve throughout its entire length, and, with fixed commodity prices, it will result in an increase in the output of both commodity X and Y. Thus we can state the following proposition.

Endowment Changes and Outputs

An increase in one specific factor increases the output of the commodity that uses that factor and reduces the output of the other industry. Increases in the supply of labor will increase both outputs.

Note the contrast to the Rybczynski theorem from Chapter 8. In the endowment model an increase in a factor will increase the output of the commodity that uses that factor intensively and reduce the output of the other industry.

A principal result of the Heckscher-Ohlin model was the factor price equalization theorem where it was shown that under certain conditions the equalization of commodity prices between two trading countries would result in the equalization of factor prices. That such a theorem does not apply to the specific factor model can easily be seen from Figure 9.4. We will reinterpret Figure 9.4 as representing two countries with identical endowments of L, identical endowments of R, but where the foreign country has a larger supply of T. Thus in Figure 9.1 the two production possibility curves will represent the two countries. Although not shown, it is clear that in a trading equilibrium country F would export commodity Y and import commodity X. In Figure 9.4 $\overline{LL}$ represents the common labor supply for the two countries, MP_x the common marginal product of labor curve for the X industry, and the marginal product curves for the Y industry in H and F are shown as MP_y and MP'_y, respectively, in quadrant II. If trade equalizes commodity prices, then VV' could represent the price line in country F and NN' the price line in country H. But while relative commodity prices have been equalized by trade, it is clear that factor prices have not been equalized. As we have already seen, the real wage will be higher in country F than in H, whereas the returns to both specific factors will be higher in H than in F. Obviously the factor price equalization theorem does not hold for the specific factor model, and we have the following proposition.

Trade and Factor Prices

The equalization of commodity prices by international trade does not equalize factor prices.

5. THE PATTERN OF TRADE

One of the principal results of the Heckscher-Ohlin theorem described in Chapter 8 is that we can predict trade patterns from the knowledge of factor endowments alone. In particular, we found that a country will export the commodity that uses its abundant factor most intensively. We now want to investigate whether a similar property holds for the specific factor model. To facilitate comparison we will begin, as we have done in the past, by assuming that our two countries, H and F, have identical endowments of labor and *total* capital in the long run. We know from our earlier discussion that in such a case, with preferences assumed identical in both countries, the two economies will be identical in every respect and there will be no possibility of international trade.

We now retain the assumption of identical long-run endowments but will assume that in the short run the capital in the two countries has been allocated differently between the two industries. In particular, we will assume that in country H there is more capital in the Y industry and that in country F more capital has initially been allocated to the X industry. In Figure 9.5 F'_y and F'_x represent the total product curves for the foreign country, while F_y and F_x represent the total product curves for the home country. These total product curves result, along with the assumption of an identical endowment of labor in the two economies, in the production

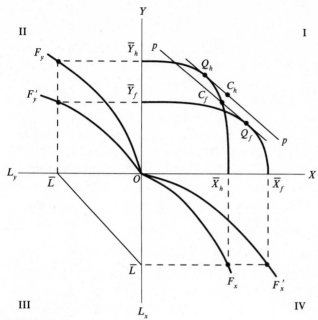

Figure 9.5

possibility curves $\overline{Y}_h Q_h \overline{X}_h$ and $\overline{Y}_f Q_f \overline{X}_f$ for the home country and the foreign country, respectively. Obviously the two countries are not identical and trade will take place. The pattern of trade is easily seen from Figure 9.5 and indeed this figure is similar to Figure 8.4 of Chapter 8. We note that the home country will export commodity Y and the foreign country will export commodity X. The production points will be Q_h and Q_f for countries H and F, respectively, with consumption at C_h and C_f. Thus in the short run the country will export the commodity that is produced with the relatively abundant specific factor.

Suppose we now consider an increase in the labor supply in country F. In Figure 9.5 this would result in a new labor constraint curve in quadrant IV farther from the origin (not shown). As we have already seen, an increase in the labor supply will shift out the production possibility curve and would result in country F producing more of both X and Y. At the new equilibrium commodity prices would differ but there is no reason to expect that the pattern of trade would change. From the long-run point of view we have now created a situation where country F is relatively well endowed with labor, and by the Heckscher-Ohlin theorem country F would export the labor-intensive commodity. In the short-run model, however, we do not obtain this result. Trading patterns depend principally on how capital is allocated between the two industries and is much less sensitive to the overall endowments of capital and labor in the economies as a whole. Thus a relative abundance of labor in one country will not imply that that country will necessarily export the labor-intensive commodity. We thus have the following proposition.

The Pattern of Trade

In the specific factor model, trade patterns cannot be predicted from knowledge of the factor endowments alone, but will depend on the nature of the production functions and on the allocation of capital between the two industries.

6. CONCLUDING REMARKS

In our discussion we have interpreted the specific factor model as being a short-run version of the Heckscher-Ohlin model discussed in Chapter 8. This approach is useful, for it allows an easy comparison of these two models in terms of the principal results. The specific factor model has a much broader interpretation, however. The specific factors need not be different kinds of capital but, rather, could be capital and land, in which case the model could be used to consider production and trade of two commodities such as manufacturers and food, where manufactured goods use capital and labor as inputs and where food requires land and labor. Alternatively, these specific factors could be resources such as iron or timber, and a model of trade for resource-rich economies would be considered. Of course, the conclusions we have reached in terms of the relationship between commodity prices and factor prices and between endowments and outputs would remain unaffected, and these alternative models could be constructed simply by renaming the variables in the earlier sections of this chapter.

The specific factor model provides an interesting contrast to the results of the Heckscher-Ohlin model described in Chapter 8. In particular, we have seen that the theorems associated with the endowment model do not carry over to the specific factor framework. Trade does not equalize factor prices and trade patterns cannot be predicted from knowledge of endowments alone. In the endowment model factor prices were uniquely determined by commodity prices and real factor rewards changed in a predictable way when commodity prices changed. In the specific factor model, although the returns to the specific factors are unambiguously related to commodity price changes, such is not the case for the return to labor. Whether labor loses or gains from a price change will depend on the consumption pattern of the representative worker. Changes in endowments also have somewhat different effects in the specific factor model. While increases in specific factors will necessarily increase the output of the commodity using this factor, an increase in labor will increase the output of both commodities, and which output increases by more will depend on the nature of the production functions and not on endowments.

PROBLEMS

1. Draw a diagram that illustrates how an increase in the labor supply will shift the production possibility curve.
2. If the labor supply increases and if commodity prices are fixed, what will determine how the relative outputs of X and Y will be affected?
3. (a) Draw a diagram similar to Figure 9.2 that shows labor gaining from an increase in the relative price of Y. (b) Show that part (a) can be done by either assuming different production functions or assuming different tastes.
*4. Use the definition of constant returns to scale to show that the total product curves derived for the same amount of the specific factor and different quantities of labor all have the same slope along a ray from the origin.
5. Show that if, after trade, the real return to labor is relatively higher in country H, then the real return to both specific factors must be relatively higher in country F.

REFERENCES

Jones, R. W. (1971). "A Three-Factor Model in Theory, Trade and History." In J. Bhagwati et al. (eds.), *Trade, Balance of Payments, and Growth;* Chapter 1. Amsterdam: North Holland.

Mayer, W. (1974). "Short Run and Long Run Equilibrium for a Small Open Economy." *Journal of Political Economy* 82: 955–967.

Mussa, M. (1974). "Tariffs and the Distribution of Income: The Importance of Factor Specificity and Substitutability and Intensity in the Short and Long Run." *Journal of Political Economy* 82: 1191–1204.

Samuelson, P. A. (1971) "Ohlin was Right." *Swedish Journal of Economics* 73: 365–384.

chapter 10

Imperfect Competition and Government Policies as Determinants of Trade

1. INTRODUCTION

Chapters 8 and 9 discussed in some detail two of the five determinants of trade described in Chapter 6, namely, production function (technology) differences, and endowment differences. In this chapter we will discuss domestic distortions as a determinant of trade, focusing in particular on taxes and subsidies, and imperfect competition. The examination of taxes and subsidies is intended as an example of the effects that a wide range of government policies can have on trade. We are not asserting that commodity and factor taxes rank with factor endowments as a cause of trade, but we do believe that collectively, government policies have a much more profound impact on trade than is suggested in most international trade textbooks.

Graphical analysis of imperfect competition is closely related to that for taxes, and so there is a simple methodological reason for putting these two quite different topics together. As before, the approach will be to neutralize other factors so that a clear understanding of the specific effects of each can be obtained. Thus throughout the chapter we will assume that there are two countries that are identical in all respects. They have identical technologies, identical factor endowments, identical homogeneous utility functions, and constant returns and perfect competition in production. Therefore, in the absence of the distortions that we introduce, the two countries would have no incentive to trade, or alternatively, the free trade equilibrium would be identical to autarky.

2. COMMODITY TAXES

In this section we consider the case in which there are distortions in the economy that prevent the free-market equilibrium from prevailing. In particular, we confine our attention to the case where the government of the home country imposes a discriminatory tax on one of the commodities. We assume that this is the only distortion in country H, the home country, and that no distortions exist in country F, the foreign country.

In Figure 10.1 TAT' represents the production possibility curve for both of the identical countries. Point A represents the autarky equilibrium for both countries before the commodity tax is imposed. Now suppose that country H imposes an *ad valorem* (percentage of value) tax on commodity Y. A sales tax that is quoted as a percentage of value is an example of an *ad valorem* tax. The tax will increase the price of Y to consumers and lower the price received by producers. At the new equilibrium there will be a "wedge" between producer and consumer prices equal to the tax. Let p_{y_1} be the price paid by the consumer, and let p_{y_2} be the price received by the producer. The relation between these two prices will be given by

$$p_{y_1} = p_{y_2} (1 + T) \qquad p_{y_1} > p_{y_2} \qquad (10.1)$$

where T is the rate of tax. Thus, if T is 10 percent, the consumer will pay $1.10 ($p_{y_1}$ = \$1.10$) for a good for which the producer receives $1.00 ($p_{y_2}$ = \$1.00$). In order to focus on trade questions, we assume that the government redistributes the tax revenue back to consumers in a lump-sum fashion (e.g., each consumer receives a check from the government each month). This simplifies matters in that the value of production and consumption will continue to be equal (connected by the world price ratio) and in autarky the production and consumption points will be the same.

Let p_1 denote the consumers' price ratio (p_{x_1}/p_{y_1}), and let p_2 denote the producers' price ratio. To find the new equilibrium with the tax, we search along the transformation curve TAT' in Figure 10.1 until we find a point where the difference between the slope of an indifference curve (the consumption price ratio) and the slope of the transformation curve (the producer price ratio) is just equal to the tax. Such a point could be E, where the consumer price ratio p_1 cuts the production possibility curve. Note that the tax equilibrium must be "downhill" from A since consumers pay more for Y than producers receive ($p_{x_1}/p_{y_1} < p_{x_2}/p_{y_2}$).

Two things are important about the tax equilibrium E in Figure 10.1. First, as we would expect, the tax has the effect of discouraging production

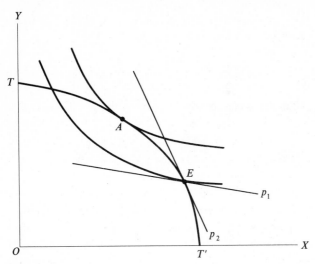

Figure 10.1

and consumption of Y. Consumers and producers substitute away from Y and in favor of X. Second, welfare is reduced in the home country. Point E is on a lower CIC than the one through A in Figure 10.1. This is due to the fact that prices no longer reflect true costs of production. The tax has made Y seem artificially expensive to consumers and artificially unprofitable to producers. Inefficient choices are made so that the equilibrium moves from A to E.

The final fact to note in Figure 10.1 is that exactly the same equilibrium could result from subsidizing X instead of taxing Y. Let S be a rate of subsidy on X so that producers of X receive the consumer price p_{x_1} plus a subsidy payment Sp_{x_1} on each unit sold. This price relationship is given by

$$p_{x_1}(1 + S) = p_{x_2} \qquad p_{x_1} < p_{x_2} \qquad (10.2)$$

where p_{x_2} is the price of X received by the producer. As in the case of a tax on Y, the subsidy implies that the two price ratios are related by $(p_{x_1}/p_{y_1} < p_{x_2}/p_{y_2})$. Thus the equilibrium E in Figure 10.1 can also represent a subsidy on X. The effect of the subsidy is to encourage more production and consumption of X, and again to reduce welfare. X is artificially cheap (i.e., cheaper than the cost of the resources needed to produce X) for consumers and artificially profitable for producers.

Until now no assumption has been made about how the tax is collected, that is, whether it is collected from consumers or from producers. In a closed model with no trade this question is unimportant, for since production must equal consumption for both goods, point E in Figure

10.1 is the only possible equilibrium. In a trading world, however, the equilibrium depends on who pays the tax. First, we assume that the tax on Y is collected at the retail level from domestic consumers only.

Now suppose we allow trade, recalling that country F is in equilibrium at A in Figure 10.1. The important point to understand is that the home country consumers face the tax-distorted price ratio, whereas foreign country consumers do not. Furthermore, domestic producers face the same prices in the foreign market as do foreign consumers and producers. Consumers in F find Y cheaper in H since they can buy at the (untaxed) producer price ratio p_2. Country H will thus export Y, which will increase the producer price of Y in country H and reduce the price of Y in country F. An equilibrium will be reached when the price ratio in F is equal to the producer price ratio in H. Such a price ratio is p_2' in Figure 10.2, where Q is the production point for both countries and C_f and C_h are the consumption points for countries F and H, respectively. Both countries produce the same bundle of goods (Q) because the countries are identical by assumption and because in the trading equilibrium producers in both countries face the same price ratio. It also follows, therefore, that factor prices are equalized by trade.

Country H exports Y, the taxed good, and imports X, and trade is balanced since C_fQ is equal to QC_h. The domestic consumer price ratio line is p_1' and is tangent to an indifference curve at C_h. It bears the same relation to p_2' ($p_1' < p_2'$) that we had at the autarky equilibrium in Figure 10.1. As in our discussion of the autarky equilibrium, exactly the same situation as that shown in Figure 10.2 would result if country H subsi-

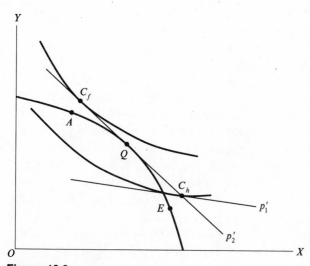

Figure 10.2

dized the consumption of X. Country H would import the subsidized good in response to the increase in demand.

This analysis shows that taxes, subsidies, or indeed any such government program can cause trade. But this trade is based on creating distortions, and thus the welfare effects of such policies and resulting trade are unclear. We now turn to an analysis of the gains from trade.

Refer again to the consumption tax/subsidy case of Figure 10.2. Recalling that A was the autarky consumption point for both countries, we can see that the decision by the government of country H to impose a consumption tax makes the consumers of this country worse off, for E, the new equilibrium, is clearly on a lower community indifference curve than A. When trade is allowed, both countries produce at Q, country F consumes at C_f, and country H consumes at C_h. C_f is on a higher indifference curve than A so country F is better off. Country H, however, may be on a higher or a lower indifference curve than E depending on where C_h is located on the line p_2'. Note that C_h is on a lower indifference curve than A regardless of where C_h is positioned, and thus country H is certainly worse off than before the tax was imposed.

The important general conclusion from this gains-from-trade analysis is that trade induced by distortions does not necessarily benefit the country with the distortion. The analysis in our gains-from-trade chapter was undertaken with the assumption that the economy was competitive and distortion free. Prices then reflect the true scarcity of resources and the true value of commodities to consumers. But distortions such as taxes or subsidies break this link, and thus prices give "false" signals about scarcity and value. Trade induced by distortions is not necessarily efficient or welfare-improving trade. We will encounter this general result a number of times throughout this book.

Now suppose that the tax on Y is collected from home country producers (or a subsidy on X is paid to home country producers of X). When trade is allowed, consumers in F will find the price of Y higher in H than in their own country since the price they face includes the tax. Consumers in H will find that Y is cheaper in F, since, by assumption, domestic consumers pay the tax only if they buy from domestic producers. Thus in this case country H will import commodity Y. In Figure 10.3 the points A and E again represent the autarky equilibrium points for countries F and H, respectively, as in Figure 10.1. With trade, country H will import Y from country F so that the price of Y increases in F and falls in country H until the consumption price ratios in the two countries are equal (remember, consumers in the two countries now face the same prices). Such a situation is shown in Figure 10.3, where p_1' is the equilibrium consumption price ratio in both countries, points Q and R are the

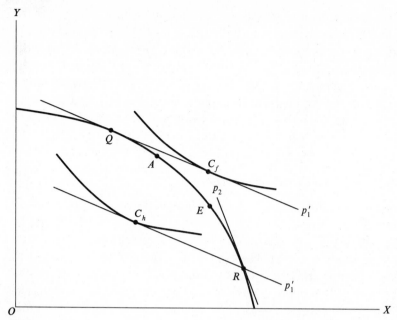

Figure 10.3

production points, and C_f and C_h are the consumption points for countries F and H, respectively. Trade is balanced since QC_f is equal to C_hR. Home country consumers face the same prices as consumers and producers in the foreign country, whereas home country producers face the distorted price ratio.

Turning to the gains from trade in the production tax case, recall that A is the pretax equilibrium production and consumption point for both countries. After the tax has been imposed by country H and trade has been allowed, country F will produce at Q and consume at C_f, and country H will produce at R and consume at C_h. For country F the consumption point C_f is superior to the consumption point A, whereas for country H the consumption point C_h is clearly inferior to A and may well be inferior to E. In the situation shown trade has made country H worse off, and autarky at E would be preferred to free trade at C_h, although this need not be the case. Again, we have the result that trade induced by distortions is not necessarily beneficial trade for the country imposing the distortion.

This last result should serve as a warning to governments that confuse production and welfare. It is true that a production subsidy can generate exports of that good. But exports are not an end in themselves as we have emphasized before. It is perfectly possible for the subsidy to generate exports yet reduce welfare.

Comparing Figure 10.2 with Figure 10.3, we see that the direction of trade is opposite in the two cases even though the tax is on Y (or the subsidy is on X) in both cases. But the result is intuitive. The consumption tax discourages consumption of Y by domestic consumers but reduces the price foreigners pay, and hence the home country will export Y in the absence of other causes of trade (Figure 10.2). The production tax discourages production of Y and permits foreign consumers to buy X at the lower tax distorted price, so the home country exports X and imports Y (Figure 10.3).

3. FACTOR MARKET DISTORTIONS

In this section we consider the effects on international trade and welfare of a factor market distortion. The particular distortion we choose is the corporate income tax. The effects of this tax are significantly different from those of a commodity tax, for the tax applies to factor returns and, as will be seen subsequently, this introduces a distortion into the production side of the model as well as changing relative commodity prices. In the following discussion we assume that the tax is imposed on one of the factors (capital) in one of the two industries (the corporate sector).

Three main effects of the corporate income tax are of interest. First, the corporate income tax, by creating a divergence between the factor-price ratios faced by producers in the two sectors, will result in production inside the production possibilities frontier. Second, the new distorted production "frontier" need no longer be concave to the origin, but could be convex or could alternate between being concave and convex. Third, in general, equilibrium price lines will no longer be tangent to the distorted production frontier. This third effect is familiar from the production tax case discussed in the previous section.

Suppose the tax on capital is in the Y industry. X producers pay r for capital, while Y producers pay $r(1 + T)$ for capital where T is the tax. The factor-price ratios faced by the X and Y industries will then bear the relationship

$$(w/r)_x > (w/r(1 + T))_y. \qquad (10.3)$$

Figure 10.4 shows the factor market allocation in an Edgeworth box. A is an initial equilibrium on the contract curve $O_x A O_y$. When the tax is introduced, the two industries will face different factor-price ratios, with that faced by the X industry being steeper than the factor-price ratio in the Y industry (equation (10.3)). A new equilibrium point must be a point like B in Figure 10.4 where the X isoquants are steeper than the Y isoquants. But note that B is not an efficient production point. At B the same amount of X is produced, but less Y than at A. B must, there-

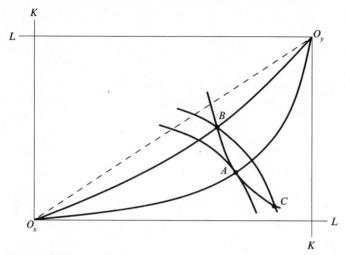

Figure 10.4

fore, correspond to a point that is interior to the efficient production frontier.

We can find all of the points in Figure 10.4 where the difference in the slopes of the X and Y isoquants is the same as at point B. Linking these distorted allocations, we have a distorted contract curve given by $O_x BO_y$ in Figure 10.4. (A larger tax could mean that the distorted contract curve lies on the other side of the diagonal, but the distorted contract curve cannot intersect the diagonal (it can lie exactly on it); these issues are not important for our purposes.)

Figure 10.5 shows the corresponding output diagram with TAT' giving the efficient production frontier. TBT' in Figure 10.5 is the distorted production frontier corresponding to the distorted contract curve in Figure 10.4. The distorted frontier need not be strictly concave from below as shown, but this is not particularly relevant for our purposes. The corporate income tax thus leads to production interior to the efficient production frontier. Note that point B in Figure 10.5 corresponds to B in Figure 10.4.

The movement from A to a point on TBT' in Figure 10.5 is not the end of the story, for the final equilibrium will not be a tangency solution. The proof is difficult, but the intuition is as follows. The slope of the distorted production frontier at a point such as B is equal to the ratio of the "true" or "social" marginal costs of producing X versus Y. But the "private" marginal cost of producing Y is greater than the true marginal cost since Y producers must pay the tax on capital. The private and social marginal costs of producing X are the same since there is no tax in that industry. Let MRT_d be the marginal rate of transformation along the

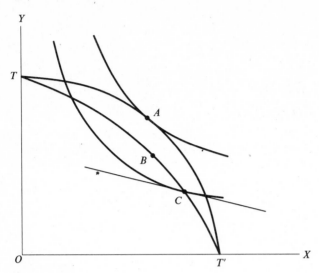

Figure 10.5

distorted production frontier TBT' in Figure 10.5. Let MC^* denote the true or social marginal cost and MC denote the private marginal cost of producing a good. The tax on capital in Y leads to the relationship

$$MRT_d = MC_x^*/MC_y^* > MC_x/MC_y \qquad (10.4)$$

since

$$MC_x^* = MC_x, \; MC_y^* < MC_y.$$

In competitive equilibrium, the ratio of private marginal costs is equal to the competitive price ratio. The inequality in (10.4) therefore implies that $MRT_d > p_1$ where p_1 is the producer price ratio. This price ratio is equal to the consumer price ratio if there are no taxes on outputs. The distorted autarky equilibrium must be at a point like C in Figure 10.5 where the CIC is flatter than the distorted production frontier. This nontangency is very much like the result obtained from the production-tax case considered in the previous section. The difference here is that the nontangency is along the distorted production frontier. The factor-market distortion thus involves two distortions: One can be thought of as the movement inside the efficient production frontier and the second as the movement along the distorted frontier.

Figure 10.6 shows the implications of the corporate income tax for the international trading equilibrium, again under the assumption that we begin with two identical countries. The initial production frontiers

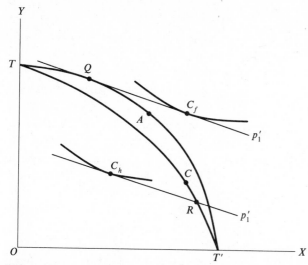

Figure 10.6

are given by TAT' with autarky equilibrium at A for each of the two countries. Country H imposes the corporate income tax with the consequences described in Figure 10.5, and in autarky consumes and produces at C. The tax discourages production of Y in country H, thus raising its price. Country F benefits from this price change, moving production to Q and exporting Y to H. Country H shifts production to R and imports Y to reach the consumption point C_h. Country H may either gain or lose from trade depending on whether the indifference curve through C_h passes above or below point C in Figure 10.6. Note that this diagram looks very similar to the production tax diagram in Figure 10.3, except for the addition of the distorted production frontier. They are indeed conceptually similar in that both taxes discourage production of Y in country H. And as before, the effect of the distortion is to create trade, but it is not necessarily beneficial trade for the country with the distortion.

Factor market distortions are a complex topic, and other types of distortions have very different effects. Other factor market distortions include the effects of unions and minimum wage laws. The preceding analysis of the corporate income tax is only one of many interesting situations. But some of the specific results we have obtained are indeed very general. First, factor-market distortions generally result in production interior to the efficient production frontier. Second, the production of disadvantaged goods (e.g., goods bearing taxes) is reduced. Third, the trade generated by the distortion is not necessarily beneficial for the country with the distortion.

4. IMPERFECT COMPETITION

The presence of monopoly in one or more of the industries in the basic model provides another type of distortion. As will be seen, the results for one of the simple cases to be discussed here are quite similar, from the point of view of trade effects, to the case of a commodity tax in one industry.

There is a variety of ways in which monopoly could be introduced. One could assume that both industries in one country were monopolized, or that monopolized industries existed in both countries. The simplest model, however, and the one that will be considered first, assumes that monopoly exists in only one industry in one country. In particular, it is assumed that in the home country commodity Y is produced by a monopolist, while X is produced under conditions of perfect competition. Both X and Y are assumed to be produced competitively in country F. The two countries have identical technologies and factor endowments and so have identical PPC's. Identical, homogeneous demand is also assumed.

The profit-maximizing rule for a producer is to increase production up to the point where the revenue gained from an additional unit sold (marginal revenue, MR) is just equal to the cost of producing that additional unit (marginal cost, MC). Small competitive firms are assumed to face fixed prices and so marginal revenue is just the price of the good: $MR = p$. The profit-maximizing rule $MR = MC$ then becomes

$$p = MC. \tag{10.5}$$

With perfect competition in both industries (as in the foreign country), equation (10.5) holds for both X and Y, and dividing one by the other, we have

$$\frac{p_x}{p_y} = \frac{MC_x}{MC_y} = MRT. \tag{10.6}$$

The right-hand side of equation (10.6) is the cost of a unit of Y in terms of a unit of X and thus is the slope of the PPC. The left-hand side is just the price ratio, and thus equation (10.6) expresses the familiar competitive equilibrium condition that the price ratio line is tangent to the PPC. This is the condition that prevails at the autarky equilibrium A in Figure 10.7.

With monopoly in industry Y, however, condition (10.5) is no longer appropriate. The monopolist faces the entire market and hence faces a downward-sloping demand curve. He cannot sell all he wants at a fixed price. To sell more units of his good he must reduce the price charged on all units (we assume that all sales are at the same price). The marginal revenue received from selling an additional unit of Y must be less than

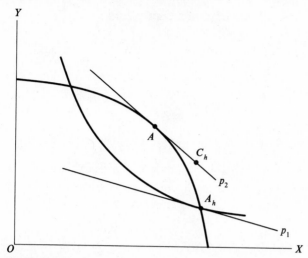

Figure 10.7

the actual price of Y because the price must be reduced on other units sold. Marginal revenue will consist of two terms: the price of the last unit sold, minus the reduced revenue on the other units sold as a consequence of the price reduction needed to sell the last unit.

The relationship between price and marginal revenue is derived as follows. Total revenue (TR) for the monopolist can be written as price times quantity:

$$TR = p_y Y. \tag{10.7}$$

Let d denote the change in a variable so that dY means "the change in Y," and so on. The change in the monopolist's total revenue can be derived from equation (10.7):

$$dTR = p_y dY + Y dp_y. \tag{10.8}$$

Students with calculus will recognize this as the rule for the differentiation of the product of two variables. Dividing equation (10.8) by dY, we obtain:

$$\frac{dTR}{dY} = p_y + Y\frac{dp_y}{dY} = MR_y < p_y. \tag{10.9}$$

Equation (10.9) is indeed marginal revenue: the change in revenue from an additional unit sold. As noted earlier, it is composed of two terms. The first is the price of the unit (p_y), and the second is the revenue lost by lowering the price on all units in order to sell the last unit ($Y(dp_y/dY)$). The latter term is the number of units sold (Y) times the price change per unit (dp_y/dY). This price change term is negative since an increase in sales

$(dY > 0)$ can only come at the expense of a decrease in price $(dp_y < 0)$. Marginal revenue is less than price.

Now multiply the second term of the MR expression in equation (10.9) by p_y/p_y and factor out a p_y from both terms:

$$MR_y = p_y \left(1 + \frac{dp_y/p_y}{dY/Y} \right) \tag{10.10}$$

$\frac{(dY/Y)}{(dp_y/p_y)}$ is just the price elasticity of demand for Y: the proportional change in Y in response to a given proportional change in p_y. Let this elasticity be denoted by e, and recall that e is less than zero because the demand curve slopes downward. Marginal revenue can now be written as

$$MR_y = p_y(1 + 1/e) \qquad e = \frac{dY/Y}{dp_y/p_y}. \tag{10.11}$$

A monopolist will only produce where marginal revenue is positive, which restricts equilibrium to sections of the demand curve where e is less than $-1 \, (> 1$ in absolute value). Demand in this region is said to be "elastic."

Given our expression for marginal revenue, the monopolist's profit-maximization rule $MR = MC$ becomes:

$$p_y(1 + 1/e) = MC_y. \tag{10.12}$$

Figure 10.8 illustrates the standard profit-maximization condition for a monopolist. With a linear demand curve D, the marginal revenue curve (MR) is also linear and steeper than D (recall that MR must be less than price at any given quantity). With marginal cost MC, the profit-maximizing output is Y_0, and this can be sold at price p_0. Clearly price is higher than marginal revenue MR_0.

Price is assumed to equal marginal cost in the X industry. The monopoly in Y (equation (10.12)) means that the economy's equilibrium condition changes from equation (10.6) to

$$\frac{p_x}{p_y(1 + 1/e)} = \frac{MC_x}{MC_y} = MRT > \frac{p_x}{p_y}. \tag{10.13}$$

The fact that $p_y > MC_y$ implies that the equilibrium price ratio p_x/p_y is less than the slope of the PPC (MRT) at the equilibrium point. This is shown in Figure 10.7, where A_h is the autarky equilibrium for the home country and p_1 is the home country's autarky price ratio.

Three facts should be noted about the monopoly equilibrium A_h relative to the competitive equilibrium at A in Figure 10.7. First, the monopolist restricts the output of Y below its competitive level at A. Second, the monopolist raises the relative price of Y above its competitive level p_2. Both effects should be familiar to students from standard partial

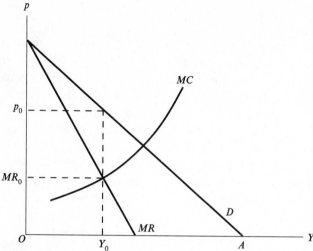

Figure 10.8

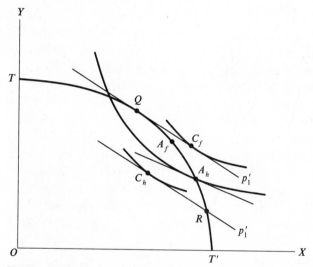

Figure 10.9

equilibrium analysis such as that in Figure 10.8. Third, welfare is reduced by the monopoly below the competitive level at A in Figure 10.7.

   The equilibrium described by equation (10.13) and Figure 10.7 looks similar to our analysis of the production tax in Section 2, and indeed, it is. If trade is opened up between the two otherwise identical economies, consumers in the home country will import the cheaper foreign Y and export X in return, much as in the case of a home country production tax on Y. This situation is shown in Figure 10.9 where the foreign country exports Y, produces at Q, consumes at C_f, and enjoys a positive gain from trade. The home country as drawn produces at R, consumes at C_h, and is worse off with trade.

This last result in Figure 10.9 that the home country is worse off with trade is not at all inevitable. Indeed, we have glossed over a key reason why we would expect trade under conditions of imperfect competition to be much more beneficial than trade with production taxes. The reason is that the variable e, the elasticity of demand, is not constant as is the fixed production tax T of the Section 2. More advanced theoretical models suggest that under a wide range of circumstances and assumptions the introduction of rival producers through trade will make the demand curve faced by the original home country monopolist more elastic. e rises or conversely $1/e$ falls in equation (10.13). The "wedge" between price and marginal cost falls with trade, and thus trade causes the economy to move toward the competitive production point. This is the subject matter of the next section.

5. PROCOMPETITIVE GAINS FROM TRADE

As just noted, the imperfect competition distortion is more complicated than the tax distortion in that the degree of distortion is endogenous in the former. But this is far from simply an annoying technical complication. In fact, it means that trade may well have additional benefits when there is imperfect competition in an economy. We will refer to these gains as "procompetitive gains from trade." This section presents a simple case, whereas the next section presents a more difficult situation.

Suppose that the economy has a monopoly producer of Y and so has an autarky equilibrium at A in Figure 10.10. The competitive equilibrium would be at B in that same diagram. To keep the example very simple, suppose that this is a small country in a very large world. Assume, in fact, that when trade is permitted, the country (and its producers) will face fixed world prices. With trade, the domestic monopolist (or former monopolist) will now face a constant p_y, and so $MR_y = p_y$ (e goes to infinity or $1/e$ goes to zero). The equality between the price ratio and the MRT will be restored. At the world price ratio p_1 in Figure 10.10 the country will produce at Q and consume at C.

Under the "small country assumption" trade takes the economy from A to C in Figure 10.10. This gain from trade can be decomposed into two separate moves: A to B and B to C. The movement from B to C is just the normal gain from trade for a distortion-free economy that we have discussed throughout this book. But now we have an additional gain from trade, which is the movement from A to B. This is what we can call the "procompetitive gain from trade" because it is equal to the gain that could

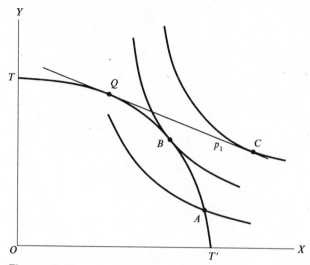

Figure 10.10

be achieved in the closed economy by eliminating the monopoly distortion.

It must be admitted that the situation shown in Figure 10.10 is rather special. As noted in Figure 10.9, trade could produce losses when there is domestic monopoly power. Nevertheless, there is a general argument in favor of the view that procompetitive gains from trade are likely to exist. This argument was outlined earlier. When trade is permitted, there will now be a larger number of Y producers in competition with any single producer. That individual producer will now have proportionately less influence over the price of the good, and therefore benefits less from restricting output. In technical terms, the individual producer usually faces a more elastic demand curve with trade. The situation shown in Figure 10.10 is just the extreme case of this more general result.

6. COURNOT-NASH COMPETITION

The purpose of this section is to present another example of procompetitive gains from trade. We assume two identical countries, and assume that each has a single monopoly producer of Y. The motivation for this example is that monopoly power often arises from the existence of scale economies and so the same industry is likely to be imperfectly competitive in all countries. Scale economies are defined and analyzed in the next chapter.

The initial autarky equilibrium for both of the identical countries is given by point A in Figure 10.11. Now suppose that we open the econo-

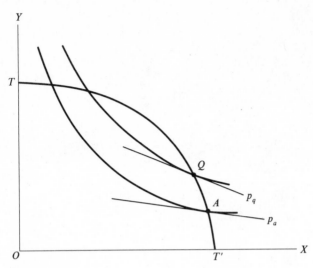

Figure 10.11

mies to trade, and assume that each monopolist (now more properly called "duopolist") views the foreign firm's output as fixed. This latter assumption is known as Cournot-Nash behavior. Now refer back to the marginal revenue expression in equation (10.9) and consider the home country Y producer. The relevant Y in this equation is now not the combined output of both producers, but rather, only the output of the home firm (and similarly for the foreign producer). MR_y for the home producer should now be written as

$$MR_{yh} = p_y + Y_h \frac{dp_y}{dY} = p_y + \frac{Y_h}{Y} Y \frac{dp_y}{dY} \qquad (10.14)$$

where $Y = Y_h + Y_f$ is the combined output of the two duopolists. Y_h/Y is the home firm's share of the "world" market for Y and can be written $s_h = Y_h/Y$. Multiplying the second term in equation (10.14) by p_y/p_y and factoring out p_y as in the previous section, we can write equation (10.14) as

$$MR_{yh} = p_y(1 + s_h/e). \qquad (10.15)$$

Equation (10.15) gives a formal demonstration of our earlier assertion. Adding producers through trade makes the demand facing any individual producer more elastic. Consider opening trade at the initial autarky equilibrium A in Figure 10.11. Can A still be an equilibrium? If both Y producers continue to produce at A, the equilibrium price p_a will remain unchanged as will the market elasticity of demand e. But with reference to equation (10.15), each firm's share of the market will fall from one (when it is a monopolist in autarky) to one-half (when it is a duopolist with trade). Recalling that the e is negative, the fall in s_h (and s_f) means that marginal revenue in equation (10.15) rises. If one firm increases output believing that the other firm will hold its output constant, some of the costs in terms of reduced price for previous units sold is borne by the rival firm. Thus the firm that is increasing its output perceives marginal revenue to be greater than if it was a monopolist bearing all of the cost of a price reduction.

When trade is opened up, each firm thus perceives MR to be in excess of MC. Each firm will thus increase output until the $MR = MC$ equality is reestablished. This could be at a point like Q in Figure 10.11 with a price ratio p_q. Curiously, there will be no net trade in this example as each country consumes and produces the same amounts of X and Y (with no trade barriers some consumers could be buying from the foreign producer and vice versa, but this trade exactly balances). Yet there is clearly a gain from the removal of trade barriers as the competition between the two Y producers generates an increase in Y production in each country. The increase in welfare shown in Figure 10.11 could be termed a "pure" procompetitive gain from trade. Note, in particular, that there is no pattern of comparative advantage in this example since the countries are identical in all respects. Yet there is a "gain from trade," which means that a pattern of comparative advantage is not a necessary condition for gains from trade. Much more will be said about "noncomparative advantage trade" in the next chapter on scale economies.

7. CONCLUDING REMARKS

This chapter has deviated substantially from traditional trade theory in which one often finds only the Ricardian and Heckscher-Ohlin models presented as determinants of trade. We believe that this narrow view is inappropriate in today's world. Governments have taken active and very major roles in most economies. Our discussion of tax and subsidy distortions is intended to provide some insight as to how various government policies can affect trade and the gains from trade, even if their intended purpose is unrelated to trade (e.g., the corporate income tax is not instituted to affect trade). One important general lesson from our analysis is that exports should never be confused with welfare. We showed cases in which a subsidy did indeed generate exports for the country, but welfare was thereby reduced.

Similarly, large corporations are a fact of great importance in today's world. To ignore these corporations and continue to assume that we live in the world of perfect competition is to miss both serious qualifications to the theory and a potentially very important source of gains from trade. The latter is particularly important for small countries that would have highly inefficient and imperfectly competitive manufacturing sectors in the absence of trade. The reason for this lies in the existence of scale economies, a subject to which we now turn.

PROBLEMS

1. Illustrate the case (similar to Figure 10.2) where, with a consumption tax in country H, trade reduces welfare (i.e., relative to E).

2. Use the gains-from-trade argument to show that country F will always be made better off by a tax in H (when the two countries are initially identical), regardless of whether the tax in H is a consumption or a production tax.

3. Suggest how our analysis of commodity taxes would change if the tax was collected by tax collectors who would have been producing X or Y in the absence of the tax (i.e., the institution of the tax reduces the effective labor supply to X and Y production). What is the relationship between the production and consumption points in autarky? Do you have a guess as to what an economist would mean by "cost of revenue-raising"?

4. With monopoly in both industries would it be possible to have the price line tangent to the production possibility curve? What condition would this require?

5. Redraw Figure 10.9 so that the home country gains from trade.

6. In the situation where only one country has the monopoly in Y and the countries are otherwise identical, could trade result in factor-price equalization?

7. With imperfect competition and/or commodity taxes, do the differences in autarky factor prices necessarily tell you anything about differences in factor endowments?

REFERENCES

Friedlaender, A., and A. Vandendorpe (1968). "Excise Taxes and Gains from Trade." *Journal of Political Economy* 76, 1058–1068.

Herberg, H., M. C. Kemp, and S. P. Magee (1971). "Factor Market Distortions, the Reversal of Factor Intensities, and the Relation between Product Prices and Equilibrium Outputs." *Economic Record* 47, 518–530.

Kemp, M. C., and H. Herberg (1971). "Factor Market Distortions, the Shape of the Locus of Competitive Outputs, and the Relation between Product Prices and Equilibrium Outputs." In J. Bhagwati et al. (eds.), *Trade, Balance of Payments and Growth*. Amsterdam: North-Holland.

Magee, S. R. (1971). "Factor Market Distortions, Production, Distribution and the Pure Theory of International Trade." *Quarterly Journal of Economics* 85, 623–643.

Markusen, J. R. (1981). "Trade and the Gains from Trade with Imperfect Competition." *Journal of International Economics* 11, 531–551.

Markusen, J. R., and A. J. Robson (1980). "Simple General Equilibrium and Trade with a Monopsonized Sector." *Canadian Journal of Economics* 13, 668–682.

Melvin, J. R. (1970). "Commodity Taxation as a Determinant of Trade." *Canadian Journal of Economics* 3, 62–78.

——(1975). *The Tax Structure and Canadian Trade.* Toronto: Economic Council of Canada. See Chapters 2, 4.

——(1979). "Short-Run Price Effects of the Corporate Income Tax and Implications for International Trade." *American Economic Review* 69, 765–774.

——(1982). "The Corporate Income Tax in an Open Economy." *Journal of Public Economics* 17, 393–403.

——, and R. D. Warne (1973). "Monopoly and the Theory of International Trade." *Journal of International Economics* 3, 117–134.

chapter *11*

Increasing Returns to Scale

1. INTRODUCTION

It has long been recognized that economies of scale provide an opportunity for trade and gains from trade. Yet very little theoretical research has been done on scale economies until recently. This is in spite of the fact that empirical research in countries as large as Canada and the Western European countries has emphasized the benefits of trade in allowing domestic firms to rationalize production. High protective tariffs in some of these countries have encouraged the manufacturing industries to produce a wide range of goods in small production runs, rather than to concentrate on larger and more efficient production of a narrower range of commodities. The more recent view is that even countries as large as the United States have not exhausted scale economies in the domestic market in some industries. Commercial aircraft and computers are two examples. U.S. consumers benefit from lower prices and higher quality in these industries because companies like Boeing and IBM can spread very high fixed costs over foreign as well as domestic sales.

The gains from trade due to scale economies can be understood fairly intuitively. Suppose, for example, that the cities and towns across the United States could not trade with one another. What do you suppose automobiles would cost if each town had to produce its own? The disadvantages of small-scale production would likely make automobiles prohibitively expensive in all but the largest cities. Trade allows production to be concentrated in a few large factories that ship to all parts of the nation. In fact, even countries as large as Canada cannot fully reap the scale economies inherent in automobile production. Thus Canada entered in the Auto Pact of 1965 with the United States in order to achieve further scale economies. As a result of the increased trade permitted by the pact, plants in both countries (but especially Canada) produced fewer varieties of cars, increased the length of production runs, and thereby lowered costs.

One reason that scale economies have not received the attention they deserve in the theory of international trade is that they are difficult to model. Scale economies are generally inconsistent with perfect competition in production, for reasons discussed in the next section. Thus some of the techniques used in earlier chapters to analyze trade are no longer useful.

2. EXTERNAL ECONOMIES

One exception to this problem of analyzing scale economies in general equilibrium occurs when scale economies are external to individual firms and, instead, occur at the industry level or at the level of industry groups (e.g., the manufacturing sector). Individual firms remain "small" so that the tools of competitive general-equilibrium theory can still be used. It should be emphasized that this is not just a technical convenience. The very first formal analysis of international trade is found in Adam Smith and the emphasis is on the increased size of the market permitting a greater degree of specialization and therefore higher productivity. It was only sometime later that Ricardo introduced the notion of comparative advantage that became the cornerstone of international trade theory. Adam Smith's view was largely forgotten until recently.

Take, for example, agriculture. Economies of scale for individual farms run out at a very small (relative to the size of the market) level of production. Yet as the size of the agricultural sector has grown, it has become profitable to produce specialized machinery and fertilizer, build railroads and handling facilities, conduct research to better seed varieties, and so forth. All of these things have meant that cost decreased, as production increased, or rather, that the industry as a whole captures scale economies, even though each individual producer may have constant returns to scale.

With external economies, there is no need to worry much about imperfect competition or monopoly pricing. Suppose that we have two absolutely identical economies whose production frontiers are both given by TT' in Figure 11.1. The production frontier is bowed in, under the assumption (as discussed in Chapter 2) that scale economies in X and/or Y outweigh any factor-intensity effects. Assume that the autarky consumption and production point for both countries is given by point A in Figure 11.1. (In general, the indifference curve will not be tangent to the *PPF* unless scale economies are equal in the two industries, but that is not important for our purposes here.) It is interesting and important to note that in this case no pattern of comparative advantage exists (autarky prices are equal), and yet there are potential gains to be had from specialization and trade. Suppose that country H specializes in Y and country F specializes in X, so that they produce at Q_h and Q_f, respectively, in Figure 11.1. Each country could then trade half of its output for half of the other country's output, so that each country would consume at $C_h = C_f$ in Figure 11.1. The utility level in each country would increase, and thus both countries would be better off, even though they were absolutely identical to start with. It is in this sense that scale economies offer gains from specialization, above and beyond those obtained from any pattern of comparative advantage.

Although the consumption point $C_f = C_h$ in Figure 11.1 could be an equilibrium, it is unlikely. An indifference curve of each country could be tangent to the cord TT' exactly at the midpoint, but only by chance.

Suppose in Figure 11.1 that when the countries specialize, each wishes to consume at point E. This cannot be a trading equilibrium since the desired exports and imports of country H exceed the desired exports and imports of country F. In order to balance trade, the price of X will

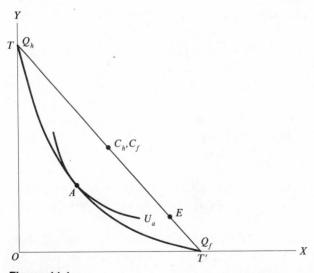

Figure 11.1

have to rise and the price of Y will have to fall. An equilibrium will eventually be reached as in Figure 11.2, where country H consumes at C_h and country F consumes at C_f. The gains from trade are shared unequally even though the countries are identical. In fact, it is just possible that in equilibrium the price of Y is so low that the price line from Q_h passes below A, resulting in losses for country H.

If country H were run by an all-knowing dictator, he would, of course, refuse to allow the country to specialize in Y in the case of Figure 11.2. He could, for example, restrict the sale of Y to keep its price higher. But the problem is that in a highly decentralized economy with external economies or imperfect competition (discussed subsequently), there is no mechanism that can ensure that the country will not inadvertently end up like country H in Figure 11.2 (or worse). The equilibrium in Figure 11.2 is stable. In country H the relative price of X in terms of Y (the slope of the price line) is less than the relative cost of producing X in terms of Y (the slope of the *PPF*). Thus H is in equilibrium specializing in Y. This demonstrates that it is possible with scale economies that the significant gains from trade could be very unevenly distributed and that one country could, in fact, lose from trade.

This simple model of scale economies provides an interesting contrast to the Hechscher-Ohlin model with respect to the effects of trade on factor prices. In the situation shown in Figures 11.1 and 11.2 factor prices are not only not equalized by trade, but they are actually driven apart by trade. At the autarky equilibrium A in Figure 11.1 the factor prices in the two identical countries must be equalized. With trade, one country spe-

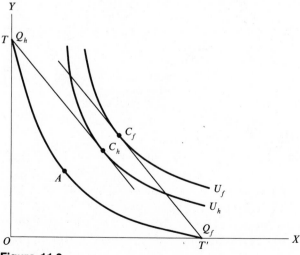

Figure 11.2

cializes in Y and the other in X. Now since the two countries have the same technologies and factor endowments by the assumption that they are identical, each has the same total bundle of factors allocated to the good that it is producing. But if X is labor-intensive relative to Y, for example, the slope of an X isoquant through a given factor bundle must be steeper than the Y isoquant through that same factor bundle (e.g., refer back to Figure 8.5). In each country, the factor price ratio w/r will be the slope of the isoquant of its good through the endowment point. Taken together, these arguments imply that if X is labor intensive, then the country specializing in X in Figure 11.1 or 11.2 will have a higher w/r ratio than the country specializing in Y. The factor-price ratios, which are equal in the absence of trade, are driven apart by trade.

Note that this last example implies that each country in Figures 11.1 and 11.2 has a relatively high price for the factor used intensively in its export industry. This has some very important implications for the effects of factor mobility, which we will discuss in a later chapter.

3. INTERNAL ECONOMIES OF SCALE

Suppose now that economies of scale are internal to the individual firm. This applies to many manufacturing firms that obtain advantages from large-scale production. It is also likely true for some extractive industries such as mining and petroleum. Internal economies may also characterize some service industries such as banking, finance, and insurance.

The problem with internal economies of scale is that they are generally inconsistent with perfect competition and competitive equilibrium. The problem is examined in Figure 11.3. Suppose a firm must incur some large fixed cost in plant or equipment in order to start production, but thereafter can produce with constant returns to scale or more precisely at a constant marginal cost. Total cost will be given by

$$C = F + mX; \qquad m = MC; \qquad AC = F/X + m \qquad (11.1)$$

where F is fixed cost, m is marginal cost, and X is output. Average cost is equal to C/X and is given by $AC = F/X + m$. The situation is shown in Figure 11.3 where MC is constant. AC falls steadily as the fixed cost is spread over a larger and larger output. AC approaches but never actually touches MC.

Could we have in this situation a competitive equilibrium in which price equals marginal cost? The answer is no, as we can show in a simple proof by contradiction. Suppose that the current market price was given by $p = p_c = MC$ in Figure 11.3, and that each firm perceived this price to be constant. At any output each firm would lose money by virtue of

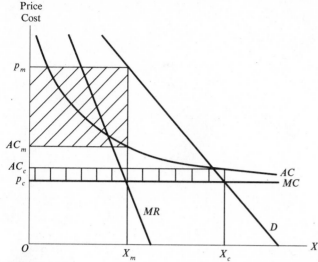

Figure 11.3

the fact that $AC > MC = p_c$ or that the average cost exceeds price no matter how much the firm produced. Thus price cannot equal marginal cost in equilibrium. If, for example, the firm produced at X_c in Figure 11.3 where demand cuts the marginal cost curve, the firm's losses (negative profits) are given by the vertically hatched rectangle. This area is the per unit loss of price minus the average cost ($p_c - AC_c$) times the number of units produced (X_c) or ($p_c - AC_c)X_c$.

Suppose, instead, that the current price exceeds marginal cost, while retaining the competitive assumption that each firm believes that it could sell all it wanted to at this price. In this case each firm would attempt to produce an infinitely large output, since at some point AC would fall below price and then keep falling. Thus no competitive equilibrium exists with internal increasing returns since either (1) the price is equal to (or below) marginal cost, in which case no firm will wish to produce anything, or (2) the price is above marginal cost, in which case each firm will attempt to produce an infinite amount.

One feasible solution to this dilemma is for one large firm to monopolize the industry and somehow manage to prevent the entry of other firms (e.g., by threatening to lower its price below average cost if another firm enters). We then have the standard monopoly outcome shown in Figure 11.3 where MR is the marginal revenue curve drawn with respect to the demand curve D. Monopoly output and price are given by X_m and p_m, respectively, where $MR = MC$. Profits are given by the diagonally hatched rectangle, ($p_m - AC_m)X_m$, or unit profit times output.

Alternatively, we could allow for free entry of firms to occur up to

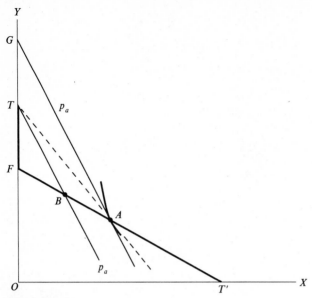

Figure 11.4

the point where the demand curve facing each individual firm is driven down to the point where it is just tangent to the AC curve at one point. But in this and indeed all possible equilibria we must be left with the situation that price exceeds marginal cost ($p > MC$). This is the key result for our purposes: Price must exceed MC or the firms will be losing money.

Figure 11.4 gives a general-equilibrium representation of this fixed cost plus constant marginal-cost technology, which we will use for the remainder of the chapter. Suppose that X and Y are produced from a single factor labor (L), which is in fixed supply ($L = L_x + L_y$). Assume further that Y is produced with constant returns to scale by a competitive industry so that units can be chosen such that $Y = L_y$. If Y is chosen as *numeraire* ($p_y = 1$), the wage rate in terms of Y will, therefore, also equal 1. p will denote the price of X in terms of Y, with the cost of producing X simply given by L_x.

It is assumed that the production of X requires an initial fixed cost, given by F, and then a constant marginal cost, m, as in the preceding example. The total cost of labor required to produce X is then $L_x = F + mX$. The production frontier for this economy is shown in Figure 11.4 as TFT'. $T = \bar{L}$ is the maximum output of Y when $X = 0$. To begin producing X, the fixed cost TF must be invested before any output is realized. Thereafter, the constant marginal cost of producing X gives the linear segment FT', which has a slope equal to m. This "kinked" production frontier is just a special case of the concave-to-the-origin PPC shown in Figures 11.1 and 11.2 and discussed in Chapter 2. Note that although the *PPC* in Figure 11.4 is composed of linear segments, it has this concavity property in that the *PPC* lies everywhere below the diagonal connecting its endpoints T and T'.

The average cost of producing X is just total cost (L_x) divided by output, or

$$AC_x = \frac{L_x}{X} = \frac{(\bar{L} - L_y)}{X} = \frac{(T - Y)}{X}. \tag{11.2}$$

Consider point A in Figure 11.4. Equation (11.2) shows, for example, that the average cost of producing the amount of X at A is simply the slope of the line passing through T and A (the dashed line in Figure 11.4). As we move along the linear segment FT', we see that the average cost of X is everywhere decreasing in the output of X, or alternatively, production of X is characterized by increasing returns to scale. The equilibrium price ratio must cut the production frontier if positive X is produced at non-negative profits. This result is just the general-equilibrium representation of the result in Figure 11.3 that price must exceed marginal cost. In Figure 11.4 the slope of the price ratio must exceed the slope of the *PPC* along FT', which is equal to m, the marginal cost of production.

An autarky equilibrium with strictly positive profits for a monopoly producer of X is shown in Figure 11.4, where the price ratio p_a through equilibrium point A is steeper than the average cost of X, given again by the slope of TA. Point G in Figure 11.4 gives the GNP of the country in terms of good Y. Workers are paid a wage of 1 in terms of Y (since the marginal product of labor in Y is 1), and so total wage income is given by $\bar{L} = \bar{Y}$ or OT in Figure 11.4. GNP is thus composed of wage income in terms of Y (OT) and profits in terms of Y (TG). The budget line of wage earners is given by a line with slope p_a through $T = \bar{L}$ as shown in Figure 11.4. Since wage earners income is fixed at $T = \bar{L}$ in terms of Y, a decrease in p always increases wage earners' utility or real income (their budget line rotates around the fixed point T). Wage income equals GNP if profits are zero (e.g., if the price ratio is given by the dashed line TA in Figure 11.4). Trade will change GNP through either changes in workers' utilities and/or changes in monopoly profits. These two components of GNP may, of course, change in opposite directions.

4. SOURCES OF GAINS FROM TRADE WITH INCREASING RETURNS

Although it is possible to lose from trade due to the distortion between price and marginal cost, there exist five separate sources of potential "noncomparative advantage" gains from trade in the presence of scale economies and imperfect competition.

1. Procompetitive Gains   This was discussed in the previous chapter so we will only briefly repeat the point here. Scale economies imply that the market can support only a limited number of firms, which will consequently be imperfectly competitive. Trade creates a larger market that can support a larger number of firms and hence a greater level of competition. A pure procompetitive gain can be shown in Figure 11.4 as follows. Suppose that the introduction of trade forces the price ratio down from p_a to the slope of the dashed line TA in Figure 11.4. Further, make the (implausible) assumption that the X producer does not change his output from that at A, so that he is now just producing at average cost. The country's budget line will now be the dashed line TA, which will cut the indifference curve through A. Consumers will be able to improve their welfare by moving down this budget line from A, importing X, and exporting Y.

2. Decreasing Average Production Cost   Suppose now that there is a monopoly producer of X in the home country but that he prices at average cost (perhaps he is threatened by the entry of new firms). Initial autarky equilibrium is given by point A in Figure 11.5 at price ratio p_a. Suppose now that we add a second identical country and assume that only one producer survives in trade due to pricing down to average cost (i.e., one firm is driven out of the market). Arbitrarily assume that the home firm survives, an assumption that makes little difference to welfare. The home firm could double its output, moving from A to Q_1 in Figure 11.5, with the foreign country now specializing in Y and producing at T. The home firm's X production is then equal to the former total production in the two countries. But the movement to Q_1 along with pricing at average cost means that the price ratio has fallen from p_a to p_1 in Figure 11.5. Consumers in each country will want to consume at C_1 in Figure 11.5, which involves consuming more X than at A. Due to the fall in price the world demand for X has increased while the total world supply of X is unchanged. Thus Q_1 and C_1 cannot be the trading equilibrium.

Equilibrium will only be reestablished after a further increase in X production. The final equilibrium could involve both countries specializing, for example, with country F at T and country H at T' in Figure 11.5. Both countries could consume at C_2, halfway between T and T'. This is an improbable outcome, but the point is that the production point will be somewhere between Q_1 and T' unless demand for X is so great that there is still excess demand for X when country H specializes. Whatever the

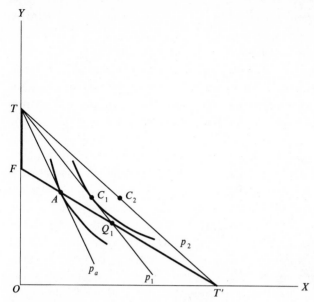

Figure 11.5

exact position of the final equilibrium, several things can be demonstrated. First, both countries must be better off with trade. Second, this gain from trade is realized by two initially identical countries and there is no "pro-competitive gain" in the sense used earlier. The gain is entirely in terms of the lower cost of production captured by having one firm serve a large international market rather than a smaller national market.

3. Exit of Redundant Firms The gain from trade described in the previous section was partly due to the fact that we replaced two firms in autarky with a single larger, more efficient firm with trade. But we could equally well have argued the point about decreasing average cost by assuming that the foreign country was too small to support X production before trade (i.e., their demand curve was everywhere below average cost). The exit of one firm was not key to the argument. Here we would like to focus more directly on the exit of firms as a source of gains from trade.

Scale economies pose something of a dilemma with respect to the number of firms in an industry. On the one hand, a small number of firms is desirable from the point of view of technical efficiency. If the average-cost curve is everywhere downward sloping (as in our current example), it is desirable to have the entire industry output produced by a single firm. But if we drop the assumption of the previous section that a firm automatically prices down to average cost, a small number of firms generally implies greater market power and correspondingly greater monopoly output restriction. This trade-off for a single economy gives rise to a third source of gains from trade. With trade, we can have simultaneously more firms competing with one another yet fewer firms in each country individually. If we combine two countries with 10 firms each, competition could, for example, drive out three firms in each country. The number of firms in each country has decreased, but the total number competing with one another is now 14 rather than the 10 that were competing in each country in autarky.

More advanced theoretical treatments have shown that this is exactly the kind of outcome we would get if there is Cournot-Nash competition and free entry of firms in each country. Free entry drives profits down to zero in each country in autarky. But the opening of trade causes each firm to perceive demand as more elastic, as was discussed in the previous chapter. Firms will increase output and some firms will exit as profits are initially negative. The trading equilibrium will have fewer firms in each country, with each firm producing a higher level of output at lower average cost. Empirical analyses for Canada have confirmed that trade liberalization has this rationalizing effect on manufacturing firms.

The situation is illustrated in Figure 11.6, where A is the autarky equilibrium for each of two identical countries. Free entry has forced price down to average cost and the vertical distance TF' is now interpreted as the combined fixed costs of the existing firms. Trade causes each Cournot-

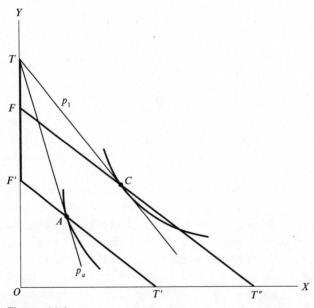

Figure 11.6

Nash firm to perceive its demand curve as more elastic, causing each to increase output. But this leads to negative profits and the exit of some firms. Equilibrium is restored at a lower price with fewer firms in each country individually, but more firms in total. Exit of the redundant firms frees up the resources that had been devoted to fixed costs and shifts the production frontier of each country out to TFT''. No trade, or more correctly, no net trade, need occur since both countries are identical and both countries attain consumption point C in Figure 11.6. Note that the two identical countries could not have reached point C in Figure 11.6 if the number of firms had remained fixed at the autarky level. The best that the two countries could have done without the exit of some firms would be to reach a point on the diagonal between T and T' in Figure 11.6 (one country specializing in X and one in Y). Point C lies to the Northwest of this diagonal and constitutes a higher consumption level for each of the countries.

4. Increased Product Diversity Gains from trade in the form of increased product diversity have been emphasized in a series of recent papers. This is usually referred to as the "monopolistic competition model" of trade, since it draws on the model of the same name used in microeconomics and industrial organization theory. The idea is that an industry is "competitive" in that there are a large number of firms, but it is also "monopolistic" in that each firm is producing a somewhat unique product. The latter assumption implies that these firms do individually face downward-sloping demand curves.

The situation is shown in Figure 11.7, where we now assume that both X and Y are produced with IRS. Production functions for X and Y are identical and the goods are symmetric but imperfect substitutes in consumption. This last assumption means that consumers are indifferent between one unit of X and one unit of Y, but that they would like to have some of both rather than more of just one. The consumer is, for example, indifferent between a stereo and a television, but would rather have one stereo and one television than have either two stereos or two televisions. Consumers prefer diversity.

In autarky, each of the identical countries in Figure 11.7 could attain consumption point A. But this is now not the best choice, even in autarky. Due to the large fixed costs, it is in a country's interest in autarky to produce only one good, specializing in either Y at point T or in X at point T' in Figure 11.7. This puts the country on an indifference curve through T and T', which is higher than the indifference curve through A. The benefits of product diversity are outweighed by the high fixed costs of starting production of the second good. With trade, each country could

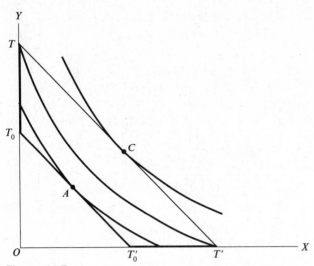

Figure 11.7

specialize in one of the goods and trade half of its output for half of the output of the other country's good, and thereby attain consumption point C in Figure 11.7 (again, this is unlikely to be the actual equilibrium). In this situation there is no change in the average cost of a good nor are there any procompetitive gains. Instead, scale economies were limiting the number of goods consumed before trade, and consumers have "decided" to take the gains from trade in the form of having more products rather than having lower costs for their existing products.

Gains from trade through product differentiation can be looked in a second way as well. While consumers may prefer diversity as just noted, consumers themselves may also have different tastes. Consumers may, for example, buy only one automobile each, but they have different views as to what is the "ideal" automobile for their tastes and income level. Due to scale economies, no country can afford to produce a unique automobile for each consumer. Germany produces Volkswagens and Mercedes, and France produces Renaults and Peugeots, all of which have somewhat different characteristics from consumers' points of view. Trade in automobiles then occurs between France and Germany due to the fact that some Germans prefer Renaults or Peugeots and some Frenchmen prefer Volkswagens or Mercedes.

This situation is shown in Figure 11.8. Suppose that automobiles have only two characteristics—size and fuel efficiency. There is a trade-off between these two characteristics such that if one wants a bigger car he or she must sacrifice some fuel efficiency. Figure 11.8 shows three possible combinations of size and efficiency, denoted X, Y, and Z, corresponding

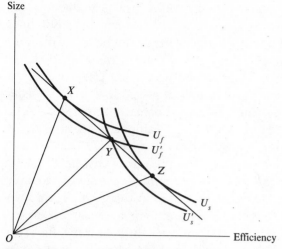

Figure 11.8

to three different types of cars. Suppose that all three models could be produced at the same average cost for the same volume of production. But due to scale economies, the average cost rises steeply as sales fall. Assume finally that societies consist of only two groups, students and faculty, and that the former have a relatively high preference for efficiency and the latter a relatively high preference for size. Indifference curves are given by U_s and U_f in Figure 11.8, respectively.

Even though the three possible models cost the same at the same level of production, scale economies force a choice. If the country produces both X and Y, giving students and faculty their "ideal" car, the volume of sales of each model will be much lower and the average cost much higher than if only the single compromise model Y was produced. Thus an entirely possible outcome is that only model Y is produced. It sells for a modest cost, but faculty are cramped and students poor from buying gas. These groups attain indifference curves U'_f and U'_s in Figure 11.8, respectively. Now if we add a second identical country through trade, one country could produce model X and the other country produce model Z, each exporting half its output for half the foreign output of the other model. Each country would be producing the same number of cars as it produced in autarky, and consequently, the cars would have the same average cost. Assuming X and Z sell for the same price that Y did in autarky, consumers pay the same for cars but attain the higher indifference curves U_f and U_s in Figure 11.8 since they now each get their most preferred model. As in the example of Figure 11.7, consumers take the gains from trade in terms of increased product diversity rather than in the form of lower prices.

5. Specialized Plants and Inputs   Increases in market size due to trade may also permit firms to build plants specialized to fewer product lines and to create specialized inputs. Machinery that is highly specialized to certain products, and business or engineering consultants who specialize in certain problems are two of many possible examples. Little theoretical work has been done on the former, although empirical analysis in Canada, for example, has emphasized plant specialization as an important source of gains from trade liberalization. Figure 11.7 can be used to convey the idea with indifference curves now interpreted as isoquants for final output. Creation of specialized inputs requires an initial fixed cost of TT. Two countries in autarky each create only one such input in the simple example of Figure 11.7. An output level corresponding to the isoquant through T and T' is attained in each country from the amount of resources devoted to producing this good. Combining the countries through trade, the creation of two specialized inputs is profitable and the output level at C can now be attained as each country trades half of the output of its specialized input for half the other country's product.

5. IMPLICATIONS FOR TRADITIONAL RESULTS

Our analysis of scale economies has produced a number of results that differ in very basic ways from those of the more traditional Ricardian and Heckscher-Ohlin models. First, there is the question of the direction of trade. In the traditional models the direction of trade is related to underlying characteristics of the economy. In the Heckscher-Ohlin model, for example, we saw that a country exported the goods that used intensively the country's relatively abundant factors. With scale economies, however, there may be some inherent arbitrariness in the pattern of specialization. This was emphasized in Figure 11.1 and in subsequent diagrams, where we noted that with scale economies, trade could arise for two identical economies or rather for two economies for which there existed no pattern of comparative advantage. Countries should specialize, but the welfare effects may depend on which country specializes in which good.

One implication of this result is that the observed pattern of trade in goods produced with returns to scale may often be determined by historical factors, such as which country entered an industry first. The first entrant gains an advantage (sometimes called "first mover advantage") by achieving low costs and perhaps technical expertise early, and may thereby discourage foreign entrants, who might have to enter initially at high cost.

Second, returns to scale have implications for the gains from trade, implications that differ in a number of ways from the more traditional results. On the one hand, scale economies offer more possibilities for gains, whereas on the other hand, there are possible complicating factors. As we showed earlier, scale economies may mean that there will be gains from trade even for two identical economies. Alternatively, gains from trade exist independently of any pattern of comparative advantage. The lower costs and increased product diversity achieved through the capture of scale economies is thus an additional source of gains, which complements the gains achieved from other bases for trade, such as differences in factor endowments.

Strong conclusions about gains from trade are, however, impossible due to the fact that scale economies are generally associated with distortions, for reasons noted before. The result is that a country's prices may not reflect accurately the underlying costs and pattern of comparative advantage. When this happens, a country could end up specializing in the wrong goods, to the point where trade actually results in welfare losses.

The third implication of scale economies for traditional results has to do with factor-price equalization. In Chapter 8 we noted that under strong assumptions (including nonspecialization and no factor-intensity reversals) trade would equalize factor prices if it equalized commodity prices. Yet even under these restrictive assumptions, factor-price equalization will generally not occur in the presence of scale economies. With scale economies, factor prices will depend upon the scale of production as well as on the other factors discussed in Chapter 8. Thus, unless countries produce at the same scale in addition to satisfying all of the other restrictive assumptions, factor prices will not be equalized by trade. This situation is reinforced by the fact that scale economies make specialization seem much more likely. We showed in connection with Figure 11.1 that the two identical countries will not have equal factor prices in the trading equilibrium. Each country will in that case have a relatively high price for the factor used intensively in its export industry. This has important implications for international factor movements, as will be discussed in a later chapter.

From an empirical point of view, many economists are coming to feel that scale economies make up a very important determinant of trade and the gains from trade for countries the size of Canada and many of the Western European nations. Empirical estimates of the gains from trade liberalization in both of these regions suggest that a major source of gains has been a rationalization of the manufacturing and certain service industries. Some would assert that these rationalization effects constituted the major source of gains from the formation of the EEC, outweighing factors having to do with comparative advantage. There is also an increasing acceptance of the view that issues involving scale economies and imperfect competition are important for as large a country as the United States. Finally, with the increased mobility of factors of production (especially capital) and technology across international borders, there is some reason to suggest that the Heckscher-Ohlin and Ricardian bases for trade may be relatively less important in explaining trade among the industrialized countries than they were even a few decades ago. The very large volume of trade among the very similar economies of North America, the EEC, and Japan seems to constitute prima facie evidence that scale economies, imperfect competition, and product differentiation are an important part of the story.

PROBLEMS

1. Show that if both countries wanted to consume at E in Figure 11.1, then there would be excess demand for X and excess supply of Y.

2. Show by redrawing Figure 11.2 that the relative price of Y could drop so low that country 1 would lose from trade.

3. Show that if a firm's price is less than its average cost, then its profits must be negative.

4. What is the largest output that the firm could produce in Figure 11.3 and still break even?

5. Draw another equilibrium in Figure 11.5 where the country loses from trade.

6. Using Figure 11.6, show that point C could not be attained by the two countries if some firms did not exit from the industry.

7. Redraw Figure 11.7 with different indifference curves such that autarky equilibrium at A is preferred to an equilibrium at either T or T'.

8. In the discussion of product diversity and monopolistic competition, we consider two different situations: (a) consumers have identical tastes but prefer diversity (Figure 11.7) and (b) consumers have heterogeneous tastes (Figure 11.8). Which approach is probably more useful in each of the following situations: (1) choosing groceries in a supermarket, (2) buying a house, (3) shopping for clothing, (4) choosing a new stereo?

REFERENCES

Helpman, E. (1981). "International Trade in the Presence of Product Differentiation, Economies of Scale and Monopolistic Competition. A Chamberlinian-Heckscher-Ohlin Approach." *Journal of International Economics* II, 304–340.

Horstman, I., and J. R. Markusen (1986). "Up the Average Cost Curve: Inefficient Entry and the New Protectionism." *Journal of International Economics* 20, 225–248.

Harris, R. G. (1984a). *Trade, Industrial Policy, and Canadian Manufacturing.* Toronto: University of Toronto Press.

———. (1984b). "Applied General Equilibrium Analysis of Small Open Economies with Scale Economies and Imperfect Competition." *American Economic Review* 74, 1016–1032.

Kemp, M. C. (1969). *The Pure Theory of International Trade and Investment.* Englewood Cliffs, N. J.: Prentice-Hall.

Krugman, P. (1979). "Increasing Returns, Monopolistic Competition, and International Trade." *Journal of International Economics* 9, 469–479.

Lancaster, K. (1980). "Intra-Industry Trade Under Perfect Monopolistic Competition." *Journal of International Economics* 10, 151–175.

Markusen, J. R. (1981). "Trade and the Gains from Trade with Imperfect Competition." *Journal of International Economics* 11, 531–551.

———, and J. R. Melvin (1981). "Trade, Factor Prices and the Gains from Trade with Increasing Returns to Scale." *Canadian Journal of Economics* 14, 450–469.

Melvin, J. R. (1969). "Increasing Returns to Scale as a Determinant of Trade." *Canadian Journal of Economics* 2, 389–402.

Wonnacott, R. J., and P. Wonnacott (1967). *Free Trade Between the United States and Canada.* Cambridge, Mass.: Harvard University Press.

chapter 12

Tastes and Per Capita Income as Determinants of Trade

1. INTERNATIONAL TASTE DIFFERENCES

Previous chapters have focused on the production side of the general-equilibrium model to describe the causes of trade and the gains from trade. This focus is representative of trade theory in general, which has devoted the overwhelming share of its attention to production, almost neglecting consumption entirely. A great many models assume that consumers have identical and homothetic utility functions, regardless of where they are located. This means that if commodity prices were equalized by trade, consumers everywhere would demand goods in the same proportions. All trade would then be due to various differences in production among countries. But there has been little empirical examination of this presumption that production differences are far more important than consumption differences. Accordingly, the purpose of this chapter is to pull a few fragments of literature together in order to examine the possible ways in which international differences in consumption patterns can influence trade flows.

Following our previous methodology, we assume that the only difference that exists between countries is in demand conditions, for only in this way can we be sure that the results derived depend entirely on differences in demand. In particular, we assume that endowments in the two countries are identical, that production functions are identical across countries, and that production takes place with constant returns and perfect competition. This implies that the production possibility curves for the two countries will be identical, so that TT' of Figure 12.1 represents the *PPC* for both the foreign and the home country. In this section we also assume that there are no distortions in the model, and that the utility functions of the two countries, while differing, are both homogeneous. The case of nonhomogeneous demand is considered in Section 2. Thus the autarky equilibrium is the point where the highest indifference curve for each country is tangent to the *PPC*. If we assume that tastes in country H are biased toward commodity Y relative to tastes in country F, then U_h and U_f could be representative indifference curves for the utility functions of countries H and F, respectively.

The autarky positions for countries H and F are A_h and A_f, respectively, and the autarky price lines are p_h and p_f in Figure 12.1. Thus in autarky, commodity Y is relatively expensive in country H, whereas commodity X is relatively expensive in country F. When trade is permitted, the residents of country H, observing that Y is relatively less expensive in the foreign country, will shift their purchases from the home country to country F. Similarly, residents of the foreign country, observing that commodity X can be purchased more cheaply in country H, will shift some of their purchases to that country. The results of these shifts in demand will be that the production point for the home country will move down the production possibility curve, whereas the production point for the foreign country will move up toward the Y axis. Such adjustments will continue until there is no longer any incentive for residents of one

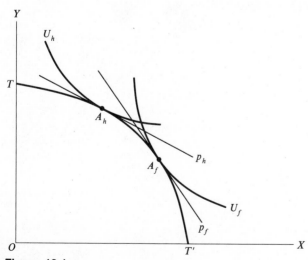

Figure 12.1

country to increase their purchases in the other, or in other words, until commodity trade has succeeded in equalizing commodity prices. Such a situation is shown in Figure 12.2, where the common world price ratio is p_w and where the common production point is Q. Figure 12.2 is drawn so that trade is balanced, or that the triangles $C_h B_h Q$ and $Q B_f C_f$ are identical.

From the analysis of Figure 12.2 we can conclude that country H, the country whose tastes are biased toward commodity Y, will import commodity Y and export commodity X, while country F, where tastes are biased toward commodity X, will import X and export Y. Thus we can conclude that when trade is caused by taste differences, the country will import the commodity toward which its tastes are biased.

In the specific example given in Figure 12.2 both countries enjoy gains from trade, and in general, the gains-from-trade theorem does apply to this particular model, since none of the assumptions required for the theorem are violated. Similarly, we can see that factor prices will be equalized by trade, for at the international trade equilibrium, both countries are producing at exactly the same point. With the same production functions, this implies that the two countries will have precisely the same efficiency locus, and the equilibrium production point will be at the same point on this locus. Thus relative factor prices must be the same in the two countries. The Stolper-Samuelson theorem also holds in this model, for in country F trade results in a relative reduction in the price of X, and if X is labor-intensive the wage-rental ratio will fall, the real return to labor will fall, and the real return to capital will rise. The opposite changes will occur in country H. Thus most of the results from Chapter 8 apply to a model where trade is due to taste differences.

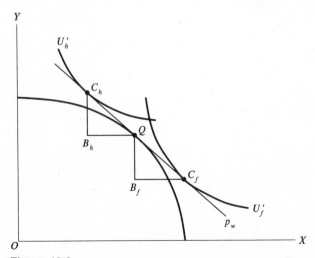

Figure 12.2

2. PER CAPITA INCOME AND NONHOMOGENEOUS DEMAND

Differences in consumption patterns among countries can also arise if individuals everywhere have identical tastes, but these tastes are non-homogeneous. In Chapter 3 we discussed a situation where tastes were nonhomogeneous, but nevertheless, aggregation of the individual into community indifference curves was possible. This occurred when income-consumption curves were linear, but did not go through the origin.

This type of "quasi-homogeneous" preference is used in Figure 12.3 to illustrate how differences in per capita income lead to differences in consumption patterns, which in turn lead to trade. Assume that we have two countries with identical populations, but that country F has uniformly superior technologies for producing both X and Y. In Figure 12.3 the PPC of country F $(T_f T_f')$ is a "radial blowup of country H's PPC $(T_h T_h')$; that is, along any ray from the origin, the slopes of the two PPCs are the same. Assume also that tastes are nonhomogeneous in that there is a "minimum consumption requirement" of Y of the type discussed in Chapter 3. The origin for a system of indifference curves is then point C_y in Figure 12.3. All consumers in both countries are assumed to have the same (nonhomogeneous) preferences.

Recalling that the populations are identical by assumption, the lower per capita income in country H implies a relatively high demand for Y in that country in autarky and vice versa for country F. The autarky equilibria will be at points like A_h and A_f in Figure 12.3, where due to the similar production structure, there is a relatively high autarky price

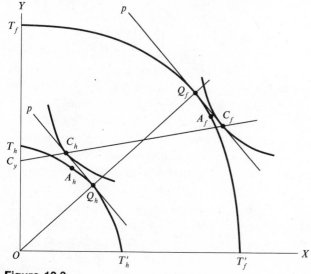

Figure 12.3

of Y in country H and a relatively high autarky price of X in country F. Each country will have a relatively high price for its "most preferred good" as in the previous section, except now "preference" derives from differences in per capita income. Underlying preferences or tastes are the same for all consumers by assumption.

The autarky price differences lead to a trading equilibrium as shown in Figure 12.3. The production points of countries H and F are Q_h and Q_f, respectively. These lie along the same ray from the origin because of our "radial blowup" assumption made earlier. Consumption points are C_h and C_f for countries H and F, respectively, at the free-trade price ratio p. These consumption points lie on a ray through C_y. Low per capita income country H imports Y and high per capita income country F imports X. As in the case of the taste differences shown in Figure 12.2, trade is due to differences in demand. In both examples the countries produce goods in the same proportions, but they consume them in different proportions at the same set of prices.

3. THE LINDER HYPOTHESIS

This analysis of the possible role of per capita income in determining trade leads naturally to a discussion of the ideas of Swedish economist Staffan Linder. Linder argued that the principles governing trade in manufacturing goods are not the same as those governing trade in primary products. He was quite prepared to support the idea that trade in primary products is determined by factor endowments. However, he argued against the notion that differences in factor endowments are the major determinants of trade in manufactured products. He chose, instead, to highlight the role of demand, beginning his argument with an observation similar to the one we made in our chapter on increasing returns to scale: A large volume of trade exists between the developed countries. These countries have very similar factor endowments and thus, according to the Heckscher-Ohlin theory, we might not expect a large volume of trade between them. We must, therefore, look for a cause of trade other than factor endowments.

Linder contended that a manufactured good is created by an entrepreneur in response to a perceived demand. A new manufactured good is, in other words, introduced only when an entrepreneur believes there is sufficient potential demand to warrant production. It is this perception of potential demand that triggers production rather than considerations of factor endowments, and so forth. The second step in the argument is that entrepreneurs are most familiar with their home market. Barriers of distance, language, and culture mean that entrepreneurs are much less familiar with foreign markets and are unlikely to be able to perceive what sort of new products could be successfully introduced into foreign markets.

The third step follows from the first two. For a manufactured product to be produced in (and therefore exported from) a country, there must exist significant home demand for the product. The range of manufactured goods produced in a country is therefore determined by domestic demand, as much as by production considerations such as factor endowments.

Suppose then that an entrepreneur perceives a home demand for a product and begins production. Where will he find export opportunities for additional sales? Linder argued that the best opportunities will be found in countries that have very similar demand patterns to the entrepreneur's home country. Thus, if an American invents the toaster and produces it for the home market, his best export opportunities will be found in Canada and in Western Europe. Similarly, entrepreneurs in Canada and Western Europe will find that their best foreign markets will be in the United States and in each other's countries.

The final step in Linder's argument is implicitly contained in this last statement. The countries with the most similar demand patterns for manufactured goods will tend to be those with similar per capita incomes. If I invent a simple toaster, people in countries with lower per capita incomes will not wish to buy the product, whereas people in countries with much higher per capita incomes may want a more sophisticated device with flashing lights, digital readout, and remote control. Thus the volume of trade in manufactured goods will be highest between countries of similar per capita income such as the United States, Canada, Western Europe, and Japan. It is thus demand, not only factor endowments, and so on, that determines the pattern of trade in manufactured goods.

4. COMBINING LINDER, NONHOMOGENEOUS TASTES, SCALE ECONOMIES, AND PRODUCT DIFFERENTIATION

Linder has often been criticized for not providing a complete general-equilibrium model. But the various elements that we have analyzed in this and in the preceding chapter can easily be combined to produce a model that helps to explain one of the stylized facts in question: the apparently large volume of trade among the industrialized countries relative to trade between the industrialized countries and the developing countries.

Suppose that there are two goods, food and manufactures, and that food is labor-intensive and manufactures are capital-intensive. Assume that food has a high minimum consumption requirement (low-income elasticity of demand), whereas manufactures have none. Let there be two blocks of countries, a capital-abundant "North" and a labor-abundant "South." The North will be relatively specialized in producing manufactures because of its capital abundance, but also relatively specialized in consuming manufactures because of its high per capita income (assume that the ownership of capital is spread over labor, so the capital-abundant country has the high per capita income). The South will be relatively specialized in producing food, but also relatively specialized in consuming food because of its low per capita income. As a result, the level of North–South trade in food for manufactures will be reduced below what it would be in a Heckscher-Ohlin world. The consumption bias in each region toward its own export good reduces both imports and exports.

Assume finally that manufactures are not a homogeneous good, but a collection of differentiated manufactured goods as discussed in the preceding chapter. Each manufacturing firm produces a somewhat unique good and sells to consumers in all the countries that make up the industrial North. This is often referred to as "intraindustry trade." In the North the taste bias toward manufactures, due to the high per capita income, now actually increases the amount of intraindustry trade among the northern countries. Relative to a Heckscher-Ohlin world with homogeneous tastes, the northern manufacturing firms switch exports from the South, where demand is low due to low per capita incomes, to other northern countries where demand is conversely high. Thus nonhomothetic demand leads to a decrease in North–South trade and to an increase in trade among the northern industrialized countries. This is the stylized fact that was to be explained. Our explanation depends, however, on a correlation between capital intensity in production and a high-income elasticity of demand in consumption, which has not yet been determined empirically.

5. THE PRODUCT CYCLE

During the 1960s and perhaps earlier some international trade economists observed that the pattern of trade in the world had undergone a gradual shift during the twentieth century. The change seemed to be particularly pronounced with respect to the manufactured exports of some developed countries. It was noted that the production of products originally developed and produced in the United States often shifted to Europe and then to less developed countries, only to be replaced by a new generation of products in the United States. This gradual and systematic pattern of change seemed to call for a new theory of international trade.

Although there is nothing particularly dynamic (having to do with changes over time) in the Linder analysis, it has been adapted quite easily to explain the shifting pattern of trade cited earlier. Consider a product such as a radio. At some point, entrepreneurs in high-income countries decided that potential demand had risen to the point where commercial public radio could be profitably introduced. Production initially occurs in the home market, where there is easy communication between the factory managers and the sales personnel. This, according to Linder, is necessary in order that critical revision, the trial-and-error learning process in the early years of production, can proceed as smoothly as possible. An increasing proportion of the output is exported to other countries as their incomes grow. The second phase of a product cycle occurs when demand in foreign countries has risen to the point where entrepreneurs there find it profitable to begin production themselves. After all, they have an advantage in terms of lower per capita incomes and thus lower wage rates. Alternatively, the original entrepreneurs in the home country establish branch plants in the foreign countries in order to maintain their market share, but in either case the point is that foreign production begins.

The third phase of the product cycle occurs when foreign producers, perhaps in Western Europe, gain the scale economies and production expertise necessary to compete successfully with the original firms, perhaps North American, in third world countries. The final phase of the product cycle finds the Europeans invading the North American market, so that the original producers are now in the position of import competitors. The process may in fact continue to the point where the original producers are driven out of the market entirely, and perhaps production begins in third world countries.

What happened to these firms as the last phase of the product cycle approached? By that time the North American firms were busy producing and exporting some new product such as televisions. A new product cycle began as the old one drew to a close. Japanese and European televisions soon began to compete with North American firms and eventually invaded the North American market. The second product cycle drew to a close and a third began. The North American electronics firms moved on to home computers, word processors, video games, and so forth.

A second example might be textile production. During the early nineteenth century Great Britain had a large share of the world export market in quality woven textiles. As the century progressed, many of Britain's export markets were lost to new producers in North America and Europe. By the middle of the twentieth century, these countries were in turn losing sales to producers in Japan. The Japanese began to experience cost increases in the 1960s, and production began to shift to countries such as Korea, Taiwan, and Mexico. By this time the Europeans, North Americans, and Japanese were beginning to specialize in new products that may some day be largely produced by third world countries.

6. PER CAPITA INCOME AND TECHNOLOGY

It may be useful to distinguish between new products, on the one hand, and new production processes or producers' goods (e.g., machinery), on the other. The product cycle described previously tends to focus on final consumption goods. Yet it seems likely that there is a closely related phenomenon with respect to production technology, which we might call the "technology cycle." Techniques of production and various types of machinery probably tend to follow a cycle from development and use in the advanced countries to eventual use in less-developed countries. Such a phenomenon is of interest insofar as production technology and producers' goods are an important export of the industrialized nations.

A simple theory of a technology cycle begins with the observation that the industrialized nations are high-income and high-wage countries. High wages create a strong incentive to invest in labor-saving production technology, since the payoff to a new innovation is the number of worker-hours saved, times the wage rate. The industrialized nations are thus the leaders in the development of new technology. This new technology improves productivity and tends to lead to further wage increases. Indeed, it would be very difficult to decide whether the development of new technology stimulates wage increases or vice versa. Presumably the causality runs both ways.

In any case, beginning with the observation of continuous technological development and wage increases, we can postulate a technology cycle similar to the product cycle. In the first phase, a new technology, such as a piece of textile machinery, is developed in an advanced country. This machine is used for production in the home country or in other advanced countries. It is not exported to less-developed countries since it is inappropriately capital-intensive. As time passes, wages rise in the developed countries to the point where the textile machine no longer permits profitable production. Simultaneously, foreign incomes rise to the point where use of the machine is justified for foreign production. The machine becomes an export of the industrialized country. In later stages of the cycle the machine may, in fact, be produced abroad.

To the best of our knowledge, this phenomenon is not well researched and thus it should be regarded as somewhat speculative at this point. Yet it does seem to offer a potentially important explanation as to the volume and direction of trade in technology and production equipment. A satisfactory theory must deal with the simultaneous causality between technical change and high per capita income.

7. CYCLE MODELS AND COMPARATIVE ADVANTAGE

At first glance, these dynamic theories seem to stand in stark contrast to our earlier discussions about the determinants of trade. Although these earlier discussions suggested a stable pattern of trade based on patterns of comparative advantage, returns to scale, and so on, the dynamic theories seem to suggest a continuously shifting pattern of trade, at least for manufactured goods. Are these two approaches irreconcilable, and are we forced to choose between them?

Much of the apparent conflict disappears if we think of goods as being composed of a number of characteristics. These characteristics include such things as quality, durability, power requirements, and so forth. Producers' equipment includes the additional characteristics of labor requirements, output rates, and so on. The product-cycle and technology-cycle notion, when looked at from this point of view, suggest that we should observe a stable pattern of trade in product characteristics, even though the goods themselves may continually change. The product-cycle theory, for example, suggests that we should find the wealthiest nations specializing in new consumer goods that cater to high-income tastes. These nations should similarly be observed to produce and export new capital-intensive, or rather labor-saving, equipment and technologies. The underlying characteristics of goods exported from a country remain the same, even though the names of the goods may change. If the types of product characteristics embodied in a nation's exports are in turn systematically related to the determinants of trade discussed earlier (factor endowments, scale economies, etc.), then the product cycle approach may not, in fact, be that different after all.

At least four reservations can be expressed about the cycle theories. The first was just mentioned. That is, it may be that the cycle theories are actually not very different after all, if we think of countries as trading the characteristics embodied in goods, rather than the goods themselves. Instead of viewing the United States as having moved from exporting radios to televisions to home computers, perhaps we should think of the United States as exporting sophisticated electronic goods, "sophisticated" being defined relative to the period in question.

Second, the product and technology cycles are based on the assumption of steadily rising real income. To the extent that real income growth has tapered off or might do so in the future, the cycles would disappear with the growth trend. Third, the product cycle theory as developed in the 1960s significantly underestimated the ability of multinational enterprises to move production abroad at little cost. As we noted earlier, the theory relies on the assumption that a new product must initially be produced at home in order to facilitate easy communication between engineers, plant managers, and sales personnel. In an era of increasingly sophisticated multinational firms this communications problem may become less of a constraint, and the firms may from the very beginning produce a new product in the location that offers the most attractive factor prices. But in this case production is determined by the usual determinants of comparative advantage, and we are back with the traditional theory.

A final reservation about the cycle theories is that they are partial equilibrium explanations of trade, and are stated in such a way that it is difficult to understand the nature of causality. They seem to assert that high per capita incomes cause the development of new products and new technologies. But, as we noted previously, would it not be equally valid to assert that new technologies cause high incomes? Until this type of problem can be fully worked out, the cycle models will have to be regarded as incomplete. A satisfactory model should give a complete or general equilibrium description of the economy, rather than treat the level of income as exogenous.

8. CONCLUDING REMARKS

In this chapter we have examined several ways in which demand influences international trade. Demand differs across countries both because people have different tastes, and because demands depend on per capita income when tastes are identical but nonhomogeneous. Empirical studies of demand tend to reject strongly the hypothesis of homogeneity (Hunter and Markusen (1987)). Differences in demand caused by differences in per capita income are in turn a cornerstone of the Linder model and the product-cycle model. Each of these latter models has other elements, such as the role of entrepreneurs in developing new products, but differences in per capita income are central to the implications of the models for international trade questions. A more satisfactory dynamic theory of trade, such as that attempted in the product-cycle theory, awaits the development of models that capture the mutual dependence of technical change and per capita income.

PROBLEMS

1. Suppose, in Figure 12.2, that over time tastes in country H shift toward commodity X. How will this affect welfare in the two countries? How will relative and real factor rewards be affected?

2. In Figure 12.2, how is the volume of trade affected by the degree of differences in tastes between the two countries?
3. In Figure 12.3, show that trade disappears as the minimum consumption requirement for Y goes to zero.
4. Try to think of several products that have undergone cycles. What are the underlying characteristics of the products in question?
5. Using the Linder hypothesis about the product cycle, explain why the United States was a leader in the development and export of automobiles. Explain why quality hockey skates were first produced in Canada.

REFERENCES

Baldwin, R. E., and J. D. Richardson (eds.) (1974). *International Trade and Investment.* Boston: Little, Brown.

Hunter, L., and J. R. Markusen (1987). "Per-Capita Income as a Determinant of Trade." In R. Feenstra (ed.), *Empirical Method for International Trade.* Cambridge, Mass.: MIT Press.

Linder, S. B. (1961). *An Essay on Trade and Transformation.* Stockholm: Almqvist & Wiksell.

Krugman, P. R. (1981). "Intra-Industry Specialization and the Gains from Trade." *Journal of Political Economy* 89, 959–973.

Markusen, J. R. (1986). "Explaining the Volume of Trade: An Eclectic Approach." *American Economic Review* 76, 1002–1011.

Vernon, R. (1966). "International Investment and International Trade in the Product Cycle." *Quarterly Journal of Economics* 80, 190–207.

———. (ed.) (1970). *The Technology Factor in International Trade.* New York: Columbia University Press.

chapter *13*

Empirical Tests of Trade Models

1. INTRODUCTION

By this stage in the book the reader will not have to be persuaded that a significant body of theoretical literature has developed in international trade. In the preceding chapters a number of models were developed to explain why trade takes place and, for each of these, propositions about trade flows and the other implications of trade patterns were also developed. Indeed, from a theoretical point of view, international trade may well be the richest area in economics.

Although the discussion of theoretical models has been extensive, and a wide variety of possible explanations for trade flows have been advanced, few of these explanations have received much attention in the empirical literature. Indeed, of the models presented in earlier chapters, only two have been investigated empirically to any significant extent, these being the Ricardian model and the Heckscher-Ohlin model. Empirical work on the Ricardian model was begun by MacDougall (1951, 1952), and only a few papers have been published using this approach since that time. Interest in testing the Heckscher-Ohlin theorem began with the publication of papers by Leontief (1953, 1956), and his results prompted a significant amount of research, at both the theoretical and empirical levels. Models that attribute trade to such things as increasing returns to scale, distortions such as taxes and imperfect competition, and taste differences have received very little attention by empirical economists. To some extent this may be due to the fact that these explanations of trade have only recently begun to attract the attention of international trade theorists. The Heckscher-Ohlin model has dominated the theoretical analysis of trade issues since the 1940s, and it is therefore not surprising that endowment explanations of trade flows have formed the basis of the vast majority of empirical studies. Perhaps in the future more work will be done on investigating other possible explanations of trade flows.

It is difficult to survey the empirical trade literature in the space available here for a variety of reasons. First, the literature is very diverse and the results of apparently similar studies are often quite different depending on the methodology, the time period used, or the countries for which the calculations were made. Volumes rather than a single chapter would be required to do justice to this extensive literature. Second, the methodology employed by empirical economists, particularly in recent years, has become quite sophisticated with the approach used depending on the investigator and the specific issue being considered. An understanding of the detail of many of these studies would require some sophistication in econometric theory. Thus the analysis of this chapter will focus on the principal approaches that have been used and on the main results that have been derived. Justice cannot be done to the many studies that have been undertaken in this area, and for more detailed information the reader is referred to more extensive treatments of the topic such as that contained in the excellent survey by Deardorff (1984). We begin with a brief discussion of some tests of the Ricardian model and then turn our attention to the approach used by Leontief. We will next review some of the work motivated by Leontief's results and then will briefly consider some of the methodological issues involved in testing trade theories.

2. TESTS OF THE RICARDIAN MODEL[1]

Recall from Chapter 7 that the Ricardian model attributes trade flows to differences in production functions. In particular, since labor is the only factor of production assumed, differences in trade flows can be associated with differences in labor's productivity among countries. Thus tests of the Ricardian theory attempt to find relationships between labor's productivity and international trade flows.

Difficulties are soon encountered, however. The first is that a strict interpretation of the Ricardian model would have countries specializing in the products they exported, and this would make comparisons of the productivity of labor difficult. We cannot compare the productivity of labor in the production of commodity X in two countries if only one country produces X. This is related to the point made in Chapter 7 that changes in productivity in one industry in a country will only affect trade patterns if, indeed, that commodity is being produced. From a practical point of view, however, this is not a major difficulty, since we seldom observe complete specialization by trading nations. Of course, this raises the issue of the appropriateness of using the Ricardian model to explain trade in such circumstances. One method of circumventing this difficulty is to suppose that distortions such as transportation costs are sufficient to allow the production of all goods in all countries even though the Ricardian technology exists.

Another difficulty encountered in applying the simple version of the Ricardian model is that we would like to compare trade between two countries, since taking all multinational trade into account would be an overwhelmingly complex problem. Bilateral trade, however, tends to be a relatively small proportion of total trade, making two-country comparisons difficult. Researchers such as MacDougall have overcome this problem by comparing how countries perform in third markets. In particular, the approach was to compare the ratio of U.S. to U.K. exports to third countries to the ratio of U.S. to U.K. labor productivity coefficients using regression analysis. The results were encouraging and indeed showed that the differences in the productivity of labor was an important explanation of trade patterns for these two countries. This has been interpreted as support for the Ricardian explanation of trade flows.

A difficulty with concluding that such tests confirm the Ricardian model as an explanation of trade flows has been noted by Deardorff (1984). Although the conclusions reached are consistent with the Ricardian model, they are also consistent with other models that could be constructed to explain trade patterns. In particular, a version of the Heckscher-Ohlin model would produce the same results. As Deardorff notes, a difficulty with such tests is that they fail to distinguish among the various possible explanations for trade flows. More will be said on this general issue in Section 4.

3. THE LEONTIEF PARADOX[2]

Leontief, using 1947 data, calculated the labor and capital content of the exports of the United States for that year. He could not, of course, measure the capital and labor contents of United States imports, for this would have required information on the production processes of all countries from which the United States was importing. Instead, he calculated what the capital and labor content of such imports would have been, had they been produced in the United States. It was assumed that the United States was capital-abundant relative to her major trading partners, and Leontief, accepting the validity of the Heckscher-Ohlin theorem as an explanation of trading patterns, expected to find that the United States exported a bundle of commodities that was capital-intensive. However, on making the comparisons between imports and exports, Leontief found that American exports were considerably more labor-intensive than the bundle of import substitutes. This result received a good deal of attention and became known as the Leontief paradox.

Leontief's work generated a flood of literature, both empirical and theoretical, which attempted to explain the result that the United States, assumed to be a country well endowed with capital, was, nevertheless, exporting a bundle of labor-intensive commodities. The subsequent empirical research was largely inconclusive, for while a few studies of other countries tended to confirm the expectations of the Heckscher-Ohlin model, most generated the same sort of paradoxical result as did Leontief's research. The theoretical explanations that were put forward can be grouped under three broad headings: (1) the theoretical model employed by Leontief, (2) the data employed in the calculations, and (3) the structure of the Heckscher-Ohlin theorem itself. In terms of (1), Leontief's theoretical model and his calculations were based on the input–output analysis he had earlier developed. This model assumed fixed coefficients in production, which means that all isoquants have corners or are L-shaped, rather than having the smooth curvature we assumed in earlier discussions. This implies that there is no substitution in production, so that the capital-labor ratio of any industry is a constant, regardless of relative factor prices. As well as assuming fixed coefficients in production, Leontief also assumed that the ratio in which the commodities were consumed was fixed, thus implying that indifference curves were also L-shaped and allowed no substitution. From a theoretical point of view, this model is capable of generating some rather strange results. For example, there is no guarantee that all factors of production will be fully employed, nor can we be sure that equilibrium prices will exist. But while Leontief's model is certainly different from the one used throughout most of this book, it is still possible, with care, to generate a Heckscher-Ohlin theorem from it, identical to that found in Chapter 8.

Criticisms of the data used by Leontief include the argument that the year for which the calculations were made, 1947, was atypical and that the investigation of other years could well produce different results. At the time the only data set available was for the United States and the year 1947, so that the importance of this argument was difficult to evaluate. As has been noted, however, later tests, for the United States as well as for other countries, were inconclusive in establishing whether the year chosen was important insofar as the results were concerned. Another criticism of the data concerned the appropriateness of the capital coefficients used in Leontief's calculations. Capital coefficients in input–output models are always somewhat suspect, for they are essentially residuals; that is, they are simply what is left over after we take account of all the other inputs that we can measure. There is also a question relating to whether we should use the flow-of-factor services or the actual physical capital stock in making the kind of calculations done by Leontief.

As for the appropriateness of the standard trade model itself, a variety of arguments were made. One of the principal criticisms was that, by considering only the two factors, capital and labor, Leontief had ignored the importance of land or resources in his calculations. It was suggested that the inclusion of resources could well have given quite different results. Another possible explanation was that the results were due to the existence of factor intensity reversals. As we saw in Chapter 8, if such reversals exist, it would be possible to find a country well endowed with capital, nevertheless exporting the labor-intensive commodity. It was also suggested that perverse demand effects could well have given rise to the paradoxical results of Leontief. Again, it is clear from earlier chapters that if demand in two countries is highly biased, its effects on trade patterns could well completely outweigh the effects of endowment differences.

The reader, having gone through earlier chapters of this part of the book, could undoubtedly provide additional reasons for the so-called paradox. For example, it could be pointed out that with increasing returns to scale, results different from those associated with the Heckscher-Ohlin model could easily be found. Distortions such as taxes could produce such results. Other deviations from perfect competition, such as monopoly, could also produce results that are not consistent with the Heckscher-Ohlin predictions.

Finally, to these various explanations as to why Leontief did not find the "expected" results, we should add Leontief's own suggestion. He noted that the labor force statistics that had been used in his calculations implicitly assumed that labor throughout the world has the same efficiency. Leontief argued that labor in the United States, being highly trained and skilled, was considerably more efficient than labor elsewhere, and one should therefore use efficiency labor units, rather than just the number of workers employed. He suggested that labor in the United States was three times as efficient as labor elsewhere, and that taking this into account the United States was shown, after all, to be exporting capital-intensive commodities. This explanation is rather unconvincing and is certainly very ad hoc in nature. The three-to-one ratio suggested by Leontief was not predicated on a careful evaluation of labor efficiency throughout the world, but was quite simply the ratio required to generate the "expected" result.

4. THE PARADOX IN PERSPECTIVE

The principal question that must be asked of the Leontief result is whether we should have expected a test performed the way Leontief performed it to confirm the Heckscher-Ohlin theorem. To put the matter somewhat more strongly, is the Heckscher-Ohlin theorem as formulated here and elsewhere a testable theorem; that is, is it subject to empirical refutation? Recall from Chapter 6 the structure of the theoretical model employed to generate the Heckscher-Ohlin theorem and the variety of other theorems developed in Chapters 7 through 12. We began by asking why trade would take place among nations and concluded that, fundamentally, such trade must be the result of differences in commodity prices. This led to an investigation of why prices would differ, and the investigation was seen to be most easily done by considering different sources of price differences, one at a time. We thus constructed a series of theoretical models in which only one determinant of trade was permitted in each. For example, for the Heckscher-Ohlin model we allowed factor endowment differences to exist between countries but assumed constant returns to scale, the same tastes among countries, no differences in production functions among countries, and no distortions. This allowed us to unambiguously identify the effects of endowment differences. In a similar fashion we considered the effects of returns to scale by considering, first, the situation in which countries were identical in every respect and where we replaced the constant returns-to-scale assumption with the assumption of increasing returns.

The point to be made is that the simple models so developed should not be seen as capable of explaining the real world. They are, if you like, theoretical experiments designed to illustrate the effects of the various possible determinants of trade. Thus it is difficult to see what a test of the Heckscher-Ohlin theorem could possibly show.

There is a related difficulty in interpreting the results derived from tests of the kind performed by Leontief. In such tests there are, of course, only two possible results. Either the data conform to the predictions of the Heckscher-Ohlin model, or they do not. Suppose, first, that they do not; this was the situation encountered by Leontief. What do we then conclude? The obvious answer is simply that not all of the assumptions made in generating the Heckscher-Ohlin theorem are satisfied in the real-world situation being investigated. This should come as no great surprise, for as we have already suggested, the assumptions made were deliberately false and were constructed so as to isolate the theoretical effects of endowment differences. No one would be very surprised to be told that the world is not perfectly competitive and that there exist distortions such as taxes.

But on the other hand, suppose the test were to confirm the predictions of the Heckscher-Ohlin model, so that a country well endowed with capital was observed to export a bundle of commodities that was capital-intensive. Could we take this as confirmation of the Heckscher-Ohlin theorem? From our earlier discussions of various trade models, we know that we could not, for a number of the other determinants of trade might well generate exactly the same observation. Recall, for example, the discussion of the model with increasing returns to scale. It can be shown that if we start with two countries that are identical in all respects, including endowments, and where these countries trade to take advantage of the increasing returns to scale, the equalization of commodity prices will not result in the equalization of relative factor rewards. Thus, even when an equilibrium trading situation is achieved, factor prices will differ, and this could well result in international factor flows. Factors will flow to the country in which their rewards are highest and this will change the relative factor endowments for the two countries. Furthermore, the rewards will be highest in the country specializing in the commodity using that factor intensively; thus, after factor flows have equalized relative factor prices we would observe that the country that is now relatively well endowed with capital will be exporting the capital-intensive commodity. This, of course, is exactly the statement of the Heckscher-Ohlin theorem, but the result has been due to increasing returns to scale and not to initial differences in endowments.

Situations similar to the one of increasing returns to scale can be derived for cases in which commodity taxes differ between countries. In more complicated models, where more than one determinant of trade is considered at the same time, a variety of situations can be constructed in which the results of the Heckscher-Ohlin theorem are observed, but where the explanation of trade flows has nothing to do with initial differences in endowments. The point is that even if the results of empirical tests conform to the predictions of the Heckscher-Ohlin model, we could not conclude that these results were generated by differences in endowments. Thus, regardless of what results are derived from a test of the kind performed by Leontief, no conclusions can be drawn about the determinants of the pattern of trade.

5. ALTERNATIVE APPROACHES TO TESTING THE HECKSCHER-OHLIN MODEL

Although some of the recent empirical work in international trade has employed the simplistic model used by Leontief—a methodology that is incapable of distinguishing among various explanations of trade—much of the more recent literature is considerably more sophisticated and is free of many of the difficulties outlined in Section 4. We can report on only a few of these studies here, and for a more detailed analysis the reader is again referred to Deardorff (1984).

One difficulty with the early studies was that the analysis focused on a single aggregate statistic calculated for a single year. Such an approach makes it difficult to distinguish cause from effect and makes any general conclusions difficult or impossible. Of course, when Leontief made his original calculations few alternatives were available, since statistics for other years did not exist and in any case the statistical techniques and the computer technology required to analyze more complex data sets was not yet available. Recent years have seen a tremendous advance, both in data collection and in computing power, and this has facilitated much more sophisticated empirical work. Regression analysis is now common and both time series and cross-sectional approaches have been used, and many studies have carried out the analysis on an industry-by-industry basis.

A pioneering study that brought more sophisticated statistical techniques to bear on the question of the determinants of trade was the paper by Baldwin (1971). After a careful review of the previous literature, Baldwin undertook a careful investigation of U.S. trade patterns using regression analysis. He worked at the industry level and ran regressions both bilaterally and multilaterally and considered a variety of possible explanations for comparative advantage. For example, in addition to capital-labor ratios, he considered skill levels and years of education. But although Baldwin's analysis was much more careful and more sophisticated than earlier research, he still found that the U.S. capital-labor ratio was negatively related to U.S. exports. Another conclusion of interest was that he found some evidence that skill levels, or human capital, were positively related to exports, suggesting that human capital may be an important determinant of trade volume.

Another important study was that of Harkness (1978), who also used regression analysis to investigate the causes of trade. Harkness used factor share variables as a measure of factor intensities and considered a variety of possible inputs, including natural resources. His results showed that, for the United States, physical capital was an important and significant determinant of exports.

Perhaps the most comprehensive analysis of the source of international comparative advantage is the book by Leamer (1984). After a careful discussion of the theoretical issues and of the econometric methods to be employed, Leamer uses a linear regression model to investigate how some 11 different resources explain 10 different trade aggregates. The results showed that the resources used provided a relatively good explanation of the trade data, and given the care with which these calculations were made, they must be regarded as very encouraging for the appropriateness of the underlying endowment model that Leamer investigated.

One of the explanations of trade patterns that most economists would regard as important but that has received almost no empirical attention is the effects of returns to scale. One body of research that does provide some insights into the effects of increasing returns to scale is numerical general-equilibrium analysis. Although these studies are not primarily concerned with determining the causes of trade, studies like that of Harris (1983) do provide some indirect evidence on this issue. Harris constructed a numerical general-equilibrium model in which the manufacturing sector was characterized by increasing returns to scale to examine the issue of how trade liberalization would affect the Canadian economy. In his model the removal of tariff barriers allowed Canadian industries to take advantage of scale economies and to sell in the larger United States market. Harris found possible gains for the Canadian economy ranging up to 8 to 10 percent of GNP. Of course, such studies are more in the nature of forecasts that use the counterfactual methodology to predict what might happen given certain policy changes than they are explanations of trade. The results of such studies are, therefore, not directly comparable to empirical studies that use historical data to identify actual changes that have taken place. The studies are, nevertheless, suggestive, for they indicate that economies of scale may have a significant role to play in the determination of trade patterns.

6. CONCLUDING REMARKS

Although there has been a significant amount of empirical work done on the causes of international trade, most of the results have been inconclusive. Many of the studies are also open to criticism on methodological grounds, and they seldom provide tests that would allow one to distinguish among the various possible determinants of trade. The results of even the more sophisticated studies could not be used, for example, to distinguish between trade *caused* by endowment differences and trade caused by increasing returns to scale that causes factor flows and *results in endowment differences*. Furthermore, almost all of the studies have concentrated attention on the endowment explanation of trade, leaving open the issue of whether such determinants as distortions or increasing returns to scale may not be equally important in the determination of trade patterns. Recent work, however, has overcome many of the deficiencies of the earlier studies, and perhaps future research will provide more balance in terms of the investigation of the whole range of possible determinants of trade.

NOTES

1. The material of this section and of Section 5 owes much to Deardorff (1984).
2. For a more complete survey of the various criticisms of Leontief's approach, see Chipman (1966).

REFERENCES

Baldwin, R. E. (1971). "Determinants of the Commodity Structure of U.S. Trade." *American Economic Review* 61, 126–146.

Chipman, J. S. (1966). "A Survey of the Theory of International Trade: Part 3, The Modern Theory." *Econometrica* 34, 18–76.

Deardorff, A. V. (1984). "Testing Trade Theories and Predicting Trade Flows." Ch. 10 in R. W. Jones and P. B. Kenen, *Handbook of International Economics: Vol. 1.* Amsterdam: Elsevier Science Publishers B. V.

Harkness, J. (1978). "Factor Abundance and Comparative Advantage." *American Economic Review* 68, 784–800.

Harris, R. (1983). *Trade, Industrial Policy, and Canadian Manufacturing.* Toronto: University of Toronto Press.

Leamer, E. E. (1980). "The Leontief Paradox, Reconsidered." *Journal of Political Economy* 88, 495–503.

———. (1984). *Sources of International Comparative Advantage.* Cambridge, Mass.: MIT Press.

Leontief, W. W. (1953). "Domestic Production and Foreign Trade: The American Capital Position Re-examined." *Proceedings of the American Philosophical Society* 97, 332–349.

———. (1956). "Factor Proportions and the Structure of American Trade: Further Theoretical and Empirical Analysis." *Review of Economics and Statistics* 38, 386–407.

MacDougall, G. D. A. (1951). "British and American Exports: A Study Suggested by the Theory of Comparative Costs, Part I." *Economic Journal* 61, 697–724.

———. (1952). "British and American Exports: A Study Suggested by the Theory of Comparative Costs, Part II." *Economic Journal* 62, 487–521.

three

ALTERNATIVES TO FREE TRADE

chapter *14*

Tariffs

1. THE WELFARE LOSS FROM TARIFFS

In Chapter 5 we contrasted a free-trade equilibrium with an autarky equilibrium, one in which a country does not trade at all. Both these extremes are fairly rare in practice. More typically a country will engage in trade but the government of that country will erect various barriers to restrict trade. The most common of these barriers are taxes levied on the importation of foreign goods. These taxes are commonly referred to as "tariffs," but it must be emphasized that they are simply a form of commodity taxation. Tariffs are sometimes levied on exports as well as on imports. This is the case, for example, with Canadian exports of natural gas to the United States. While there are other forms of trade restriction as well, this chapter will concentrate on tariffs. (Other barriers, such as quotas, will be discussed in the following chapter.)

Assume for the remainder of this section that we are a small economy facing fixed world prices; that is, we can trade as little or as much as we want at a fixed world price ratio, p^*. In this case, tariffs will affect the equilibrium price ratio facing domestic producers and consumers but will not affect p^*. Assume also that the pattern of comparative advantage is such that our country exports X and imports Y. Our government then places an *ad valorem* tax of T on each unit of Y imported into the country. Since p^* is fixed, the domestic price will rise by the full amount of the tax.

Let $p = p_x/p_y$ be the domestic price ratio. Since exports are not taxed, the domestic and world prices will be related by $p_x = p_x^*$ and $p_y = p_y^*$ $(1 + T)$ or $p = p^*/(1 + T)$. Due to the import tariff on Y, the domestic price ratio will be less than the world price ratio $(p < p^*)$.

The second fact to note is that domestic producers and consumers will base their decisions on domestic prices. It is these domestic prices, rather than world prices, that consumers must pay and producers will receive. Third, trade must, of course, still be balanced at the world price ratio, because p^* remains the price ratio at which we do business with the rest of the world. These three equilibrium conditions can be summarized as follows:

$$MRS = MRT = p = p^*/(1 + T) < p^* \tag{14.1}$$

$$p_x^*(X_c - X_p) + p_y^*(Y_c - Y_p) = 0 \quad \text{or} \quad p^* = \frac{(Y_c - Y_p)}{(X_p - X_c)} \tag{14.2}$$

where subscripts p and c again denote the amounts of a good produced and consumed, respectively. Equation (14.1) notes that domestic consumers and producers will equate the domestic MRS in consumption and MRT in production to the domestic price ratio, which is in turn less than the world price ratio. Thus, at the post-tariff equilibrium, the slopes of the community indifference curve and the production frontier will be equal and less than the slope of the world price ratio. Equation (14.2) requires that the domestic production and consumption points be linked by the world price ratio.

These equilibrium conditions imply that the post-tariff equilibrium must be as shown in Figure 14.1. In that diagram, A refers to the autarky equilibrium, whereas C_f and Q_f refer to the free-trade consumption and production points, respectively. A tariff on imports of Y will result in production at a point like Q_t and consumption at a point like C_t. Points Q_t and C_t are linked by the world price ratio as required by the balance-of-payments constraint (equation (14.2). Q_t and C_t also satisfy equation (14.1) in that we have $MRS = MRT < p^*$.

Several characteristics of the post-tariff equilibrium are clear from Figure 14.1. First, the post-tariff level of welfare (U_t) is less than the free-trade level (U_f) but more than the autarky level (U_a). The tariff thus leads to a welfare loss relative to free trade but certainly not relative to autarky. Second, the tariff causes production to move from the free-trade point (Q_f) back toward the autarky point (A).

These effects on welfare and production reveal the essential nature of tariffs, which is to move the country back from free trade in the direction of autarky. The country specializes less in the good in which it

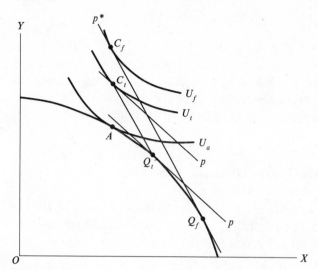

Figure 14.1

has a comparative advantage and thus sacrifices some of the gains from trade. If the tariff were raised higher and higher, eventually the country would find it unprofitable to import any Y in Figure 14.1 and would be driven all the way back to the autarky equilibrium at A.

Tariffs accomplish this movement by distorting domestic prices and, since domestic producers and consumers respond to domestic prices, by distorting domestic decision making. By raising the price of Y, the tariff makes it seem that Y is more valuable than it actually is and thereby encourages domestic producers to produce more Y. Resources are diverted from the true pattern of comparative advantage by this misrepresentation, and thus gains from specialization are lost. Consumer prices are similarly distorted, and thus gains from exchange are also lost. (More will be said about gains from exchange in Section 3 of this chapter.)

The final important point to note is that tariffs can significantly redistribute income, in addition to reducing overall income. In Figure 14.1 the tariff raises the domestic price of Y and shifts production from Q_f to Q_t. We know from our earlier analysis that this will generally change factor prices. In the Heckscher-Ohlin model the increase in the price and production of Y will increase the real income of the factor used intensively in the production of Y and decrease the real income of the other factor (the Stolper-Samuelson theorem). Thus in this case the losses shown in Figure 14.1 are shared very unevenly, and one factor is, in fact, made better off. The other factor suffers a welfare loss in excess of the entire welfare loss due to the tariff.

2. ARGUMENTS IN FAVOR OF TARIFFS

If the arguments of the preceding section are true, why is it that we, nevertheless, have many tariffs and other forms of import restrictions? Why would a government deliberately take actions that lower the welfare of the country? In this section we briefly examine a number of arguments in favor of tariffs that seem to be largely false, or true only under very special assumptions or interpretations.

Protection of Domestic Labor It is sometimes argued that we need import tariffs to protect our workers from cheap products produced with cheap foreign labor. Now this argument could have a theoretical basis in a Stolper-Samuelson type of result: If imports are relatively labor-intensive, then a tariff will raise the real income of labor and lower the real income of capital.

In actual fact, the cheap labor argument probably has little to do with Stolper-Samuelson–type phenomena and is probably generated instead by taking a very partial view of the problems of a handful of industries that are experiencing difficulties. U.S. manufacturing industries such as textiles, clothing, and footwear are having difficulties competing, but this is because the U.S. does not have a comparative advantage in these goods. Just because an industry is having difficulties competing does not mean that a tariff will raise the U.S. wage rate. Indeed, as just pointed out, the empirical evidence seems to suggest the opposite.

The cheap labor argument also seems to confuse cause and effect. It seems to assert that expensive U.S. labor is the *cause* of difficulties in certain industries. This is true only in a very indirect sense. Actually, U.S. labor is expensive as the *result* of the fact that labor is highly productive in those industries in which the U.S. does have a comparative advantage. To place import tariffs on industries such as textiles and footwear is to encourage labor to move out of industries in which it is highly productive into industries in which it is much less productive.

Adjustment Costs It is true that a lowering of tariffs on certain goods would cause temporary difficulties, perhaps even severe hardships for labor and other factors employed in those industries. Laborers may face long periods of unemployment and/or expensive retraining. Capital owners may experience bankruptcy as the values of specialized machinery and buildings fall drastically. Small towns where the factories are located would be especially hard hit as plants close down.

It would be frivolous to suggest that this argument should be disregarded on the grounds that the tariffs should not have been there in the first place. The relevant question is what should be done, given that the tariffs are already there. Most economists believe that adjustments to tariff changes will generally improve aggregate welfare and therefore make everyone better off (or at least no worse off), if some redistribution scheme is used to accompany the reduction of the tariffs.

The argument runs something like this. Eliminating inefficient tariffs causes adjustment problems in the short run, as factors of production leave the import-competing industries. These costs, for example, include the lost output due to workers being unemployed during the transition process. However, these adjustment costs must be balanced against the (present value of the) future stream of income that will be earned from increased efficiency in production, once the transition is complete. If the present value of the benefits outweighs the costs, then adjustment will improve welfare in the present value sense. If industries are competitive and there are no significant distortions in the economy, then private agents (firms and workers) will evaluate these costs and benefits in an efficient fashion and make the socially correct decision. Note especially that factor owners have the option of continuing production in the import-competing industries at lower wages. Thus there is no need for the government to worry about the adjustment problem strictly from the point of view of efficiency. Private agents will behave efficiently on their own.

Two qualifications should be noted. First, redistribution is certainly an important issue, since the gains from increased efficiency are spread very unevenly. Some groups of factor owners will certainly be made worse off in the present value sense. (The Stolper-Samuelson theorem states that some groups will be made worse off even in the static sense.) All that we can say is that the fact that there are aggregate gains means that there will exist some redistribution scheme that will make everyone better off. Such a scheme could include unemployment benefits and retraining programs for displaced workers and tax write-offs for capital owners, for example.

Second, the argument that private agents will choose a socially efficient adjustment program is conditional on the assumptions of competition and no distortions. If these assumptions do not hold, then of course the conclusions do not hold. Indeed, as we will note in a subsequent section, in the presence of domestic distortions, a small open economy might not wish to engage in free trade.

Unemployment It is sometimes suggested that tariffs can be used to reduce domestic unemployment. The argument seems to be that tariffs will induce people to shift their spending from imported goods to domestically produced goods. This will create jobs in domestic industries and reduce unemployment.

Throughout this book, we have been assuming full employment, and under this assumption the argument that tariffs can increase employment is trivially false. Tariffs merely shift employment from the export sector to the import-competing sector. But even if we allow for unemployment due to various causes, the argument is still generally false, particularly over the long run. Since we have just dealt with unemployment due to structural adjustment, let us focus on Keynesian-type unemployment, due to deficient demand.

The argument that tariffs will shift spending from imports to domestic goods suffers from a partial equilibrium view of the economy. As we have noted earlier in the book, the economy faces a balance-of-payments constraint, which equates domestic spending on foreign goods and assets to foreign spending on domestic goods and assets. The two are brought together in the balance-of-payments constraint. If tariffs have the effect of reducing domestic spending on foreign goods (imports), then the system will initiate changes that reduce foreign spending on domestic goods (exports) or foreign investment in our economy. The exact mechanism by which this occurs is more the subject matter of international finance, but nowadays the balance of payments is generally maintained through changes in exchange rates.

In any case, balance-of-payments constraint implies that any reduction in imports caused by tariffs will be met by corresponding reductions in exports or foreign investment. Although the reduction in imports does supposedly give an expansionary stimulus to domestic demand, the reduction in exports and investment constitutes a contractionary force. Increased employment opportunities in import-competing industries as a result of tariffs may be balanced or even outweighed by job losses in export industries. Thus, when we take a general-equilibrium view of the economy, the employment argument cannot be supported.

Uncertainty   Especially since the Arab oil embargo of 1973, we have heard the argument that free trade leaves us open to fluctuations and instabilities arising abroad. These instabilities disrupt the domestic economy, causing alternating periods of inflation and unemployment.

While there is certainly some truth in this argument, it must be emphasized that it cuts both ways. The counterargument is that free trade can help stabilize the economy against the disruptive effects of domestic fluctuations. One example might be labor strikes. If domestic consumers and producers have the opportunity to import good X, then workers in the X industry have far less ability to disrupt the economy by striking. It might be instructive to note in this regard that the most militant unions are often found in the nontraded-goods industries, such as postal service, transportation and communications, public service, and so on. Trade helps to protect the rest of the population in the case of traded-goods industries, by limiting union militancy.

Other examples can be found. Domestic petroleum supplies are uncertain, as well as foreign supplies. Proven domestic reserves bounce up and down with the vagaries of exploration success. Thus instability of supply can arise from domestic as well as from foreign fluctuations. The ability to trade reduces the impact of fluctuations arising in the domestic economy, at the expense of increasing the impact of fluctuations arising in foreign economies.

The same argument can, of course, be applied to capital markets. The domestic demand and supply of investment funds rises and falls over business cycles. The ability to borrow and lend internationally is probably just as important in helping to stabilize domestic interest rates and investment as that ability is occasionally harmful to us.

National Defense A variation of the instability argument is that we need to have certain industries because their outputs are vital in time of war, when foreign supplies are unavailable. This argument has been used extensively in the United States, where, according to some, it has been used to gain protection for industries such as textiles and footwear (soldiers need uniforms and boots). This argument is not easy to assess since it involves evaluating the probability of war and the probability that there will be any need for anything in the event of nuclear war. We leave it to the reader to speculate on the problem.

High Technology Goods In the United States, there has in recent years been the suggestion that we will somehow be better off (if not now, at least in the future) if we produce something called high technology goods. The notion apparently is that we will have a higher income if we produce these "high tech" goods than if we continue to rely on other traditional export strengths in primary industries. We know of no careful analysis of this idea or even a rough outline of what this proposition is supposed to mean. If it asserts that our income or GNP will be high if we deliberately move away from our comparative advantage, then the proposition is almost certainly false. The development of new high technology products is an expensive and highly uncertain affair.

The United States has, of course, succeeded in the high technology field with many types of products. The issue here is whether artificial encouragement through tariffs or subsidies will benefit the United States. We know of no argument that provides a convincing reason as to why private markets are failing to respond in an efficient fashion. It is simply the case that glamour goods are not necessarily profitable goods.

Tariffs for Revenue   Tariffs constitute a source of revenue for the government of a country. Revenues are, of course, necessary for the operation of government activities. Is it possible to justify tariffs on the grounds that they are just another method of financing government expenditure? Economists tend to believe that tariffs are a very poor means of raising revenue, due to their distortionary effects (discussed in the first section of this chapter). Figure 14.1 is, for example, derived under the assumption that all tariff revenue is simply given back to consumers in the form of lump-sum grants. In a more realistic model, there might be additional goods provided to consumers on the basis of the tariff revenue raised. But the principle remains the same: Tariffs distort production and consumption decisions and thereby cause a welfare loss. Governments should seek other methods of raising revenue that are less distortionary (although there may exist no feasible taxes that are truly nondistortionary).

Sometimes tariffs are, in fact, one of the few methods available to governments for collecting revenue. This seems to be true, for example, in developing countries where the economic and social structures make it very difficult to collect income taxes and other types of taxes. In these cases, using tariffs for revenue may make some sense. In the case of the United States, however, the argument makes little sense, and indeed to the best of our knowledge, it has not in fact been used in recent decades in defense of tariffs. Tariffs are in any event a very small proportion of total federal government revenues in the United States.

Miscellaneous   Other wild claims are sometimes made in defense of or in advocacy of tariffs and you will simply have to analyze these arguments for yourself. We have heard, for example, that tariffs will encourage Americans to "keep their dollars at home." We have even heard the argument that restricting imports will lower the rate of inflation. Proving this one false will be left to you as an exercise.

3. THE INFANT-INDUSTRY ARGUMENT

One argument that deserves somewhat more thorough comment is known as the "infant-industry argument." It states that it may be unprofitable to start up certain industries in a situation of free trade, but if they were given time to develop behind tariff protection, those industries would eventually prove profitable and the tariff could later be dropped. Protection given while the industry is "infant" will yield rewards when the industry becomes "mature."

For a competitive, distortion-free economy, most economists generally do not believe this argument is valid. The reason is that in such an economy, any industry that is unprofitable from a private point of view is unprofitable from a social point of view. The infant-industry argument is clearly made with respect to industries that are unprofitable from a private point of view, otherwise private entrepreneurs would be willing to start up such industries without the benefit of a tariff. These entrepreneurs would calculate the present value of the profits that would occur over time and make a decision on entering the industry, based on that present value. It is quite possible that entrepreneurs would be willing to begin production even if they expected significant losses in the first few years of operation. Indeed, the expectation of such losses is typical, rather than the exception to the rule, in most industrial ventures. If entrepreneurs do not enter an industry, it is not because they fear current losses, but rather, because they believe that the discounted value of possible future profits will not compensate for current losses.

If a government is assessing whether a proposed industry might be socially beneficial to the country, the same considerations will enter into the government's calculations. If the economy is competitive and distortion-free, a government interested in purely economic considerations will, in fact, make the calculation in exactly the same way as a private entrepreneur would. If the industry is not profitable from a private point of view, it will not be profitable from a social point of view. In such a situation the infant-industry argument is invalid.

There are, however, several possible situations in which the infant-industry argument could be valid. First, the industry might be characterized by external economies (discussed in Chapter 11). Some industries, for example, consist of independent but interdependent firms that supply services, parts, or other inputs to other firms. In such a situation it may not be profitable for a single firm to begin production, given that all the complementary firms do not exist. Yet if all the firms could somehow be started simultaneously, the industry would, in fact, prove profitable.

Suppose, for example, that we wished to start a textile firm in a very backward country. We would find cheap labor, but we would also find that (1) there were no skilled mechanics to repair our machinery, (2) the electricity supply was unreliable or nonexistent, (3) there were no cost accountants to monitor production, (4) there existed no distribution network to market our output, (5) all inputs such as thread, dye, and so on, had to be imported at considerable cost in time and money. In such a situation we might well decide not to build a textile plant, even though production could be profitable if entrepreneurs in activities (1) to (5) could somehow begin production simultaneously. This would be a case in which the infant-industry argument might be valid and a tariff or other form of assistance might be justified.

A second possibility arises when there are capital market imperfections. Suppose that the rate of interest that a firm must pay to borrow funds exceeds the true opportunity cost of funds in the economy. This problem, like the previous one, is particularly acute in developing countries with underdeveloped financial institutions and capital markets. Private firms will, of course, evaluate the present value of profits using the market rate of interest they must pay, rather than the true opportunity cost of capital. This will bias these firms toward not undertaking the investment necessary to begin a new industry, since the distorted high interest rate will reduce the present value of future profits, while leaving present costs of investment unchanged. This decision not to enter an industry may be made in spite of the fact that the industry would be profitable from a social point of view. The government would then be justified in imposing a tariff or some other form of support to develop the industry.

Finally, a variety of other distortions could possibly mean that the profit-maximizing decisions of private firms were not consistent with welfare-maximizing choices. We examined several instances of this in Chapters 10 and 11. In any of these situations governments may be justified in assisting in the development of new industries. It does not necessarily follow, however, that a tariff is the best method of assistance.

4. TARIFFS, TAXES, AND DISTORTIONS[1]

As we noted earlier, tariffs are simply a special kind of tax. The purpose of this section will be to expand on the notion of tariffs as taxes and to analyze the relationship of tariffs to other types of taxes. Recall from Figure 14.1 that an import tariff on Y has the effect of raising *both* the price charged to the consumer and the price received by the producer. This hurts the consumer of Y and helps the producer of Y. The tariff acts like a tax on consumers and a subsidy to producers of Y. In fact, any tariff is exactly equivalent to a combined consumption tax and production subsidy. Looking only at the information in Figure 14.1, we would find it impossible to tell if the equilibrium at C_t was caused by an import tariff or by a combined consumption-tax/production-subsidy on Y.

A point somewhat more difficult to grasp is that an import tariff on Y is exactly equivalent to some export tax on X.[2] Restricting imports is, in other words, equivalent to restricting exports, which seems to contradict an old prejudice that we should try to restrict imports and encourage exports. Referring back to Section 1 of this chapter, recall that an import tariff on Y in Figure 14.1 raises the domestic price of Y above the world price ($p_y > p_y^*$), while leaving the domestic price of X equal to the world price ($p_x = p_x^*$). In ratio terms, the effect of the tariff is to set $p < p^*$ ($p = p_x/p_y$). But an export tax lowers the domestic price of X below the world price ($p_x < p_x^*$) while leaving the domestic price of Y equal to the world price ($p_y = p_y^*$). In ratio terms, the effect of the export tax is to set $p < p^*$. Thus an import tariff and an export tax have the same effect on the domestic price ratio, and since it is only the ratio that matters, both have the same effect on production and consumption. Again looking only at the information in Figure 14.1, we would find it impossible to tell if the equilibrium at C_t was generated by an import tariff or by an export tax.

Export taxes and import tariffs are equivalent, in that they tend to raise the relative domestic price of imports and to lower the relative domestic price of exports. Both tend to shift resources out of export industries into import-competing industries. The suggestion that we should restrict imports by tariffs and simultaneously encourage exports by subsidies is probably wrong on two accounts. First, we should not do either in a small economy since free trade is optimal and, second, the two proposed policies have exactly opposite effects.

This last point brings up the issue of subsidizing exports in a small open economy; this is analyzed in Figure 14.2. Suppose that S is an *ad valorem* subsidy rate on X. Then $p_x = p_x^* (1 + S)$ and $p = p^* (1 + S) > p$. Equation (14.1) must be replaced by

$$MRS = MRT = p = p^* (1 + S) > \mathrm{p}^*. \qquad (14.3)$$

The balance-of-payments constraint in equation (14.2) must, of course, continue to hold.

Figure 14.2 shows that the effect of the subsidy is that the country produces more X and less Y (point Q_s) than at the free-trade equilibrium (point Q_f). Consumption occurs at C_s where the MRS in consumption equals the distorted price ratio. The country trades more with the rest of the world (both exports and imports increase) but welfare is reduced from U_f to U_s.

Distorted prices thus lead to an inefficient allocation of resources in the export subsidy case, just as in the import tariff case. In the latter case Figure 14.1 shows that the tariff leads to too little production of X and too little trade. In the export subsidy case Figure 14.2 shows that the subsidy leads to too much production of X and too much trade. Distorted prices lead to welfare losses in both cases.

Now let us return to the notion that an import tariff (or export tax) is equivalent to a consumption tax and a production subsidy. Suppose that for some political reason the government is determined to increase pro-

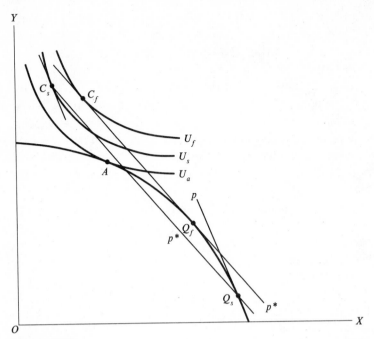

Figure 14.2

duction in the import-competing sector. Given this objective, the important economic question is, what is the least-cost method of achieving this
objective? The problem with an import tariff is that it acts as a tax on
consumption, in addition to serving as a subsidy to production. Might it
not be better to use a direct subsidy instead? The answer is definitely yes,
as is shown in Figure 14.3. If the government uses an import tariff to shift
production from Q_f to Q_t, consumption will move to C_t resulting in a
welfare level of U_t.

Suppose instead that the government simply subsidizes the production of Y. In this case production will still shift to Q_t. But consumers will
not face distorted prices and will instead be allowed to trade at world
prices. This will allow consumers to attain consumption bundle C_s and
utility level U_s in Figure 14.3. The intuitive explanation of this result can
be expressed by using the terminology of gains from exchange and gains
from specialization, developed in Chapter 5. The tariff in Figure 14.3
distorts both consumer and producer prices, thereby causing a loss of
gains from exchange as well as gains from specialization. The subsidy
distorts only producer prices and thereby causes a loss only of gains from
specialization. Unfortunately, politicians and the general public seem to
find tariffs acceptable but subsidies somehow unacceptable. Despite the
argument of Figure 14.3, tariffs are by far the more common method of

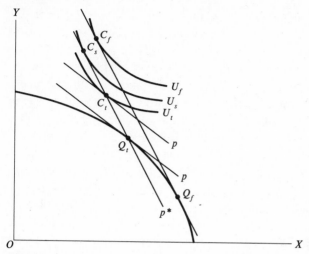

Figure 14.3

protection. More will be said about this in the concluding section of this chapter.

A final point concerning tariffs and taxes is explored in Figure 14.4. As we noted earlier in this chapter, the result that tariffs are harmful for a small open economy relies on the assumption that there are no distortions in the economy. If there are distortions, it may be the case that tariffs could be used to offset these distortions and thereby increase welfare. This is an application of what is known in economics as the "theory of the second best." This theory states that in the presence of distortions (such as domestic taxes or monopoly), welfare is not necessarily improved by

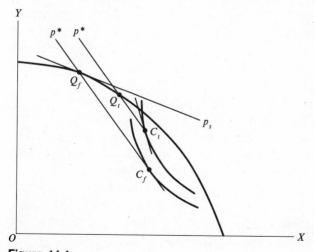

Figure 14.4

removing a single distortion (such as an import tariff). An equivalent statement is that in the presence of distortions, adding an additional distortion may improve welfare.

An application of the latter form of the theory of the second best is shown in Figure 14.4. Suppose that for some political reason the producers of Y have managed to obtain a subsidy from the government, and the government is unwilling to take the political risk of removing the subsidy. Free-trade production will take place at a point like Q_f in Figure 14.4, where the domestic producer price ratio p_s (the slope of the production frontier) is flatter than the world price ratio. Consumers can trade at world prices and so consumption is given by point C_f. Even though the government cannot remove the subsidy, it can improve welfare by introducing an additional distortion, namely, an import tariff on X. This will raise the domestic price of X and, with the subsidy on Y constant, encourage the production of X and move production in Figure 14.4 from Q_f to Q_t. The consumer prices will then be distorted by the tariff on X $(p > p^*)$, so consumption will occur at a point like C_t. Welfare is thus improved by the tariff, even though the country trades at fixed world prices. The tariff accomplishes this by influencing production in a direction opposite to the influence of the distortionary subsidy. The tariff in effect pushes the economy back in the direction of its efficient pattern of specialization.[3]

5. MONOPOLY POWER

In what has been said so far, we have assumed that the country is small, so that it faces fixed world prices (i.e., the country is essentially a perfect competitor on world markets). But suppose now that the country is large enough that world prices will be influenced by what the country wishes to buy and sell. More specifically, the world price of our export good will fall as we export more, and the world price of our import good will rise as we import more. The more we wish to trade, the worse our terms of trade become.[4]

Figure 14.5 depicts two countries in a trading situation, with OC^h and OC^f representing the free-trade offer curves of countries H and F. Country H exports X and imports Y and vice versa for country F. The offer curves intersect at F, establishing a free-trade price ratio of p_f^*. Now refer back to Figure 14.1 to see what happens when country H imposes an import tariff on Y. The tariff raises the domestic price of Y, thereby discouraging consumption and encouraging production of Y. Both effects combine to result in a decrease in imports and exports at a constant world price ratio. The tariff, in other words, causes the country to desire to trade less at given world prices. This is represented in Figure 14.1 by the fact that C_tQ_t is shorter than C_fQ_f.

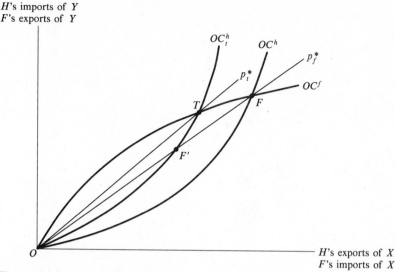

H's imports of *Y*
F's exports of *Y*

OC_t^h OC^h p_f^* OC^f

T p_t^* *F*

F'

O

H's exports of *X*
F's imports of *X*

Figure 14.5

The information contained in Figure 14.1 is easily transferred to Figure 14.5. As noted in Figure 14.1, the tariff causes country *H* to want to trade less at the current world price ratio. Thus at p_f^* in Figure 14.5 country *H* will now wish to trade a smaller amount such as *F'*. If we repeat this argument at all possible terms of trade, we will conclude that the effect of the tariff is to shift OC^h inward; that is, the tariff will cause country *H* to wish to trade less at every price ratio. The tariff will thus have the effect of shifting country *H*'s offer curve from OC^h to OC_t^h.

The new trade equilibrium following the imposition of the tariff by country *H* will be at *T* in Figure 14.5, where OC_t^h and OC^f cross. Note that the terms of trade will have changed from p_f^* to p_t^*. This represents an increase in the relative price of *X* (*H*'s export good), and thus represents an improvement in the terms of trade for country *H*.

Figure 14.6 illustrates the possibility that this improvement in the terms of trade can be so strong that country *H* is actually made better off by the tariff. The tariff raises the price ratio from p_f^* to p_t^*, resulting in post-tariff production and consumption at Q_t and C_t, respectively. Welfare increases from U_f to U_t following the imposition of the tariff.

The economic intuition of this possibility is fairly simple. While a country would like its firms to behave competitively when selling at home, it would be beneficial for the country to behave as a monopolist when selling abroad. Since we have assumed that individual firms are competitive, there is scope for the government to move in and essentially make the country behave as a monopolist. The tariff causes the country to restrict its "output" (exports) like a monopolist and also restrict its "de-

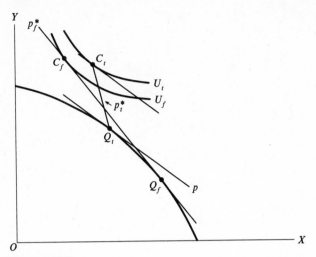

Figure 14.6

mand" (imports) like a monopsonist, thereby moving prices in the country's favor.

*6. THE OPTIMUM TARIFF

When a country can gain by imposing a tariff, we might ask what the best possible tariff level is. This is known as the "optimal tariff" issue.[5] The key to deriving the optimal tariff was contained in our preceding discussions, where we noted that a tariff could allow a country to exert its monopoly power in the supply of its export good, or monopsony power in purchases of its import good.

Since we are usually talking about tariffs on imports, let us take the latter approach and think of the country as exercising its monopsony power in the purchase of imports. Figure 14.7 depicts the situation for our country, which is again assumed to import Y. E_y^f is the foreign supply curve (technically, excess supply curve) and I_y^h is the home country's (excess) demand curve for Y. Free-trade equilibrium would be given by the intersection of the two, establishing a free-trade price of p_{yf}^* and imports equal to I_{yf}.

But this free-trade equilibrium is not an optimum for country H. An optimum requires that country H equate the domestic price of Y to the marginal cost of imports. The foreign supply curve gives the price of imports for each quantity of imports, and price is simply the average cost. Let C_y denote the total cost of imports. We have

$$C_y = p_y^* I_y; \qquad AC_y = C_y/I_y = p_y^*; \qquad I_y = (Y_c - Y_p)\,(14.4)$$

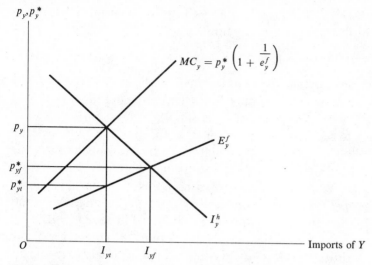

Figure 14.7

where AC_y is the average cost of imports. Free trade thus equates the domestic price of Y to the average cost of Y ($p_y = p_y^*$).

Marginal cost is defined as the change in cost (ΔC_y) in response to a change in the quantity of imports (ΔI_y). ΔC_y can be approximated as follows:

$$\Delta C_y = p_y^* \, \Delta I_y + I_y \, \Delta p_y^*. \tag{14.5}$$

Dividing (14.5) by ΔI_y, we have

$$\frac{\Delta C_y}{\Delta I_y} = p_y^* + I_y \frac{\Delta p_y^*}{\Delta I_y} = p_y^*\left(1 + \frac{I_y}{p_y^*}\frac{\Delta p_y^*}{\Delta I_y}\right). \tag{14.6}$$

Let e_y^f be defined as country F's elasticity of supply of exports. Since $\Delta C_y/\Delta I_y = MC_y$, equation (14.6) can be rewritten as:

$$MC_y = p_y^*(1 + 1/e_y^f), \; e_y^f = \frac{p_y^*}{I_y}\frac{\Delta I_y}{\Delta p_y^*}. \tag{14.7}$$

Since the supply curve slopes upward, e_y^f is positive and marginal cost is greater than average cost ($MC_y > AC_y = p_y^*$). The marginal cost curve is shown by MC_y in Figure 14.7.

Country H maximizes its welfare by equating p_y to MC_y. Thus in Figure 14.7 the country should import quantity I_{yt}, resulting in a domestic price of p_y. This restriction on imports drives down the world price of Y from p_{yf}^* to p_{yt}^* and results in a welfare gain for country H, as discussed in the previous section. We also know that an import tariff will lead to the relationship $p_y = p_y^*(1 + T)$, where T is the *ad valorem* tariff rate. Thus the optimal tariff rate will be the rate that solves the equation

$$p_y = p_y^* (1 + T) = p_y^* (1 + 1/e_y^f); \qquad T = 1/e_y^f. \qquad (14.8)$$

The optimum tariff is thus equal to the inverse elasticity of supply. The more inelastic foreign excess supply is, the larger the optimum tariff will thus be (i.e., T will be large when e_y^f is small).

It is easy to see that the optimum tariff formula covers the special case of a small open economy. If a country can trade as much or as little as it wishes at fixed world prices, this means that the supply curve facing the country is horizontal or infinitely elastic. In this situation e_y^f is infinite and $1/e_y^f$ is zero. Thus the optimal tariff for a small economy is zero and free trade is indeed the optimal policy as discussed in section 14.1.

Two qualifications to this discussion should be noted. First, the optimal tariff formula is deceptively simple in that it seems to tell us exactly what the tariff should be. But in actual fact e_y^f is generally a variable that changes its value as we move along the foreign excess supply curve. $T = 1/e_y^f$ is unfortunately no more than an equilibrium condition and does not by itself tell us what the numerical value of T should be. The optimal value of T must be found by first estimating E_y^f and I_y^h and then using E_y^f to construct MC_y or e_y^f. It is only after this has been done that the *formula* can be applied to find the optimal *value* of T. Note especially in this regard that T will depend on domestic factors, even though the optimal tariff formula seems to rely only on the foreign elasticity. T will equal $1/e_y^f$ evaluated at the point where the domestic excess demand curve crosses MC_y. Since e_y^f generally varies along MC_y, the actual value of e_y^f and therefore T will depend on where I_y^h crosses MC_y. Thus domestic factors do indeed help determine the value of the optimum tariff, and the simple formula does not, in fact, provide a shortcut to this value.

The second qualification is a much more important one. The optimal tariff discussed here is based on the assumption that the foreigners will not retaliate when we institute the tariff. Suppose, however, that the foreigner will exactly match any tariff we impose. In Figure 14.5 this will cause OC^f to shift inward and move the terms of trade back against country H. Indeed, it is quite possible that we could end up with exactly the same world price ratio that prevailed with free trade. The volume of trade would be lower, and therefore, since neither country had succeeded in improving its terms of trade, both countries would be unambiguously worse off.[6]

Due to the high probability of foreign retaliation, the term "optimal tariff" is very misleading. It is optimal only under the very special assumption of no retaliation. If all countries pursued this so-called optimal strategy simultaneously, it is quite likely that everyone would be worse off—

hardly an optimal outcome. If countries cooperate instead of myopically pursuing their self-interests, it is likely that they will find that relatively free trade constitutes the optimal policy.

7. CONCLUDING REMARKS

Tariffs, like other forms of commodity taxes, tend to raise prices and reduce quantities. Import tariffs raise the price of imports and so reduce their quantity. If a country is small and thus faces fixed world prices, this reduction causes an unambiguous reduction in the gains from trade, and so reduces national welfare. Tariffs simply move the country back in the direction of autarky.

We examined many of the arguments commonly made in favor of tariffs and found most to be invalid. Those that are at least potentially valid are the ones based on domestic distortions such as external economies, distortionary taxation, or monopoly. In the presence of such distortions, free trade is not necessarily optimal, and a tariff may be useful in counteracting a distortion and may thereby lead to an increase in welfare. But even in these situations we noted that a tariff is not necessarily the best instrument for counteracting a distortion. Production distortions are, for example, best dealt with by production taxes and subsidies that directly attack the problem. Tariffs are indirect and have the undesirable effect of distorting consumer prices, thereby causing a loss of gains from exchange.

Another situation in which a tariff can be beneficial occurs when the country has some monopoly power in trade. The tariff allows the country to exploit this monopoly power by shifting world prices in the country's favor. But this argument is greatly undermined by the likelihood that other countries will retaliate against the tariff-imposing country. The noncooperative scenario of tariff imposition and retaliation is unlikely to be beneficial to any country. The probable outcome is that the volume of world trade will be reduced without any country gaining a significant terms-of-trade advantage. Gains from trade are lost with the reduction in world trade.

In a cooperative scenario, countries are likely to find therefore that the so-called optimal tariffs are not, in fact, optimal at all. By cooperatively reducing their tariffs, countries can expand trade without suffering adverse terms-of-trade effects and thereby increase their welfare.

Why then do we still have significant tariffs in the United States? At least three reasons are of importance. First, we noted that tariffs have significant income redistribution effects. Thus certain industries will find it very much in their interests to lobby vigorously for tariff protection, using whatever concocted arguments or political threats they can muster. Typically, a tariff will lead to a very large income gain for the industry in question, while the losses will be spread very thinly across the rest of the population. This population is therefore unlikely to mount any opposition to a particular tariff. Thus, even though the losses to the general population as a whole probably well outweigh the gains to the industry, the government may find it can have its political cake and eat it too, by granting the industry tariff protection.

It is interesting to note in this respect that industries are more likely to ask for, and governments more likely to grant, tariff protection than subsidies, even though we have shown the latter to be less distortionary. The explanation is probably that both the industry in question and the government perceive that tariffs can be instituted with less *political* opposition than subsidies. Many voters will not oppose tariffs and can, in fact, be talked into believing they are beneficial. The same voters, however, probably react adversely to subsidies, which are viewed as unfair giveaways and likely to result in high taxes.

Second, we noted that many protariff arguments are based on a partial view of the economy. One example is the notion that tariffs will increase employment by encouraging consumers to shift from foreign to domestic goods. To the extent that people in power are economically naïve, they may be persuaded by such arguments. Alternatively, the government may not believe these arguments, but if the general population does, then the government may be forced to institute protective tariffs.

Third, the fact that many inefficient tariffs remain in place is partly due to the substantial adjustment costs that would be incurred following their removal. Theory suggests that the rest of the economy should be able to compensate adequately the losers from trade liberalization, but this would probably involve additional government programs and expenditures. In many situations it is probably easier simply to stay with the status quo, rather than force an adjustment. The ultimate benefits from adjustment are thinly spread out among consumers, and thus, as we noted earlier, there may be little political payoff from removing many inefficient tariffs.

PROBLEMS

1. Is it possible for a tariff to make a country worse off relative to free trade?
2. Redraw Figure 14.1 for the case in which the country exports Y and imports X.
3. In the Heckscher-Ohlin model the prices of labor and capital always move in opposite directions. Yet, in practice, workers and capital owners in import-

competing industries lobby for protection together. Can you think of reasons as to why this might make sense in the short run, even though the Heckscher-Ohlin model is a valid long-run description of the economy?

4. Comment on the argument that tariffs can help reduce the rate of inflation. You should be able to prove that the opposite is true.

5. Imagine that you are the owner of a textile plant in South Carolina and are having difficulties due to cheap imports. Write a paragraph arguing why you should be given tariff protection. Then write a paragraph arguing the opposite.

6. Suppose that you are a government official and some businesspeople approach you with an infant-industry argument to ask for protection to start a new industry. What sort of questions would you ask to assess the validity of their request?

7. For the past several years, the United States has been subsidizing exports of grain. Analyze the welfare effects of this policy.

8. Suppose that instead of instituting an optimal import tariff, the government decides to use an optimal export tax. Using a methodology similar to that of Figure 14.7, can you derive the optimal export tax formula?

NOTES

1. A comprehensive treatment of the effects of various taxes on trade and welfare is given by Melvin (1975).
2. This point is credited to Lerner (1936).
3. Certain aspects of trade policy in the presence of domestic distortions are discussed in Bhagwati (1967, 1971), Johnson (1965), and Melvin (1975).
4. The original argument is due to Bickerdike (1906) and was formalized and generalized by a number of authors including Graaff (1949).
5. Again, see Bickerdike (1906) and Graaff (1949).
6. See Johnson (1954) for a full discussion of the tariff war outcome and Markusen (1981) for an analysis of the opposite problem: cooperative tariff reduction.

REFERENCES

Bhagwati, J. N. (1967). "Non-Economic Objectives and the Efficiency Properties of Trade." *Journal of Political Economy* 75, 738–742.

——. (1971). "The Generalized Theory of Distortions and Welfare." In J. Bhagwatti et al. (eds.), *Trade, Balance of Payments and Growth: Essays in Honor of Charles P. Kindleberger,* Amsterdam: North-Holland.

Bickerdike, D. F. (1906). "The Theory of Incipient Taxes." *Economic Journal* 16, 529–535.

Graaff, J. de V. (1949). "On Optimal Tariff Structures." *Review of Economic Studies* 16, 47–59.

Johnson, H. G. (1954). "Optimal Tariffs and Retaliation." *Review of Economic Studies* 21, 142–153.

———. (1965). "Optimal Trade Intervention in the Presence of Domestic Distortions." In R. Caves et al. (eds.), *Trade, Growth and the Balance of Payments: Essays in Honor of G. Haberler.* New York: Rand McNally.

Lerner, A. (1936). "The Symmetry Between Import and Export Taxes." *Economica* 11, 306–313.

Markusen, J. R. (1981). "The Distribution of Gains from Bilateral Tariff Reduction." *Journal of International Economics* 11, 553–572.

Melvin, J. R. (1975). *The Tax Structure and Canadian Trade.* Ottawa: Economic Council of Canada.

chapter *15*

Quotas and Other Nontariff Barriers

1. QUOTAS

We noted in Chapter 14 that tariffs are the most common form of trade restriction, and that tariffs are simply a form of tax. Tariffs thus allow consumers to import as little or as much as they wish, subject to paying the tax. Tariffs directly affect the price of imports and only indirectly affect the quantity of imports via the effect of price increases on consumer and producer decisions.

After tariffs, the second most common form of trade restriction is quotas. *Quotas* are ceilings on the quantities of imports and particular goods. A quota might, for example, state that no more than 500,000 square meters of cloth can be imported, or no more than 100,000 automobiles. Quotas are in a sense opposite to tariffs, in that quotas directly affect the quantities of imports and only indirectly affect prices. Yet tariffs and quotas are fundamentally similar, in that each ultimately restricts the quantity and raises the prices of imports. Under certain circumstances discussed later, tariffs and quotas have identical effects.

The effect of an import quota is illustrated in Figure 15.1, where OC^h and OC^f are the free-trade offer curves of countries H and F, respectively. Free-trade equilibrium occurs at point F where OC^h and OC^f cross. Suppose now that the government of country H imposes a quota on the imports of Y, equal to $\bar{I}_y$. This is shown by the horizontal line $\bar{I}_y$ in Figure

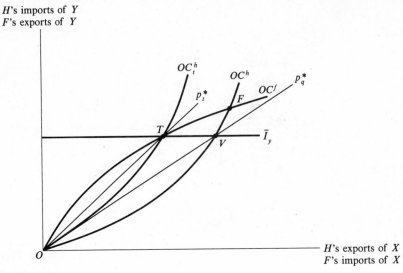

Figure 15.1

15.1. Any trading equilibrium is restricted to being on or below this line. Thus the free-trade equilibrium at F is no longer feasible; in other words, the quota is a binding constraint on trade.

The binding quota $\bar{I}_y$ on imports of Y by country H will create a disequilibrium situation that will lead to price and quantity changes. These changes will depend on exactly how the quota is instituted, as we will explain shortly. First, we can use Figures 15.1 and 15.2 to analyze the

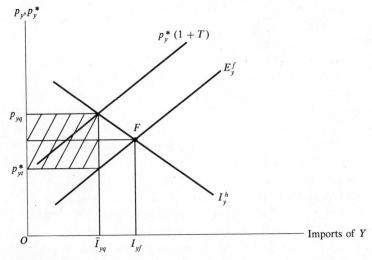

Figure 15.2

range of possible outcomes. Let I_y^h in Figure 15.2 represent country H's demand for imports of Y and E_y^f represent country F's supply of exports of Y. These curves cross to establish a free-trade equilibrium at F, corresponding to F in Figure 15.1. The quota on imports is shown by the vertical line at $\overline{I}_y$ in Figure 15.2. The import demand curve I_y^h gives the maximum amount that citizens of country H are willing to pay for Y, whereas E_y^f gives the minimum price that producers in country F are willing to accept. Thus p_{yq} and p_{yt}^* in Figure 15.2 are the prices that H is willing to pay and F is willing to receive, respectively, when the quota $\overline{I}_y$ is imposed. The difference between these prices, $(p_{yq} - p_{yt}^*)$, will be captured by one country or the other depending on how the quota is instituted. The total value of capturing this difference is the price difference times the quantity of imports or $(p_{yq} - p_{yt}^*)\,\overline{I}_y$. This is equal to the area of the hatched rectangle in Figure 15.2.

The general-equilibrium representation of this problem is given in Figure 15.1. p_q^* is the price ratio that country H is willing to pay for imports under the quota; that is, p_q^* is given by the point on country H's offer curve where imports equal $\overline{I}_y$ (point V). Similarly, p_t^* in Figure 15.1 gives the price ratio that country F is willing to receive. p_t^* is given by the point on F's offer curve where exports equal $\overline{I}_y$ (point T). An equilibrium at T in Figure 15.1 will correspond to the situation where country H captures the price difference shown in Figure 15.2. At T, the world price ratio has increased (the relative price of Y has fallen) so that country H has moved the terms of trade in its favor. Point V in Figure 15.1 is the case in which country F captures the price difference created by the quota. At V, the world price ratio has fallen relative to free trade (the relative price of Y has increased) so that country F is receiving a higher price for its exports of Y despite the quota. Thus country F is capturing the price difference if the equilibrium occurs at V.

Suppose that country H polices the quota by issuing licenses to import Y. If the government of H auctions off the licenses or simply gives them to domestically owned firms, country H will capture the price difference shown in Figure 15.2, and the trading equilibrium will occur at point T in Figure 15.1. In either case country H holds the licenses, so that competitive supply by firms in country F will drive the world price ratio to p_t^*. There is, of course, a distributional difference between auctioning off the licenses and giving them away to domestic firms. In the former case the government captures the revenue (the hatched rectangle in Figure 15.2), whereas in the latter case the revenue goes to the owners of the domestic firms.

Suppose instead that country H asks the government of country F to restrict exports to the quota level $\overline{I}_y$. This is sometimes known as "voluntary restraint" on the part of the exporting nation. In this case country F will capture the revenues discussed in Figure 15.2 and the trading equilibrium will occur at V in Figure 15.1. Competition by importing firms in country H for the limited supply of Y will drive the relative world price of Y up and the world price ratio down to p_q^* in Figure 15.1.

The amount of Y imported by country H is the same (the amount of the quota) under each of these quota systems. But the world price ratio and hence the amount of country H's exports will differ, depending on whether residents of H hold the licenses or a voluntary restraint is used. In the former case the world price of Y is forced down and country H has to export a relatively small amount of X to pay for Y (equilibrium at T in Figure 15.1). In the voluntary restraint case the world price of Y is bid up and country H has to export a relatively large amount of X to pay for Y (equilibrium at V). This is simply another way of showing that country H is better off at T than at V, and vice versa for country F. Country H is, in fact, unambiguously worse off at V relative to free trade, since both its volume of trade and its terms of trade have deteriorated. It is interesting to note that country F could actually be better off at V in Figure 15.1 relative to free trade, if the improvement in its terms of trade outweighs its loss in volume of trade. Thus the voluntary restraint quota of country H could actually make country F better off, while it unambiguously makes country H worse off.

Why then would country H ever institute a voluntary restraint quota? The answer probably lies with the politics of world trade. Suppose country H is worried not so much about overall GNP, but with the employment level in a particular industry. This was more or less the situation of the U.S. government with respect to the automobile industry in the early 1980s. The federal government wanted to preserve jobs in the industry and was not interested in the arguments we have presented in Figures 15.1 and 15.2. If it had instituted a tariff or quota against Japanese automobiles, with licenses distributed domestically, the Japanese may well have retaliated against U.S. products. But by asking the Japanese for voluntary export restraint, the U.S. government was essentially introducing a policy that was less damaging and therefore more acceptable to the Japanese. Jobs could be preserved without greatly damaging Japanese trade profits, by voluntary restraint. There are, of course, losers from such a policy—the American auto buyers.

*2. THE RELATIONSHIP BETWEEN TARIFFS AND QUOTAS

In the simple static competitive model presented in the previous section a quota may have effects identical to a tariff, depending on how the quota is administered. If the government auctions off import licenses, there will exist some tariff that exactly duplicates the quota. Consider again the import quota $\bar{I}_y$ in Figure 15.1. We noted in the previous section that the equilibrium would occur at point T if the government auctioned off import licenses or gave the licenses to domestic firms. We noted in Chapter 14 that the effect of a tariff would be to shift country H's offer curve inward. Thus there will exist some import tariff for country H that exactly shifts H's offer curve from OC^h to OC^h_t in Figure 15.1. The post-tariff offer curve OC^h_t intersects OC^f at T in Figure 15.1, and thus the tariff and the quota have identical effects on world trade and prices. If the quota is auctioned off instead of distributed to domestic firms, the revenue created by the price difference is captured by the government, as in the tariff case, and thus the quota and tariff are identical from a distributional point of view as well.

The same results can be derived from Figure 15.2. The effect of the tariff is to shift the foreign supply curve upward by the amount of the tariff. Thus to duplicate the quota, we find the tariff rate T that shifts E^f_y upward to $p^*_y(1 + T)$ so that the latter curve intersects the home country's import demand curve I^h_y at $\bar{I}_y$. The value of the tariff revenue will be $(p_{yq} - p^*_{yt})\,\bar{I}_y$ (the price difference times the quantity of imports), which is the hatched rectangle in Figure 15.2. This is, of course, the same amount of revenue discussed earlier with respect to the quota.

Even when the government auctions off licenses, there is a wide variety of circumstances in which quotas and tariffs are not equivalent. Rather than attempt to provide an exhaustive list, we will just analyze a few examples in order to give the flavor of the problem.[1]

Economic Growth   Suppose that we have an initial situation in which we solve for the tariff that is equivalent to some quota. The situation is shown in Figure 15.3, where I^h_y is country H's initial demand curve for imports. $\bar{I}_{yq}$ is an import quota. E^f_y is country F's export supply curve. Tariff rate T shifts the supply curve upward to $p^*_y (1 + T)$, resulting in the same equilibrium achieved by the quota. Now suppose that country H experiences economic growth. With income higher, consumers will wish to spend more on imports, and thus the import demand curve will shift out to $I^{h'}_y$ in Figure 15.3.

If the quota is in effect, no additional imports are permitted, and thus the price must rise far enough so that demand remains constant at $\bar{I}_{yq}$. Thus the quota causes growth to result in a price increase from p_{yq} to p'_{yq} in Figure 15.3. If the tariff is in effect, the new equilibrium will be found at the intersection of $I^{h'}_y$ and $p^*_y (1 + T)$ in Figure 15.3. The tariff allows imports to increase from $\bar{I}_{yq}$ to I_{yt} and results in a price rise that is more moderate (p_{yq} to p_{yt}) than the price rise under the quota. This can

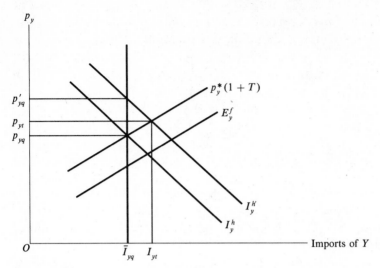

Figure 15.3

be summarized by saying that quotas become more and more restrictive as an economy grows, and thus become more and more distortionary. For a quota to be equivalent to a tariff, the quota must be periodically loosened as the economy grows, to permit growth in imports.

Price Fluctuations   The argument that tariffs and quotas are nonequivalent in the presence of growth probably generalizes to trade under any sort of changing economic conditions. Quotas are rigid with respect to quantities, and thus all changes must be absorbed by price changes. Tariffs permit quantities of imports to change so that adjustment will occur in quantities as well as prices. (Of course, some changes such as a recession could cause the demand for imports to fall so far that the quota becomes nonbinding, resulting in changes in the quantities of imports.) It is tempting to conjecture that economic changes will, therefore, lead to larger domestic price fluctuations under quotas than under tariffs. However, this is true with respect to domestic price responses to domestic changes (as in Figure 15.3) but not with respect to changes that are foreign in origin. The argument proceeds as follows.[2]

The domestic and foreign price ratios are related by

$$p_x/p_y = p_x^*/(p_y^* (1 + T)) \qquad T > 0. \qquad (15.1)$$

If there is an import tariff, T is the fixed value of the tariff. If there is an import quota, let T be a sort of "implicit tariff" that gives the difference between what domestic consumers are willing to pay and the foreign price. T is, in other words, the amount the government can collect per unit of imports by auctioning off the licenses. Suppose that we are a small open economy facing a perfectly elastic foreign supply curve. Suppose also that the foreign supply curve shifts up and down randomly. If we have a tariff, the domestic price ratio will fluctuate in the same proportion as the foreign fluctuation, since T is fixed in equation (15.1).

But if we have a quota, T varies with the world price; that is, an increase in the foreign price p_y^* will narrow the gap between the domestic demand price and p_y^*. Alternatively, an increase in p_y^* will mean that domestic importers are willing to bid less for the import licenses, and thus the "implicit tariff" T is reduced in value. The effect of this can be seen from equation (15.1). If any increase in p_y^* causes a fall in T, these changes will be partially offsetting, with the result that the domestic price ratio fluctuates less than the world price ratio. Thus the quota provides better insulation from foreign fluctuations, whereas the tariff provides better insulation from fluctuations that are domestic in origin. This result should, however, be interpreted with care insofar as the stabilization of domestic prices does not necessarily constitute a welfare criterion that the government should pursue.

Monopoly   Another interesting case of nonequivalence of tariffs and quotas occurs when there is domestic monopoly.[3] Let Figure 15.4 represent the home country's market for Y. D_y^h is the domestic demand curve (not excess demand curve) and MC_y^h is the marginal cost curve of the domestic Y industry. The foreign supply of Y is infinitely elastic at price p_y^*. $p_y^*(1 + T)$ gives the foreign supply curve when there is an import

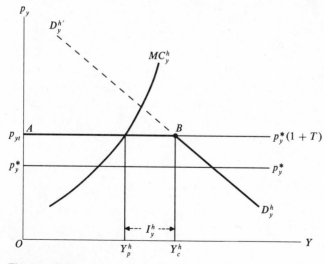

Figure 15.4

tariff. The effective demand curve facing the domestic Y industry is ABD_y^h in Figure 15.4 when the tariff is in place. Consumers can always buy Y at the tariff-inclusive price of $p_y^*(1 + T)$ so that the demand curve facing domestic producers is perfectly elastic at price $p_y^*(1 + T)$ up to point B, where the price that domestic consumers are willing to pay drops below $p^*(1 + T)$. Equilibrium with the tariff in Figure 15.4 will have domestic producers supplying Y_p^h where domestic price $p_{yt} = p_y^*(1 + T)$ equals marginal cost. Consumers will purchase quantity Y_c^h where D_y^h is equal to $p_y^*(1 + T)$. Imports will equal $I_y^h = (Y_c^h - Y_p^h)$.

The important fact to note about Figure 15.4 is that the equilibrium just discussed will occur regardless of whether or not the domestic Y industry is competitive. With foreign supply infinitely elastic at p_y^* and therefore at $p_y^*(1 + T)$, marginal revenue for a monopolist will equal price, and thus both the monopolist and the competitive industry will choose to produce at Y_p^h in Figure 15.4.

Suppose instead that a quota is imposed, with the size of the quota being equal to the amount of imports I_y^h following the imposition of the tariff in Figure 15.4. The effect of the quota is shown in Figure 15.5. At a domestic price above p_y^*, domestic consumers will wish to buy as much foreign Y as possible, but this is limited to I_y^h. Thus at prices above p_y^*, the demand curve facing domestic producers is D_y^h minus (shifted left) the amount of the quota I_y^h. This "residual demand curve" is given by $A'B'$ in Figure 15.5. At prices below p_y^*, the domestic consumers will not wish

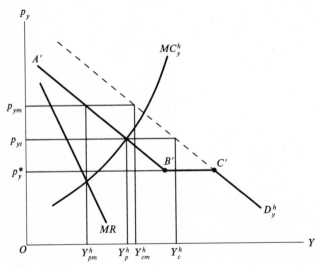

Figure 15.5

to buy any foreign Y and thus the quota is nonbinding. The demand curve facing domestic producers of Y is thus given by $A'B'C'D_y^h$ in Figure 15.5.

If the domestic Y industry is competitive, it will produce where MC_y^h cuts the demand curve $A'B'C'D_y^h$ in Figure 15.5. This results in an output of Y_p^h at price p_{yt} and a consumption of Y_c^h. Since the quota shifted domestic demand to the left by the exact amount that was imported under the tariff, you should be able to verify that the competitive outcome with the quota is exactly the same as the tariff outcome.

But now suppose that the Y industry is monopolized. With the quota, domestic demand is no longer perfectly elastic as it was with the tariff. The segment of the residual demand curve $A'B'$ is downward sloping, and thus marginal revenue will be less than price. The monopolist can raise the domestic price above p_{yt} in Figure 15.5 without losing all his sales to imports (as would happen with the tariff) since consumers are already importing the maximum permissible amount of Y. Let MR in Figure 15.5 be the marginal revenue curve associated with the demand curve $A'B'$. The monopolist will produce quantity Y_{pm}^h where marginal revenue equals marginal cost. The domestic price will be driven up to p_{ym} and consumption will be reduced to Y_{cm}^h.

Relative to the tariff, the quota makes domestic demand more inelastic, thus creating a better environment for the profitable exploitation of monopoly power. Since there is almost certainly a welfare loss associated with this exercise of monopoly power, tariffs would seem to be a preferable form of import control in the presence of domestic monopoly power in import-competing industries.

Retaliation A final case of nonequivalence between tariffs and quotas occurs when countries attempt to institute "optimal" trade restriction schemes, such as the optimal tariff that we discussed in Chapter 14.[4] Recall that the so-called optimal tariff was $T = 1/e$, where e was the elasticity of export supply by the foreign country. Thus the more inelastic foreign supply was, the higher was the optimal tariff. It turns out that the imposition of a quota by a country affects its offer curve in a significantly different way from a tariff. When the other country retaliates, its optimal quota restriction is quite different from its optimal tariff, due to the fact that the foreigner has used a quota. The argument is fairly long and technical, and thus we will not present it here. Basically, the result is that a "trade war" of quotas and retaliation will result in an ultimate equilibrium with less trade and larger welfare losses than would a tariff war. Under certain assumptions the quota war leads to a complete elimination of trade, and countries are reduced to their autarky level of welfare.

3. OTHER NONTARIFF BARRIERS

Tariffs and quotas are not the only methods of restricting trade. There is a large number of other policies that can act directly or indirectly to restrict imports or exports. There are corresponding measures that artificially stimulate exports, but in order to limit our discussion, we will just focus on import restrictions. This should be sufficient to give the reader an understanding of the issues. Several of these nontariff barriers are as follows.[5]

Import Licensing It is often the case, particularly in developing countries, that importers must obtain licenses to import certain goods. These licenses may be "free" and potentially unlimited in number (i.e., there is no quota), but require the importer to spend time filing forms and waiting for permission. These activities represent very real costs even though they do not appear in any official accounting figures. These costs include the opportunity costs of the importer's time, interest costs due to time delays, the cost of uncertainty over whether or not a license will be granted, the costs of additional bureaucrats, and so on. Import licenses also have the potentially unfavorable effects of permitting bureaucrats to engage in arbitrary and unfair practices in issuing licenses (e.g., bureaucrats could discriminate in favor of friends or those willing to pay bribes).

Exchange Control A restriction closely related to import licensing is termed "exchange control." With exchange control, importers face restrictions not on imports per se but on their ability to buy the foreign currency needed to pay for imports. Exchange control is very common in developing countries and communist nations but is not very common in the West. Exchange control suffers from the same problems as import licensing and is generally frowned upon by economists. In many cases exchange control is initially imposed as an emergency measure to deal with severe balance-of-payments problems, but then somehow persists long after the emergency has passed.

Other Assorted Red Tape Import licensing and exchange control are only two of a virtually endless number of ways in which governments can interfere with international commerce. Other ways include diverse methods such as slow customs procedures, complicated forms, packaging and labeling requirements, requirements to comply with domestic industrial codes and specifications, and so forth. In some cases these requirements make perfect sense and do not discriminate against foreign goods per se. An example might be the U.S. requirements concerning safety and emission controls for automobiles. But in other cases there would seem to be little purpose in the regulations other than to harass importers.

Red tape is perhaps even more common with respect to foreign investment. The problems a foreign company would face in trying to set up a plant in Canada are generally far greater than the problems faced in simply exporting to Canada.

Government Purchasing   It is not uncommon for governments to discriminate deliberately and systematically in favor of domestic suppliers when purchasing goods and services. Often governments are required to do this by law. This is, in fact, not a trivial issue, since in many countries the various levels of governments add up to a sizable proportion of GNP. Purchasing more expensive domestic goods instead of cheaper foreign goods raises costs to consumers and distorts the allocation of resources, just as tariffs do.

Discriminatory Domestic Taxation   Anyone who has had no involvement with tax laws other than filling out a yearly income tax return has seen only the tip of the iceberg, for domestic tax policies are highly complex. There is a great deal of scope in such laws to discriminate against foreign goods and firms and all countries avail themselves of those opportunities to some degree. There was, for example, a great deal of controversy between Canada and the United States in the early 1980s when Canada introduced highly discriminatory taxation laws dealing with oil and natural gas.

A slightly different version of this problem arises with government-owned corporations, which are often given implicit or explicit competitive advantages over foreign firms. A common example of this in recent decades might be the favorable treatments given to government-owned airlines.

Propaganda Campaigns   Governments, corporations, and labor unions often run advertising campaigns to encourage consumers to buy domestic goods. The messages delivered range from simple flag-waving to unambiguously false economic arguments. Insofar as these arguments are successful, they shift spending to import-competing goods and distort production away from our most efficient pattern of specialization. There is a distributional difference from tariffs, however; if consumers can be induced by propaganda to buy more expensive domestic goods, then the government collects no revenue. In fact, if the government spends money on advertising, the difference is even greater.

4. CONCLUDING REMARKS

Nontariff barriers are similar to tariffs in a very basic sense. Nontariff barriers restrict trade, raise prices of imports, and redistribute income just as tariffs do. The most common nontariff barriers are probably quotas, which impose quantitative restrictions on imports. We noted that there are circumstances under which quotas are identical to tariffs. Circumstances in which quotas and tariffs are *not* equivalent include: (1) the issuing of quotas by methods other than license auction, (2) domestic growth, (3) domestic or foreign fluctuations, (4) domestic monopoly power, and (5) retaliatory trade "warfare."

Other nontariff barriers to trade include such things as import licensing, exchange control, other red tape, government purchasing policies, tax policies, and propaganda campaigns. These measures affect prices and the distribution of income differently from tariffs, and sometimes in highly arbitrary and uncertain ways.

If a country is determined to have trade barriers, most international trade economists would probably prefer to see tariffs used instead of nontariff barriers, for several reasons. First, tariffs are direct and measurable. It is easy to look at a tariff schedule and assess the level and distribution of protection. Measures such as discriminatory tax treatment, government purchasing, and import licensing are indirect and hard to measure. It is not very clear how they affect the pattern of trade, the volume of trade, and income distribution. It is interesting to note in this regard that economists generally try to convert nontariff barriers to tariff equivalents, when trying to assess the impact of the nontariff barriers on various domestic variables.

Second, tariffs are visible, whereas the exact structure of nontariff barriers can be hidden behind the bureaucracies' walls. It is very difficult for foreigners to know exactly how import licensing works and whether or not various rules and regulations are being instituted for legitimate reasons or simply to harass importers. This visibility and measurability is important in helping to simplify trade liberalization negotiations. It is probably far easier to negotiate mutual tariff reductions than to negotiate and enforce reductions in nontariff barriers. Indeed, it is partly for this reason that many trade analysts feel that nontariff barriers represent a greater problem than the remaining rather low tariffs between industrialized nations.

Third, tariffs are considered to be fairer than nontariff barriers. Any surplus value (economic rent) created by tariffs tends to find its way into the government treasury. Nontariff barriers (except auctioned quotas) generally leave this rent in the hands of private companies and individuals in a highly arbitrary way. One hears stories of developing countries in which the distribution of import licenses is a method of distributing political patronage, for example.

Fourth, tariffs probably lead to less wasting of resources than nontariff barriers. Red tape, for example, tends to lead to a waste of time and effort on the part of importers working their way through the bureaucratic process. It is almost as if some percentage of imported goods were simply blown up, thus wasting the resources needed to produce those goods, whereas tariffs simply transfer income without wasting resources.

PROBLEMS

1. Draw a diagram such as Figure 15.1 in which both countries have binding import quotas. What is the equilibrium terms of trade if both countries auction off import licenses?
2. Consider how the terms of trade are determined in problem 1 when both countries use voluntary restraint quotas.
3. Using Figure 15.3, show what happens in the tariff versus quota case when domestic demand falls below I_y^h.
4. We know from earlier chapters that domestic factor prices depend on domestic commodity prices and outputs. Suppose Y is labor-intensive. Discuss the effects on the real wage under tariffs versus quotas as the economy grows, as in Figure 15.3.
5. In light of our analysis of monopoly, discuss the use of tariffs versus quotas with respect to encouraging domestic competition.

NOTES

1. See Bhagwati (1965) for more discussion.
2. See Fishelson and Flatters (1975) and Young (1979).
3. See Bhagwati (1968).
4. See Rodriguez (1974).
5. Baldwin (1974) presents a good general discussion.

REFERENCES

Baldwin, R. E. (1974). "Nontariff Distortions of International Trade." In R. E. Baldwin and J. D. Richardson (eds.), *International Trade and Finance.* Boston: Little, Brown.
Bhagwati, J. N. (1965). "On the Equivalence of Tariffs and Quotas." In R. Caves

et al. (eds.), *Trade, Growth and the Balance of Payments: Essays in Honor of G. Haberler.* New York: Rand McNally.

——. (1968). "More on the Equivalence of Tariffs and Quotas." *American Economic Review* 58, 142–146.

Fishelson, G., and F. Flatters (1975). "The (Non) Equivalence of Tariffs and Quotas under Uncertainty." *Journal of International Economics* 5, 385–393.

Rodriguez, C. A. (1974). "The Non-Equivalence of Tariffs and Quotas Under Retaliation." *Journal of International Economics* 4, 295–298.

Young, L. (1979). "Ranking Optimal Tariffs and Quotas for a Large Country under Uncertainty." *Journal of International Economics* 9, 249–264.

chapter *16*

Imperfect Competition, Increasing Returns, and Strategic Trade Policy

1. INTRODUCTION

An interesting and important phenomenon occurs when governments are observed to act as agents in support of large domestic firms in the international marketplace. Certain actions by the governments in question are designed to give domestic firms important advantages over foreign rivals in competing for international business. These actions often involve some direct or indirect form of subsidy, which lowers the costs of the domestic firms relative to their competitors.

Figure 16.1 considers again the case of a production subsidy that we discussed in Chapter 10. In free trade the country exports X, producing at Q and consuming at C, with the world price ratio given by p^*. Now suppose that the government puts a production subsidy on X, which implies that the producer price ratio now exceeds the consumer price ratio. Producers will now increase the production of X to a point like Q', with consumption occurring at C'. Exports increase, but this is at the expense of a deterioration in welfare.

This may not be the end of the story. Note in Figure 16.1 that the country is now both importing more and exporting more at the price ratio p^*. If the country has some influence over world prices, this will force up the price of Y and force down the price of X. A new equilibrium might occur at a price ratio p', with production and consumption at Q'' and C'',

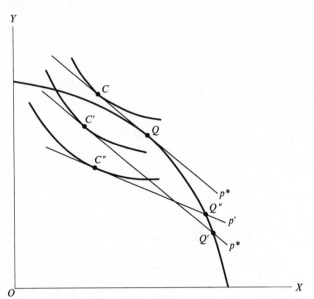

Figure 16.1

respectively. There has been a further deterioration in welfare due to the deterioration in the terms of trade.

   Figure 16.1 thus gives us the standard view of a production subsidy, and similar results hold for an export subsidy as we noted in Chapter 14. In the standard competitive trade model, production or export subsidies are never optimal. Note further that the deterioration in the terms of trade for the country imposing the subsidy must conversely constitute an improvement in the terms of trade for the foreign country. The foreign country's welfare improves as a consequence of the home country's subsidy. The intuition is that the home country is now selling its export good more cheaply to the foreign country. In this model the home country should not want a production subsidy on the export good while the foreign country should welcome it.

2. INCREASING RETURNS AND IMPERFECT COMPETITION

Recent theoretical work has pointed out that the conclusions of Figure 16.1 break down if there are increasing returns and/or imperfect competition in production. The argument is shown in Figure 16.2. We use the type of technology discussed in the chapter on increasing returns. Y is a competitive good produced with constant returns to scale, while X is produced with increasing returns in the form of a fixed cost ($\overline{Y}F$ in Figure 16.2) and

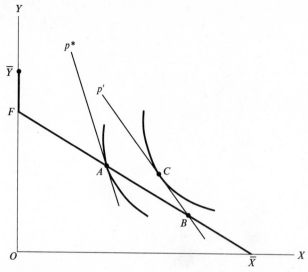

Figure 16.2

a constant marginal cost. This marginal cost in terms of good Y is given by the slope of $F\overline{X}$ in Figure 16.2.

Suppose that we initially have two identical countries, and that a single X producer in each country is engaged in Cournot competition with the X producer in the other country (see Chapter 10, Section 5). The price must exceed marginal cost due to the scale economies (Chapter 11) and so equilibrium in each country could be at a point like A in Figure 16.2 with a price ratio $p*$. No net trade takes place by virtue of the fact that the countries are identical, so each country consumes at A and produces at A in Figure 16.2.

Under reasonably general demand assumptions, a small production subsidy will have the effect on the subsidizing country (call it the home country) shown in Figure 16.2 and the effect on the foreign country shown in Figure 16.3. In the home country the effect of the production subsidy is to stimulate production to point B in Figure 16.2 and to cause the home country to export X. The increased production of X also causes the world price of X to fall to a new level shown by p' in Figure 16.2. Consumption occurs at point C, which constitutes a welfare improvement over A.

Note the contrast between Figures 16.1 and 16.2. The reason for the welfare improvement in Figure 16.2 is that the initial price ratio exceeds marginal cost. With price (the value of X to consumers) greater than marginal cost, there is a welfare gain to stimulating the production of X. It does not follow that an even larger subsidy will continue to improve welfare, and, in fact, it can be shown that the deteriorating terms of trade

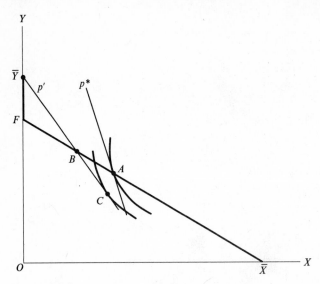

Figure 16.3

will eventually outweigh the favorable production expansion effect. Nevertheless, Figure 16.2 makes it clear that there does exist a case for a small production subsidy when there are scale economies and/or imperfect competition and initial exports are zero.

Welfare effects on the foreign country are shown in Figure 16.3. The increased production by the home country means that it captures a larger share of the world market, or alternatively, that the demand curve facing the foreign firm shifts left at each price of X. The foreign firm will reduce production, moving to a point like B in Figure 16.3. The price ratio has fallen to p' as it has in the home country, so foreign consumers import X to arrive at the consumption bundle C in Figure 16.3. Foreign welfare has deteriorated. This last result is not inevitable. We could have drawn Figure 16.3 so that the price ratio p' cuts through the indifference curve passing through A, in order to achieve a higher utility level in the foreign country. But the point is that the home country subsidy could make the foreign country worse off, which contrasts with the result in the constant returns, perfect competition model that the home country subsidy must make the foreign country better off.

3. RENT SHIFTING

A few more words should be said in connection with the result of Figure 16.3 that the foreign country may lose as a consequence of the home country subsidy. The basic intuition is that in the initial equilibrium at

A the foreign X producer was earning positive economic profits. (Recall from Chapter 11 that the average cost of producing A in Figure 16.3 is the slope of the chord connecting A and $\overline{Y}$. If the price line p^* is steeper than this chord as it is in Figure 16.3, then price exceeds average cost and profits are positive.) When the home country subsidizes its X producer, the resulting fall in the price of X robs the foreign producer of some of these profits. In Figure 16.3 profits fall to exactly zero at price p' (p' is the slope of the chord connecting B with $\overline{Y}$, and thus price equals average cost).

It can similarly be shown that the profits of the X producer in the home country must increase as a consequence of the subsidy (if they did not, the firm could refuse the subsidy). What has thus happened in Figures 16.2 and 16.3 is that some of the profit or "rent" in the world market for X has been shifted from the X producer in the foreign country (and thus from foreign total income) to the X producer in the home country (and thus to home income). This phenomenon is known as "rent shifting." The existence of positive rents in the world market creates an incentive for a government to subsidize strategically its firms in those markets in order to capture a larger share of world rents. The existence of rents in the market for large commercial airliners may, for example, provide some rationalization for the subsidization (often indirect) of Boeing and Airbus by their respective governments.

4. FREE ENTRY

The argument that a country can gain through the use of a production subsidy when there are scale economies and/or imperfect competition turns out to be very fragile. Different assumptions to those used to produce the case shown in Figure 16.2 can reverse the conclusion. Several examples of this have been shown in the literature, but we will examine just one alternative assumption.[1] Suppose now we assume that, instead of there being just a single firm in each country, there is free entry of firms in each country up to the point where profits are zero. This certainly seems to be a realistic assumption for many if not most manufacturing industries.

Figures 16.4 and 16.5 show a special case from Horstmann and Markusen (1986). In addition to assuming free entry, they assume that firms behave in a Cournot fashion (as in Chapter 10) and that consumers have linear demand curves. The technology of production in the X sector is the same as we have been assuming in this chapter: fixed cost plus constant marginal cost, and a single factor of production. Given these assumptions, the authors show that a specific production subsidy results simply in the entry of additional firms in the home country, with each firm

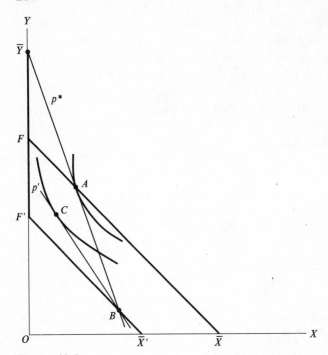

Figure 16.4

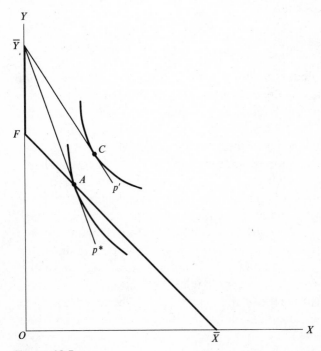

Figure 16.5

continuing to produce the same output at the same average cost as was produced prior to the subsidy.

The equilibrium is shown in Figure 16.4, where point A is the initial equilibrium and $p*$ is the initial price ratio. Figure 16.4 is similar to Figures 16.2 and 16.3 except that the initial equilibrium involves average-cost pricing as a consequence of the free-entry assumption ($p*$ equals the slope of the chord connecting A with $\overline{Y}$). The production subsidy creates profits that lead to the entry of new firms. These firms use additional resources for fixed costs, so the production frontier shifts inward to $\overline{Y}F'\overline{X}'$ in Figure 16.4. Horstmann and Markusen show that the new equilibrium involves each firm producing the presubsidy output at presubsidy average cost, and hence the new production point is point B in Figure 16.4 (the average cost of production is the same at A and B).

The subsidy does, however, imply that the consumer price ratio is less than the producer price ratio, and so the consumer price ratio is shown by p' in Figure 16.4. The home country will export X to arrive at a consumption bundle C in Figure 16.4. Production of X has increased, but welfare has deteriorated. The reason is that the increased production of X has not resulted in the capture of scale economies, but has come from the inefficient entry of new firms, each producing at the old scale. The possible gains that we saw in Figure 16.2 are now dissipated by entry and the use of scarce resources to finance fixed costs.

The situation for the foreign country is shown in Figure 16.5. The initial equilibrium at A and price ratio $p*$ is identical to the equilibrium for the home country at A in Figure 16.4. From the point of view of the foreign country the home country subsidy forces down the price of X, and so the foreign firms now make negative profits. Because the firms in each country have identical costs and because trade is free, the unsubsidized firms in the foreign country cannot compete against the subsidized firms in the home country (remember that the latter make zero profits). The foreign X producers are driven entirely out of business and the foreign country specializes in Y. Production occurs at $\overline{Y}$ and consumers import X to reach the consumption bundle C. The trade vector $\overline{Y}C$ in Figure 16.5 is equal and opposite to the trade vector CB in Figure 16.4, so that trade balances as is required for an equilibrium.

Figure 16.5 shows that the foreign country is better off as a consequence of the home country subsidy. The home country is worse off, so this combined result is much like that obtained from a constant returns, perfect competition model. The comparison is appropriate. In the case of free entry (at least under the specific assumptions used here), scale economies are not captured as a consequence of the subsidy, but rather, new firms are added at constant scale almost as if the industry had constant returns. With reference to the previous section of this chapter, it is also true that no rents are transferred to the home country since, with free entry, there are no rents being earned (profits are always zero in equilibrium).

5. IMPORT PROTECTION AS EXPORT PROMOTION

Another interesting example of the strategic use of export subsidies occurs when the marginal costs of production are decreasing (Krugman, 1985). Suppose that a U.S. firm and a Japanese rival are each selling in their own markets, exporting to their rival's market, and perhaps selling in third countries. Assume that marginal cost decreases with the amount produced. Now assume that the Japanese erect a trade barrier (a tariff or quota) to imports of the American product.

The effect of the Japanese trade barrier is to restrict the Japanese home market to the domestic firm, or at least to give that firm a larger share of the domestic market. Output of the Japanese firm increases and that of the U.S. firm falls, given constant levels of sales by each firm in other markets. But that is not the end of the story. This change in output levels implies a decrease in the marginal cost of production for the Japanese and an increase in marginal cost for the American firm. Thus there will be further ramifications of the Japanese trade barrier in that the Japanese firm will now be more competitive in the U.S. market and in third country markets. Conversely, the U.S. firm will be less competitive in its home and third country markets.

The equilibrium condition of marginal revenue equals marginal cost will now imply that the Japanese firm will expand sales in the United States and in third countries and that U.S. sales will shrink. Rents in these markets will be shifted to the Japanese firm as described in the previous section and the prices charged could even fall in the Japanese market, providing a benefit to consumers in that country. Import protection by the Japanese thus becomes export promotion.

Krugman also shows that this argument holds up when the scale economies are in the form of dynamic learning-by-doing, in which marginal costs of production fall with accumulated sales experience. Protecting or reserving the home market for the domestic firm allows that firm to lower its costs more quickly and therefore to compete more effectively in export markets. Krugman has suggested that this is exactly what the Japanese did with their domestic semiconductor industry. By reserving their domestic market for domestic firms, the Japanese developed a semiconductor industry that could not have existed independently. On the basis of accumulated experience, the Japanese are now leading exporters of semiconductors.

As in the case of the production subsidy discussed earlier, this argument may be weakened by the inefficient entry of new firms in response to the introduction of protection. Nevertheless, it again illustrates why the existence of scale economies and imperfect competition may imply radically different policy implications from those of traditional theory as discussed in the introduction to this chapter.

6. CONCLUDING REMARKS

This chapter has presented some examples of why scale economies and imperfect competition may give governments an incentive to assist strategically their domestic firms in international markets. By "assist," we mean actions such as direct or indirect subsidies that lower the costs to domestic firms of doing business abroad.

Section 1 noted that such subsidies are not optimal in models based on constant returns to scale and perfect competition. Domestic welfare deteriorates as a consequence of production or export subsidies and the only beneficiaries are foreign consumers who can buy cheaper imports. But scale economies and imperfect competition imply an excess of price (the value of a good to consumers) over marginal cost (the value of resources needed to produce an additional unit). In such a situation there is an incentive for governments to stimulate production. Furthermore, the existence of monopoly profits or rents in world markets may imply that a government can transfer more of those rents to domestic firms by subsidizing domestic production. It was also noted that, since these firms are often producing differentiated products, firms may be both exporting and import-competing. Protecting or reserving the domestic market for domestic firms may thus allow the latter to lower their marginal production costs and to become more competitive in export markets.

These are important findings, but it must be remembered that their validity rests on fairly specific assumptions. We demonstrated this in Section 4 where we showed that the entry of new firms in response to subsidies destroyed the validity of prosubsidy arguments based on the existence of domestic monopoly and positive monopoly rents. Arguments in favor of subsidies must, therefore, be very carefully evaluated in light of industry structure and other variables.

PROBLEMS

1. In Figure 16.2, convince yourself that as long as production of X increases, the production subsidy always leads to a welfare improvement.
2. Redraw Figure 16.3 to show that the home country subsidy could make the foreign country better off.

3. With reference to Figures 16.4 and 16.5, is it valid to suggest that the subsidy makes the home country worse off because it is selling its export good for less than it costs to produce it?

NOTE

1. For other qualifications to the results of Section 3, see Dixit and Grossman (1986) and Eaton and Grossman (1985).

REFERENCES

Brander, J. A., and B. J. Spencer (1985). "Export Subsidies and International Market Share Rivalry." *Journal of International Economics* 18, 227–242.

Dixit, A. K., and G. M. Grossman (1986). "Targeted Export Promotion with Several Oligopolistic Industries." *Journal of International Economics* 21, 233–250.

Eaton, J., and G. M. Grossman (1985). "Optimal Trade and Industrial Policy Under Oligopoly." *Quarterly Journal of Economics* 101, 383–406.

Horstmann, I., and J. R. Markusen (1986), "Up the Average Cost Curve: Inefficient Entry and the New Protectionism." *Journal of International Economics* 20, 225–248.

Krugman, P. R. (1984). "Import Protection as Export Promotion: International Competition in the Presence of Oligopoly and Economies of Scale." In H. Kierzkowski (ed.), *Monopolistic Competition in International Trade*. Oxford: Oxford University Press.

Spencer, B. J., and J. A. Brander (1983). "International R & D Rivalry and Industrial Strategy." *Review of Economics Studies* 50, 707–722.

Venables, A. J. (1975). "Trade and Trade Policy with Imperfect Competition: The Case of Identical Products and Free Entry." *Journal of International Economics* 19, 1–20.

chapter 17

Effective Protection

1. THE CONCEPT OF EFFECTIVE PROTECTION

The basic argument of the effective protection literature is that if tariffs are not uniform for all imports, then the nominal tariff rates[1] do not give an accurate indication of how the tariff structure influences the domestic economy. The domestic manufacturer of a particular commodity, for example, is influenced not only by the tariff on the good he produces, but also by whether or not there are tariffs on the inputs that he imports. The manufacturer will be better off the higher the tariffs are on his outputs, for such tariffs presumably allow him to charge higher prices, and worse off the higher the tariffs are on his inputs, for these tariffs tend to raise his costs. The term "effective protection" is applied to the formula that attempts to indicate the net effect of these influences.

We can illustrate the effective protection argument with a simple example. Suppose a particular industry produces a product that we call commodity 1 with a very simple process that involves only labor and some intermediate good, commodity 2, as inputs.[2] We let X_1 represent the amount of output of commodity 1, X_{21} represent the amount of input of commodity 2 into the production of commodity 1, and L_1 represent the amount of labor used to produce commodity 1. We assume that there are constant returns to scale. Now in this simple example the revenue received from the sale of the product must be allocated either to the producers of commodity 2 or to labor, and so if we denote the price of commodity 1 as p_1, the price of commodity 2 as p_2, and the wage rate as w, we have:

$$X_1 p_1 = X_{21} p_2 + L_1 w. \tag{17.1}$$

That is, total revenue equals total cost. Now suppose we are interested in how each dollar of receipts is allocated to the two inputs. We can find this by dividing all terms of equation (17.1) by $X_1 p_1$ to obtain:

$$1 = a_{21} + v_1 \tag{17.2}$$

where $a_{21} = \dfrac{X_{21} p_2}{X_1 p_1}$ and $v_1 = \dfrac{L_1 w}{X_1 p_1}$. We can rewrite equation (17.2) as

$$v_1 = 1 - a_{21}. \tag{17.3}$$

This equation tells us, for given prices, the proportion of each dollar spent on commodity 1 that goes to labor, and if we think of labor as the residual claimant, we can think of equation (17.3) as determining labor's share. Let us assume, for example, that 60 percent of cost is due to the intermediate factor, that is, $a_{21} = .6$, so that in the initial situation $v_1 = .4$. One interpretation of the concept of effective protection relates to how much labor's share is changed by a tariff structure if the industry is to remain just competitive with foreign producers.

We now examine how labor's share will be affected under a variety of assumptions about the tariff structure. Let us first suppose that there is a 20 percent tariff levied on commodity 1. Let us further suppose that the domestic producer responds to this tariff by increasing his price by 20 percent.[3] Thus the return on what used to be a dollar's worth of output is now \$1.20, and so in equation (17.3) we replace 1 with 1.2. Since the cost of the intermediate product has not changed, we have:

$$v_1' = 1.2 - a_{21} = 1.2 - .6 = .6.$$

Thus a 20 percent tariff on commodity 1 allows labor to increase its share from .4 to .6, which is a gain of 50 percent. More formally, with g the effective tariff rate, we have:

$$g = \frac{v_1' - v_1}{v_1} = \frac{.6 - .4}{.4} = .5 \quad \text{or} \quad 50 \text{ percent.}$$

In this case, whereas the nominal tariff on commodity 1 is 20 percent, the effective protection afforded the labor employed in this industry is 50 percent.

Now suppose that as well as the 20 percent tariff on commodity 1 there is a 20 percent tariff on commodity 2, the intermediate good. Under the assumption that all units of this input increase in price by 20 percent to our producer, the cost of this input will increase by 20 percent, and we must increase a_{21} by 20 percent, that is, replace it by $a_{21} (1 + .2)$. Equation (17.3) now becomes

$$v_1' = 1.2 - a_{21} (1 + .2) = 1.2 - .72 = .48.$$

The effective protection in this case is

$$g = \frac{v_1' - v_1}{v_1} = \frac{.48 - .4}{.4} = .2 \quad \text{or} \quad 20 \text{ percent}$$

and the effective protection is equal to the nominal protection.

Suppose that we now keep the same tariff on the output but increase the tariff on the intermediate good from 20 to 30 percent. Then from equation (17.3) we have

$$v_1' = 1.2 - a_{21} (1 + .3) = 1.2 - .78 = .42$$

and the effective protection is

$$g = \frac{v_1' - v_1}{v_1} = \frac{.42 - .4}{.4} = .05 \quad \text{or} \quad 5 \text{ percent.}$$

The effective protection is thus less than the nominal tariff.

As a final example, suppose that there is no tariff on commodity 1 but that there is a 20 percent tariff on the intermediate good. In this case there is no increase in receipts but only an increase in cost. We thus have

$$v_1' = 1 - a_{21}(1 + .2) = 1 - .72 = .28$$

and the effective tariff is thus:

$$g = \frac{v_1' - v}{v} = \frac{.28 - .4}{.4} = - .3 \quad \text{or} \quad - 30 \text{ percent.}$$

As we can see, in this case the effective protection is negative, which means that if, as we have supposed, labor is the residual claimant, wages must decrease by 30 percent if the industry is to remain competitive, even though the price of the output has not been affected.

From the preceding examples we can now draw the following conclusions:

1. If the tariff on the output is higher than the tariff on the input, the effective protection will be higher than the nominal tariff.
2. If all tariffs are equal, then the effective protection is equal to the nominal tariff.
3. If the output tariff is lower than the tariff on the input, then the effective protection will be less than the nominal tariff.

4. Effective protection can be negative if the tariff on the input is sufficiently higher than the output tariff, or if there is no tariff on the output.

This last point makes it clear that any tariff system will be a serious disadvantage to export industries, which must in general sell at world prices. For an export industry, tariffs will raise costs but cannot be expected to increase revenue. Thus we might expect that a general reduction in tariffs would be a substantial stimulus to export industries, as their competitive position would be substantially improved.

2.   THE ASSUMPTIONS OF THE MODEL

In this section we list and explain the reasons for the assumptions that underlie the effective protection concept. We also indicate how the relaxation of these assumptions might be expected to influence calculations of rates of effective protection.

Perhaps the most crucial assumption is that all production functions exhibit constant returns to scale. This assumption is important because it allows us to consider value added per unit of output without being concerned with the absolute level of output. In other words, given the technology and the price structure, value added per unit of output is invariant to the scale of operation, and we do not have to worry about how a change in the tariff structure might affect the level of output in the industry under consideration.

It is of some interest to consider how the analysis would be affected if constant returns to scale were not assumed. Referring again to the simple model given by equation (17.1), if we think of labor as the residual claimant, we can write:

$$L_1 w = X_1 p_1 - X_{21} p_2. \qquad (17.4)$$

We divide all terms by $X_1 p_1$ and obtain

$$v_1 = 1 - \alpha_{21} \qquad (17.5)$$

where

$$v_1 = \frac{L_1 w}{X_1 p_1} \quad \text{and} \quad \alpha_{21} = \frac{X_{21} p_2}{X_1 p_1}.$$

Equation (17.5) has the same form as equation (17.3), but cannot be used in the same way unless we are sure that output will not change. For example, suppose the imposition of a new tariff structure doubles the output of the first commodity. Then unless X_{21} also doubles, α_{21} will change, and unless we have constant returns to scale there is no reason to expect X_{21} to double. Thus, if we were to observe a change in v_1 it could be a combination of changes due to the new tariff structure and changes in α_{21}. The effective protection concept is concerned with isolating the changes due to tariffs, and therefore it seems reasonable to eliminate these other influences by focusing on the constant returns-to-scale case.

A second assumption is that production coefficients are fixed. The production coefficients give the amount of an input required per unit of output, and thus this assumption means that inputs are always combined in the same proportions, regardless of factor prices or scale of output. This assumption is associated with the work of Leontief (1941) and implies that the isoquants have "corners," or, in other words, that the elasticity of substitution among inputs is zero.

This assumption is made to facilitate the analysis by allowing us to abstract from changes that could be brought about by changes in the relative price of factors. If the production functions allow for substitution in production, then any change in factor prices would be expected to change the production coefficients. Such changes would be expected to affect observed value-added changes in the same way as changes in scale could affect these calculations in the absence of constant returns to scale.

Dropping the fixed-coefficient assumption has two main effects. First, allowing substitution in production results in lower calculated rates of effective protection and, second, taking account of substitution may change the ranking of effective protection rates. It has been shown, however, that ranking changes are not very great even when substitution elasticities as high as 2 are assumed. Thus, although estimates may be somewhat higher than they would be if no substitution were assumed, the ranking of the rates will probably not be much different.

A third assumption is that the tariff represents the difference between domestic prices and free-trade world prices. This implies that domestic producers set their price equal to the foreign price plus the tariff. This permits us to interpret effective protection as the increase in the value added that is associated with the tariff. Changing this behavioral assumption about firms would necessitate an alternative interpretation of the effective protection concept.

A fourth assumption is that production and trade take place in the protected industries both before and after the tariff. This assumption is necessary to ensure that calculated rates do, in fact, measure an increase in value added due to the tariff. Imagine, for example, that before the tariff there was no domestic output of a particular product due to high costs. When a tariff is imposed, however, the price may be increased sufficiently to make domestic production profitable. But in this case it will not in general be true that a calculation comparing domestic, tariff-ridden prices with free-trade prices will accurately represent an increase in the returns to the fixed factors. Some of the increase in price goes toward making the industry competitive. Observe that if for a particular industry this assumption fails to hold, then effective rate calculations will give an overestimate of the increase in value added due to the tariff.

A final assumption is that the elasticities of foreign demand for our exports, foreign supply of our imports, and domestic supply of nontraded inputs are infinite. These assumptions eliminate the possibility of price changes other than those associated with the imposition of tariffs. With perfectly elastic foreign demand for our exports we need not worry about our attempts to sell more (or less) causing prices to fall (or rise). Perfectly elastic foreign supply of imports and domestic supply of nontraded inputs means that domestic producers do not have to be concerned about input price changes due to shifts in demand.

These assumptions on elasticities are perhaps the most severe limitation of studies on effective tariffs. While it is recognized that finite elasticities could change calculated rates significantly, there seems to be no simple way of correcting this deficiency. While it is easy enough to develop formulas that contain elasticity terms, no reliable information is available on the values of these elasticities. It has been found that relaxing the assumption of a perfectly elastic supply of domestic nontraded inputs tends to reduce the effective protection calculations.

3. THE FORMAL MODEL

The model used to calculate effective protection is just an extended version of the model we derived in Section 1; we now allow for more than one intermediate input. In general, since total cost is equal to total revenue we can write, for the jth industry,

$$X_j p_j = X_{1j} p_1 + X_{2j} p_2 + \ldots + X_{nj} p_n + L_j w$$

or

$$X_j p_j = \sum_{i=1}^{n} X_{ij} p_i + L_j w \qquad (17.6)$$

where X_{ij} is the amount of commodity i used to produce commodity j, where L_j represents the amount of the fixed factors (i.e., labor and capital) necessary to produce commodity j, and where p_i is the world price of the ith commodity. From (17.6) we can write

$$L_j w = X_j p_j - \sum_{i=1}^{n} X_{ij} p_i .$$

Dividing by $X_j p_j$, we have

$$v_j = 1 - \sum_{i=1}^{n} a_{ij} \qquad (17.7)$$

where

$$v_j = \frac{L_j w}{X_j p_j} \quad \text{and} \quad a_{ij} = \frac{X_{ij} p_j}{X_j p_j}.$$

Equation (17.7) gives us the value added per unit of output for the no-tariff situation. In the tariff situation, that is, in the domestic economy, in place of equation (17.6) we have

$$X_j p_j (1 + t_j) = \sum_{i=1}^{n} X_{ij} p_i (1 + t_i) + L_j w. \qquad (17.8)$$

This shows that all prices (except the prices of fixed factors) are higher by the amount of the tariff. Then rearranging and dividing by $X_j p_j$, we have

$$v_j' = (1 + t_j) - \sum_{i=1}^{n} a_{ij} (1 + t_i) \qquad (17.9)$$

where v_j' is the value added in terms of tariff-ridden prices.

The rate of effective protection, g, is defined as the percentage increase in the value added per unit in an economic activity that is made possible by the tariff structure, relative to the situation in the absence of tariffs. Thus we have

$$g_j = \frac{v_j' - v_j}{v_j} = \frac{(1 - t_j) - \Sigma \; a_{ij}(1 + t_i) - 1 + \Sigma \; a_{ij}}{1 - \Sigma \; a_{ij}}$$

or

$$g_j = \frac{t_j - \Sigma \; a_{ij} t_i}{1 - \Sigma a_{ij}}. \qquad (17.10)$$

Recalling the definition of a_{ij}, we see that it is in terms of world prices, and thus this is the formula that would be used to calculate effective protection if our information were in terms of free-trade prices. If the data available are in terms of domestic prices that already include the tariff, a slightly different formulation is required.

4. SOME EXAMPLES FOR THE CANADIAN ECONOMY

Table 17.1 gives some examples of nominal and effective rates of protection for the Canadian economy for the year 1963. Tariffs were quite high in this time period, and these calculations indicate quite clearly how nominal and effective rates can differ. These industries have been chosen to show the range of rates possible, and are not meant to be representative of the rates in Canada. There were 134 industries considered in the study from which Table 17.1 is derived, and for these the simple average of nominal rates was 17.7 and of effective rates was 36.9. Thus, in general, the effective rate was over twice the nominal rate.

The industries in Table 17.1 show the relationships among nominal and effective rates illustrated in Section 1. Flour mills and petroleum refineries have effective rates that are much higher than nominal rates, indicating that tariffs on inputs are relatively low. These industries also illustrate that even for relatively low nominal rates, the actual protection can be quite high. Thus, although the nominal rates for flour mills and structural metals are both low and almost the same, the effective protection that the tariff structure provides for flour mills is five times that provided to structural metal. Structural metal also provides an example of a case where the nominal and effective rates are almost the same, indicating that tariff rates on inputs are not much different from the rates on outputs. Several of the industries show negative effective rates and

Table 17.1 A SAMPLE OF NOMINAL AND EFFECTIVE TARIFFS IN CANADA FOR 1963

Industry	Nominal Rate	Effective Rate
Dairy factories	7.1	−13.8
Flour mills	8.8	38.1
Sugar refineries	24.2	−6.9
Synthetic textiles	30.3	64.0
Auto fabrics	30.3	90.9
Publishing	1.3	1.7
Iron and steel mills	6.7	11.1
Fabricated structural metal	8.0	7.3
Boiler and plate works	9.7	10.4
Agricultural implements	0	−7.5
Motor vehicle parts	10.2	14.4
Household radio and TV	20.7	51.4
Petroleum refineries	5.3	30.3
Industrial chemicals	6.8	8.8
Jewelry, silverware	3.1	−4.1

Source: J. R. Melvin and B. W. Wilkinson, "Effective Protection in the Canadian Economy." (See References this chapter.)

positive nominal rates, indicating that although there is a tariff on the output, the combined effect of both input and output tariffs makes these industries worse off than they would be with free trade. Thus the tariff system acts to the disadvantage of such industries.

5. CONCLUDING REMARKS

The concept of effective protection rests on some quite restrictive assumptions, and thus too much confidence should not be placed on the tariff rate estimates. The concept does very clearly indicate, however, the importance of input tariffs and the fact that nominal rates by themselves may give quite a misleading indication of the actual protective effects of a tariff structure.

PROBLEMS

1. Suppose a commodity is produced only after the introduction of a tariff. Will the usual effective protection calculation be the correct one?
2. Suppose the production functions for an industry differed in the foreign country such that they were more efficient than in the home country. Would this affect the interpretation of effective protection?
3. For industry X_1 with inputs X_{21} and X_{31}, suppose $t_1 = 30\%$, $t_2 = 20\%$, and $t_3 = 10\%$. If $a_{21} = .2$ and $a_{31} = .5$, calculate g_1.
4. Find tariff rates for problem 3 such that
   (a) $g_1 < 10\%$,
   (b) $g_1 < 0$.

NOTES

1. By "nominal tariffs" we simply mean the listed tariff rate, as found in the Tariff Manual for example.
2. By "intermediate good" we mean a good that is produced by some other industry and used as an input for the industry in question.
3. In other words, we are assuming that the price of commodity 1 goes up 20 percent whether it is produced domestically or in the foreign country, that is, that the domestic producer prices up to the tariff.

REFERENCES

Basevi, G. (1966). "The United States Tariff Structure: Estimates of Effective Rates of Protection of United States Industries and Industrial Labour." *Review of Economics and Statistics* 47, 147–160.

Corden, W. M. (1966). "The Structure of a Tariff System and the Effective Protection Rate." *Journal of Political Economy* 74, 221–237.

Johnson, H. G. (1965). "The Theory of Tariff Structure, with Special Reference to World Trade and Development." In H. G. Johnson and P. B. Kenen. *Trade and Development.* Etudes et Travaux de l'Institut Universitaire de Hautes Etudes Internationales. Geneva: Librairie Droz.

Jones, R. W. (1971). "Effective Protection and Substitution." *Journal of International Economics* 1, 59–81.

Leith, J. C. (1968). "Substitution and Supply Elasticities in Calculating the Effective Protective Rate." *Quarterly Journal of Economics* 82, 588–601.

Leontief, W. W. (1941). *The Structure of American Economy, 1919–1939.* Cambridge, Mass.: Harvard University Press.

Melvin, J. R., and B. W. Wilkinson (1968). "Effective Protection in the Canadian Economy." Toronto: University of Toronto Press for the Economic Council of Canada.

Wilkinson, B. W., and K. Norrie (1975). *Effective Protection and the Return to Capital.* Toronto: University of Toronto Press for the Economic Council of Canada.

chapter 18

Customs Unions

1. INTRODUCTION

Previous chapters dealing with tariffs and quotas have generally assumed a two-country model. In the real world, however, there are many countries, all of which, potentially at least, have the ability to impose their own tariffs, quotas, and other trade impediments. Thus it is natural to ask whether cooperation among some subset of these countries could make all members of the union better off. The theory of customs unions investigates this question, or in other words, asks whether some sort of geographical discriminatory change in trade barriers could be of benefit to those countries that are party to the cooperation.

Such cooperation could take a variety of forms. One could consider a free-trade area where a number of countries agrees to eliminate all tariffs or other trade barriers among themselves and continue to impose their existing tariffs against outside countries. A slightly stronger form of cooperation would eliminate all tariffs and trade barriers among member nations and impose a *common tariff* against outside countries. Such an association is what we commonly refer to as a customs union. Of course, cooperation need not be confined simply to the area of trade restrictions. In the European Economic Community, for example, member nations have agreed to coordinate tax policies and various other sorts of domestic policy variables as well. As a final step in this sort of cooperation, we might imagine the elimination of all barriers, including barriers to factor mobility, and the institution of a single government that would determine policy for all member countries. This latter alternative would, at least from a theoretical point of view, be equivalent to redefining the member nations as a single new country. While issues of political cooperation are doubtless important and interesting, we will confine our attention here to cooperation at the economic level. In particular, we will concentrate on the customs union case, in which a group of countries eliminates all tariffs and other trade restrictions among member nations, and imposes a single common tariff against all outside countries.

From the discussion of the trade models presented in Section 2 it is clear that the benefits associated with customs unions could come from a number of sources. First, there could be gains from trade associated with specialization to take advantage of intercountry differences in endowments or tastes. Second, a union may allow its members to reap the benefits of increasing returns to scale. Third, by forming a union, a group of countries may be able to affect the terms of trade between themselves and the rest of the world and reap benefits associated with the optimum tariff. Fourth, by forming a union, domestic industries will face increased competition, and losses due to the existence of monopolies may be eliminated. There is no obvious presumption as to which of these effects are likely to be more important than others, and any complete analysis of customs union theory should take all of them into account. Traditionally, however, the economic literature on customs unions has concentrated attention almost entirely on the first and to a limited extent the third. The discussion of this chapter will follow that tradition.

The classical presumption in customs unions theory was that, because customs unions reduce tariffs and therefore move countries toward free trade, such cooperation would be welfare-improving. Previous chapters have, however, presented numerous examples of situations where this proposition is not true. As one example, consider the case where a country has imposed both tariffs and domestic commodity taxes. In such a case it was established that the removal of the tariff alone would not necessarily improve welfare. This was seen as an application of the "theory of the second-best," which states that in a system with several distortions the removal of any one of them cannot be presumed to be welfare-improving. Furthermore, even in a world in which tariffs are the only distortion, if tariffs have improved the terms of trade and if something like an optimum tariff is being levied, then certainly the removal of such a tariff will make the economy worse off. It is, therefore, clear that the simple proposition that tariff removal, by moving a country toward free trade, makes the economy better off is at best simplistic. The development of the customs union literature can be seen as an attempt to identify particular circumstances in which the formation of customs unions will necessarily increase welfare.

Before we proceed it is worthwhile pointing out that the issues in the customs union debate are complex, and many of the questions still remain unsettled or ambiguous. The analysis to be presented here is particularly simplistic and is meant only to identify some of the parameters that will determine whether or not certain forms of economic cooperation could be welfare-improving. The analysis will more or less follow historical lines, but no particular attempt will be made to identify the ideas with specific authors. There is a good deal of disagreement about what specific authors actually said or meant, and no consensus exists as to who is really responsible for the advances (or the errors) that are to be found in the discussion. The arguments themselves, however, have a well-documented history and certainly deserve consideration.

2. TRADE CREATION AND TRADE DIVERSION

The simplest model of a customs union considers a single commodity X whose money price in three countries A, B, and C (adjustment having been made for exchange rates) is as shown in the first line of Table 18.1. Country A, with a price of 35, is the high-cost producer and with free trade would clearly import from country C. Now suppose that country A imposes a 100 percent tariff, implying that imports from country B would now cost 52 and imports from C, 40. Clearly such a tariff is prohibitive for, faced with these alternatives, the domestic economy finds it more efficient to produce commodity X at home. If country A were to form a customs union with either B or C, welfare would be improved, for commodity X could be obtained at a price of 20 or 26 as opposed to the cost of 35 implied by domestic production. The formation of a union with either B or C results in trade, and this situation is referred to as trade creation.

Alternatively, suppose that country A has been imposing a 50 percent tariff, which has given rise to the relative costs shown in the third line of Table 18.1. With this tariff rate country A still finds it cheaper to buy

Table 18.1

Country	A	B	C
Price	35	26	20
100% tariff		52	40
50% tariff		39	30

commodity X from country C than to produce it at home, and the tariff is, therefore, not prohibitive. Furthermore, even though domestic consumers must pay a price of 30, the economy as a whole is paying only 20, the difference being the amount collected by the domestic government. Now suppose country A forms a customs union with B. Domestic consumers will now observe a price of 26 in B and a price of 30 in C and therefore will divert their purchases from C to B. Such a situation is referred to as trade diversion, and in the simple case shown reduces domestic welfare, for consumers must pay 26 units whereas formerly they effectively paid only 20.

The simple argument surrounding Table 18.1 led to the conclusion that customs unions that resulted in trade creation would be expected to increase welfare, whereas trade-diverting customs unions would be welfare-reducing. It is easy to show, however, that these results depend on some very special assumptions. In particular, it is implicit in the argument that the production possibility curve is linear and that there is no substitution in consumption (in other words, the indifference curves are rectangular). We will now consider the effects of relaxing these two assumptions.

3. SUBSTITUTION IN CONSUMPTION

The situation of Table 18.1 can be represented geometrically as in Figure 18.1, where the costs of commodity X are now measured relative to commodity Y. Thus the relative cost of X in terms of Y for country C is represented by the line AC and for country B by the line AB. Suppose preferences for consumers in country A are represented by isoquants such as I_0, implying that consumption must always be along the line OZ. With free trade, country A would purchase commodity X from country C and would consume at point E. Furthermore, a nonprohibitive tariff would increase the domestic price of X and result in a domestic terms of trade such as p, but consumption would remain at point E in Figure 18.1.

Now suppose country A forms a customs union with country B and imposes a prohibitive 100 percent tariff on country C. This will cause consumption to shift to point F in Figure 18.1 and welfare is clearly reduced. Thus trade diversion has resulted in a welfare loss.

That the result of Figure 18.1 depends crucially on the fact that the indifference curves are rectangular, or in other words, exhibit zero elasticity of substitution, can easily be seen from Figure 18.2, which represents the same situation, except that now the indifference curves illustrate substitution in consumption. With free trade, consumption will take place at E, but now a nonprohibitive tariff that increases the domestic price ratio to P will move consumers to point H, where there is a tangency between

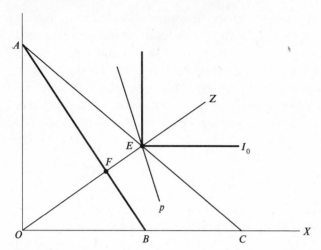

Figure 18.1

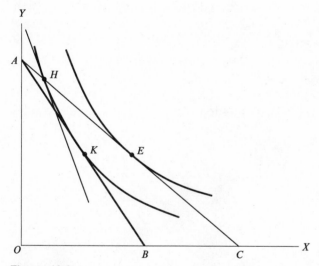

Figure 18.2

this new domestic price line and the highest indifference curve along the terms of trade line AC. Now consider the formation of a customs union between countries A and B. With a prohibitive tariff on C, domestic consumers will buy X from B at the price ratio line AB, and will thus consume at point K. Point K, because it is on the same indifference curve as point H, implies that the formation of a customs union has neither reduced nor improved welfare, even though the customs union has been trade-diverting. Of course, this is a very special case and is certainly not to be expected. The point is that the relative cost ratio for country B could lie either above or below AB of Figure 18.2, and there is, therefore, no clear presumption that trade diversion is either welfare-improving or welfare-reducing. Thus with substitution in consumption, a customs union that diverts trade from the most efficient to a less efficient producer could, nevertheless, increase welfare. Note, however, that the optimum in terms of this model is free trade, moving consumption back to point E. A customs union with B represents a second-best solution in this example, whether or not the trade diversion increases or reduces welfare relative to point H.

4.   A HECKSCHER-OHLIN APPROACH

In the last section we relaxed the assumption that there was no substitution in consumption, but retained the assumption that the production possibility curve was linear. We now examine the effects of trade creation and trade diversion for the traditional Heckscher-Ohlin type model with a production possibility curve illustrated by TAT' of Figure 18.3. With free trade, production is at A and consumption at C_0, so that the price line p represents the terms of trade with country C. With a nonprohibitive tariff, production would move to Q with consumption at C_1. The question now is whether a customs union with country B, with a relatively higher price of X than exists in country C, could make the domestic economy better off than the tariff-ridden situation of C_1. The answer clearly de-

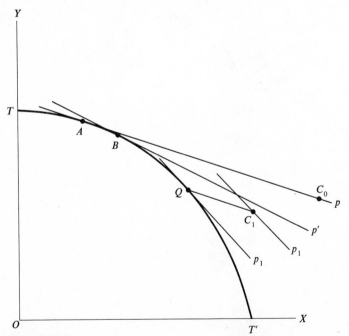

Figure 18.3

pends on the price line in B. Suppose the domestic economy could buy at the price ratio p'. This price line passes above C_1 and thus necessarily intersects the indifference curve tangent to p_1 at C_1, and the equilibrium consumption point for p' must, therefore, necessarily be on a higher community indifference curve. The switch from trading with country C to trading with country B at prices p' is an example of trade diversion, and thus it is clear that trade diversion may be welfare-improving.

It is interesting to note that the possibility of trade diversion improving welfare illustrated in Figure 18.3 is independent of whether or not there is substitution in consumption, the situation that gave rise to trade-diverting welfare improvements of Figure 18.2. This can be easily seen by supposing, in Figure 18.3, that community indifference curves are rectangular as in Figure 18.1. Even in this case, as long as the terms of trade p' with union partner B pass above point C_1, the union will be welfare-improving. Thus it is clear that the proposition that trade diversion reduces welfare depends on the assumption of both no substitution in consumption and a linear production possibility curve.

Figure 18.4 represents the same free-trade situation of Figure 18.3, but now assumes that when a nonprohibitive tariff is imposed, the terms of trade with the rest of the world are improved and become p'' with consumption point C_1. This is a situation in which a tariff, by improving the terms of trade, increases welfare, and is an example of the optimum tariff discussed in Chapter 14. Again it is assumed that, in the initial tariff situation, trade takes place with country C.

We now ask whether a customs union with country B could be

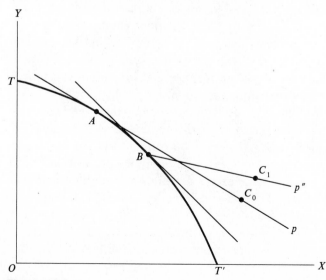

Figure 18.4

welfare-improving. The answer is clearly no. Indeed, if the situation of Figure 18.4 represents the optimum tariff, then no customs union of any kind, including free trade, could make the country better off. In other words, if we are already pursuing the optimum policy, then no change, whether trade-diverting or trade-creating, could possibly make us better off.

5. CONCLUDING REMARKS

As was suggested in our introduction, the gains associated with any form of economic cooperation could come from a variety of sources. The analysis described here has concentrated almost entirely on production differences, and thus is a very incomplete analysis of possible gains associated with customs unions. The discussion in the literature has focused on the question of whether customs unions are trade-creating or trade-diverting, and on circumstances under which trade diversion may make a country better or worse off. In the final analysis, however, it may well turn out that these issues are not the fundamentally important ones. Kemp and Wan (1976), for example, have provided a convincing argument that any sort of customs union, if properly defined, could be welfare-improving. Their argument runs as follows. Consider a situation in which any number of countries, M, produce and exchange any number of commodities, N, and in which each country is allowed to have any kinds of tariffs, domestic taxes, or other distortionary policies. Now consider the possibility of some subgroup, S, of these countries forming a customs union. Suppose it were actually possible to combine this subgroup S physically into a single economy whose resources were equal to the sum of those of the individual union members. Suppose further that this fictitious single country were now faced with the same excess demands and supplies that subgroup S was faced with before the union. The question now is whether this new economy can organize itself in such a manner that individual consumers are better off than they were before the union. Unless by chance it turns out that the initial situation had been the optimum, then the answer is clearly yes. After all, when faced with the same excess demands and supplies from foreigners and given that the initial situation contained distortions, there will clearly be a preferred equilibrium position. Note finally that ensuring that the same excess demands and supplies face this union as existed in the initial situation can be done simply by defining a system of external taxes, subsidies, and so on, so that the initial world terms of trade for all commodities is maintained.

The situation described earlier would almost certainly involve redistributions of income among consumers and, more importantly, would very likely involve redistributions among countries. Thus to ensure that this customs union is welfare-improving would almost certainly involve international transfers—transfers that might very well be difficult in practice to implement. It is also clear that what can be said for the customs union among the S countries described previously must also apply to $S + 1$ countries, and indeed, by logical extension we would end up with free trade. It is interesting to note that this argument leads back to the classical proposition that a customs union, because it moves us closer to free trade, will be presumed to be welfare-improving. We have seen that while this is not generally true, if the appropriate kinds of redistributions are carried out, keeping in mind that some of these redistributions would be international in nature, then any customs union certainly has a potential for improving the welfare of member nations.

PROBLEMS

1. In Table 18.1 suppose that the cost of production in A had been 29. What will be the effect of a 50 percent tariff?
2. Draw Figure 18.2 to illustrate the case in which trade diversion is welfare-improving.
3. It is not always reasonable to suppose that, in Figure 18.2, the terms of trade (slope of line AB) is unchanged after A begins to buy goods from country B. How would you take this into account? How would it change the conclusions concerning the welfare effects of trade diversion?
4. In Figure 18.4, if C_1 were moved far enough to the right on p'', could it be on a lower CIC than C_0?
5. Redraw Figure 18.3 to show the case in which trade diversion reduces welfare.

REFERENCES

Kemp, M. C., and H. Y. Wan (1976). "An Elementary Proposition Concerning the Formation of Customs Unions." *Journal of International Economics* 6, 95–97.

Krauss, M. B. (1972). "Recent Developments in Customs Union Theory: An Interpretive Survey." *Journal of Economic Literature* 10, 413–436.

Lipsey, R. G. (1960). "The Theory of Customs Unions—A General Survey." *Economic Journal* 70, 496–513.

——, and K. Lancaster. (1956–57). "The General Theory of the Second Best." *The Review of Economic Studies* 24, 11–32.

Melvin, J. R. (1969). "Comments on the Theory of Customs Unions." *Manchester School of Economic and Social Studies* 36, 161–168.

Michaely, M. (1963). "On Customs Unions and the Gains from Trade." *The Economic Journal* 75, 577–583.

four

FACTOR MOVEMENTS, GROWTH, AND THE THEORY OF DIRECT FOREIGN INVESTMENT

chapter *19*

Factor Movements

1. EFFECTS ON PRODUCTION

Up to this point, we have assumed that countries may trade commodities but that factors of production are immobile among countries. We noted in the Introduction that it is this immobility of factors that has traditionally distinguished the study of international trade from interregional trade. Yet anyone who has read history is aware of many examples of human migrations, such as those from Europe to North America in the nineteenth century. Those familiar with more contemporary business events are aware of the high level of capital movements and foreign investment that have characterized the world economy since World War II.

It is thus apparent that some factors of production are mobile. What are the effects of such factor movements on world trade and welfare? This question is of particular interest in the United States, where there has been a long-standing controversy surrounding the effects of U.S. investment in foreign countries and much more recently of foreign investment on the American economy.

International trade economists generally distinguish between several types of factor movements: (1) direct foreign investment, (2) portfolio investment, and (3) labor migration. A direct foreign investment is defined as an investment in which the investor acquires a substantial controlling interest in a foreign firm or sets up a subsidiary in the foreign country. Direct foreign investment thus involves ownership and/or control of a business enterprise abroad. Companies that engage in direct foreign investment are known as multinational enterprises or transnational corporations. (Direct foreign investment will be the subject of the following chapter.)

This chapter will be confined to the discussion of portfolio investment and labor migration. Portfolio investment occurs when an individual or company buys foreign bonds or purchases foreign stocks in quantities too small to gain control of a foreign firm. We will assume throughout the chapter that portfolio investment and labor migration occur in response to differences in wage and rental rates between two countries. (The motives behind direct foreign investment are more complex; thus an analysis of this type of investment is postponed until the next chapter.) Of course, portfolio investment and labor migration occur for reasons other than differences in factor prices. These reasons might include escape from war or repression in the case of labor migration, or uncertainty over future economic conditions in the case of capital mobility. With this caveat in mind, we restrict our discussion to factor movements motivated by factor-price differences.

Portfolio capital movements and labor migration have very similar effects on production and trade. Thus we analyze the two together, generally referring arbitrarily to capital as the mobile factor. The two may differ with respect to the repatriation of earnings. Capital owners generally tend to remain in their home country, repatriating their foreign earnings and consuming at home. Migrants generally spend most of their earnings in their new country. Yet migrants often repatriate substantial sums (e.g., guest workers in Europe, Mexican and West Indian farm workers in the United States) and capital owners sometimes move with their funds (e.g., Canadians retiring to Florida, employees sent abroad to work on a company investment project). Thus we treat capital and labor movements as being essentially similar and simply note, where appropriate, how repatriation affects the results.

The preceding chapters have shown a number of cases in which trade does not equalize factor prices. We emphasized in Chapter 8 that the conditions under which trade in commodities leads to the equalization of factor prices are very restrictive, and thus equalization should, in fact, be regarded as the exception rather than the rule. The incentives for factors to migrate due to unequal factor prices between countries can arise from the following types of situations. (1) If production technology differs between countries (Chapter 7), it is unlikely that trade will equalize factor prices even if it equalizes commodity prices. (2) If some goods are produced with increasing returns to scale (Chapter 11), then trade will not equalize factor prices. (3) If tariffs or transport costs prevent trade from equalizing commodity prices, factor prices will differ between countries. (4) If there are production taxes or imperfect competition in some sectors, marginal costs and therefore factor prices will not be equated between countries.

With these considerations in mind, let us consider the effects of factor movements within the context of a Heckscher-Ohlin two-factor production model. Suppose that in free-trade equilibrium a country has a higher wage rate and lower rental rate than its trading partners. Suppose also that good X is labor-intensive. Assume finally for the sake of clarity that world prices are such that initially the country does not find it advantageous to trade. The production frontier for this country is shown by $\overline{YX}$ in Figures 19.1 and 19.2. The initial equilibrium in each diagram is at point A, where world prices (p^*) are such that there are no gains from trade.

With the domestic wage rate higher than the foreign rate, labor will flow into the country, shifting the production frontier to $\overline{Y'}\ \overline{X'}$ in Figure 19.1. Since X is labor-intensive by assumption, the Rybczynski theorem (Chapter 8) tells us that the production of Y will fall and the production of X will rise at constant prices. Thus holding p^* constant, production shifts from A to Q in Figure 19.1. Consumption will occur at point C if no earnings are repatriated (i.e., without repatriation, the value of domestic consumption at world prices will equal the value of domestic production). An inflow of labor thus leads the country to export the labor-intensive good.

This will always be the pattern of trade regardless of whether or not the migrants repatriate their earnings, or, if they do, whether they repatriate them in terms of X or in terms of Y. Suppose that the foreign workers are able to capture all of the increase in income shown in Figure 19.1 (the distance between the "budget line" p^* through Q and p^* through A). If all of the migrants' earnings are repatriated, domestic factors will be forced back to the budget line p^* through A, and they will choose to trade along p^* until they reach point A, their original consumption bundle. In other words, if income and prices do not change, the domestic factors consumption bundle will not change. The country will thus produce at Q and consume at A in Figure 19.1. The line connecting Q and A gives the net trade including repatriation. Since Q lies to the southeast of A, the country is a net exporter of X (importer of Y) regardless of whether or not the foreign labor repatriates its earnings.

The case of capital outflow is shown in Figure 19.2. The Rybczynski theorem tells us that in this case the production of Y (the capital-intensive good) must decrease and the production of X (the labor-intensive good)

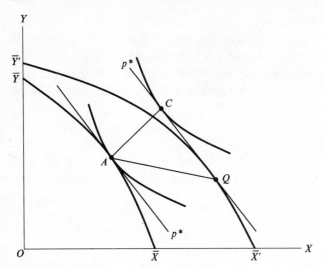

Figure 19.1

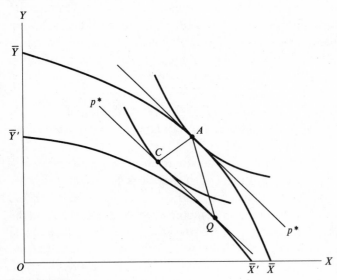

Figure 19.2

must increase. As in the case of labor inflow, capital outflow moves the production point from A to Q in Figure 19.2 at constant prices. With no repatriation, consumption occurs at C and the country thus imports Y (the capital-intensive good) and exports X. With full repatriation of income earned abroad, consumption occurs at A and the net trade including repatriated earnings is given by AQ. In either case there are net exports of X and imports of Y.

The analysis of Figures 19.1 and 19.2 can be summed up as follows.

If a country has a higher wage rate and a lower capital rental rate than its trading partner, then either a labor inflow and/or a capital outflow will have the same effect on production and trade. At constant prices, the country will produce more of the labor-intensive good and less of the capital-intensive good, exporting the former and importing the latter, regardless of whether or not earnings are repatriated.

This analysis is limited by two assumptions: (1) commodity prices and therefore factor prices do not change as a result of factor movements; (2) there are no tariffs. A full welfare analysis of factor movements requires us to drop these restrictive assumptions, which we will do in the next section.

2. WELFARE EFFECTS OF FACTOR MOVEMENTS

Factor movements affect domestic welfare in a number of ways, depending on the circumstances leading to the movements, whether or not prices change in response, and so forth. In this section we simply categorize the possible ways that factor mobility can affect welfare; in the subsequent section we will show which of these effects will dominate in specific situations. Four welfare effects can be identified and are discussed in arbitrary order, as follows.[1]

Inframarginal Gains (IMG) Suppose that a country has a capital rental rate that exceeds that of the rest of the world. Suppose further that an inflow of foreign capital drives down the domestic return on capital to equal the world rate. The situation is shown in Figure 19.3, where VMP_k is the value-of-marginal-product curve for capital (VMP_k equals the price of some good times the marginal product of capital in producing that good). The VMP_k curve slopes downward, reflecting the assumption that there are diminishing returns to capital. Let $\bar{K}$ in Figure 19.3 denote the economy's stock of capital and r^0 the competitive rental rate under the assumption that capital is paid the value of its marginal product.

Suppose now that an amount of foreign capital, K^*, is imported so that the capital stock is now $\bar{K} + K^*$. The domestic rental rate will be driven down to r^1 and the foreign capital will earn r^1 on each unit or a total of $r^1 (K^*)$. The payments to the foreign capital will thus equal the diagonally hatched rectangle $bcde$ in Figure 19.3.

But these payments are less than the total output of this capital. Consider starting at the initial capital stock $\bar{K}$ and just importing a small amount of foreign capital. The output produced by this capital will be its VMP_k times the quantity. This can be approximated by drawing a narrow rectangle under the VMP_k curve as is done in Figure 19.3. If we then add

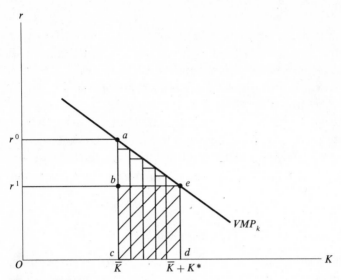

Figure 19.3

a second small amount of foreign capital, its contribution to output is again found in the same fashion by constructing a second narrow rectangle under the VMP_k curve. Repeating this procedure until we arrive at $\bar{K} + K^*$ in Figure 19.3, we see that the total change in output (or domestic income) produced by the foreign capital is given by adding up all of the little rectangles or, more exactly, by the area under the VMP_k curve between $\bar{K}$ and $\bar{K} + K^*$. The total change in output is thus given by the trapezoid *acde* in Figure 19.3.

Thus, although the foreign capital is paid the value of its marginal product, this marginal product is less than its average product so that some gains in income accrue to domestic citizens. This domestic income gain is given in Figure 19.3 by the area of the triangle *abe*, which is the difference between the total contribution of foreign capital (*acde* in Figure 19.3) and the payments to foreign capital (*bcde* in Figure 19.3). This is sometimes referred to as an "inframarginal gain" in the sense that while no benefits are captured from the marginal unit of foreign capital, gains are captured on each inframarginal (within the margin) unit.

It should be noted that the question of whether or not foreign capital owners migrate with their capital is of minor importance here. The inframarginal gains shown in Figure 19.3 are the gains to existing residents. If foreign capital earnings are repatriated, then the total increase in domestic consumption is just the inframarginal gain. If foreign owners accompany their capital (or if this were an issue of labor mobility), then national income would increase by the full amount of increased production, but the welfare change of existing residents would still, of course, be limited to the inframarginal gain.

Differential Rate of Return (DRR)   A second type of potential gain is more straightforward. Suppose that foreign factors, whether they be capital or labor migrants, must pay a tax that reduces the amount they receive below the value of their marginal product. The situation is shown in Figure 19.4, where we again assume a capital inflow of K^*, resulting in a VMP_k of r^1. Now, however, it is assumed that a tax is paid on these earnings, so that the foreign capital is left with a return of only r^2 to repatriate (or for foreign migrants to consume). Now in addition to the inframarginal gain, abe, the existing residents are able to capture the further amount, $bcde$, in tax in Figure 19.4. We call this the "differential rate of return" since it relates to the difference (or differential) between what the factor produces and what it is paid after tax.

It should be emphasized that the IMG and the DRR are not in general independent, since the imposition of a foreign investment tax will generally decrease the amount of foreign investment and thus reduce the inframarginal gains. More will be said of this below.

The situation for a capital-exporting country is only slightly different, as shown in Figure 19.5. The original capital stock is again given by $\overline{K}$ and an amount K^* is exported to give a smaller capital stock of $\overline{K} - K^*$. r^1 is assumed to be the foreign rental rate, and thus the country is assumed to export capital up to the point where the domestic rental rate is equal to the foreign rate. The total earnings of the domestic capital

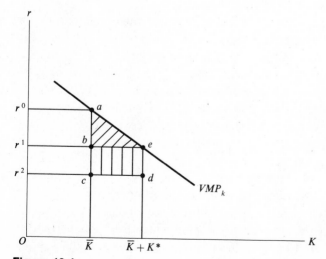

Figure 19.4

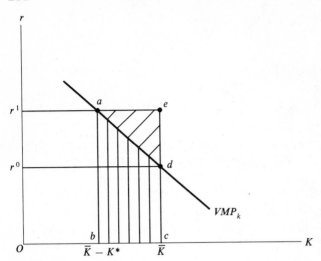

Figure 19.5

invested abroad are $r^1(K^*)$ or the area of the rectangle *abce* in Figure 19.5. The total area under the VMP_k curve (*abcd*) gives the total value of domestic production lost by exporting capital. The triangle *ade* thus gives the country's inframarginal gains from exporting capital (*abce* − *abcd*). A DRR gain can similarly be defined for the capital-exporting country if a capital export tax or income tax on foreign earnings is imposed. In this case the DRR gain arises from the fact that domestic capital earns a higher rate of return abroad than at home.

Terms-of-Trade Effects (TOT)   Since factor movements change factor endowments and thus production, they should be expected to have some effect on trade and prices. Welfare changes due to changes in commodity prices are referred to as "terms-of-trade effects." The pure effects of commodity price changes are shown in Figure 19.6, where I_y^h and E_y^f are the domestic import demand curve and the foreign export supply curve, respectively. In order to focus on the effects of price changes, we have assumed that E_y^f is perfectly vertical (inelastic). The initial equilibrium is at quantity I_{y0}^h and price p_{y0}^*.

Suppose that factor mobility results in an inflow of the country's scarce factor (factor used intensively in the import-competing industry). Production will shift toward the import-competing industry and consumers will wish to import less at each price ratio. The import demand curve shifts left to $I_y^{h'}$ in Figure 19.6. This has the effect of driving down the price of imports to p_{y1}^*, which constitutes an improvement in the terms of trade.

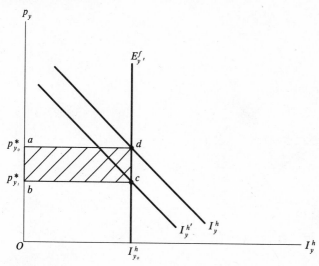

Figure 19.6

The country's total savings or welfare improvement is given by the fall in price times the quantity of imports $(p_{y0}^* - p_{y1}^*)I_{y0}^h$. This is given by the hatched rectangle *abcd* in Figure 19.6.

This TOT effect would be zero if we took the opposite extreme assumption, that the foreign export supply curve was perfectly elastic (the small-country assumption), but more will be said of this later. Note also that this analysis is essentially the same for a factor-exporting country and is indeed *exactly* the same if the country exports its abundant factor (factor used intensively in the production of its export good).

Volume-of-Trade Effects (VOT)   A fourth and final effect of factor movements has been called the "volume-of-trade effect." This only occurs when a country has tariffs in effect, but since tariffs often induce factor movements (discussed subsequently), this is an important case. Figure 19.7 abstracts from terms-of-trade effects (much as Figure 19.6 abstracts from volume-of-trade effects) by assuming that the foreign supply of exports is perfectly elastic at price p_y^*. The effect of a domestic tariff is to raise the import price and thus the domestic price to $p_y = p_y^*(1 + T)$ in Figure 19.7. I_y^h continues to give the domestic import demand curve, and equilibrium imports are thus I_{y0}^h at price $p_y = p_y^*(1 + T)$.

Suppose as in Figure 19.6 that factor movements (whether imports or exports) cause the country to desire to trade less at each world price. The import demand curve shifts left from I_y^h to $I_y^{h'}$ and imports fall from I_{y0}^h to I_{y1}^h in Figure 19.7. This shift at constant prices causes a welfare loss due to the fact that the domestic price of the import is more than the

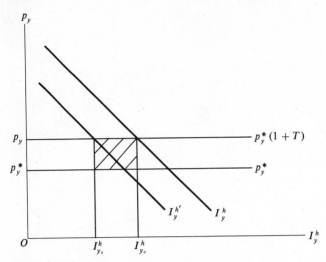

Figure 19.7

foreign price. The domestic price p_y gives the value of Y to domestic consumers, whereas the foreign price p^* gives the cost of obtaining Y. Thus with $p_y > p_y^*$ the value of Y is greater than the cost of obtaining Y. The economy is collecting a "surplus" of $(p_y - p_y^*)$ on each unit of imports. If factor movements reduce imports, they reduce this surplus by $(p_y - p_y^*)$ times the change in imports $(I_{y0}^h - I_{y1}^h)$. This is called the volume-of-trade effect (VOT) and is given by the hatched rectangle in Figure 19.7.

It follows from this discussion that the VOT will be zero if the country engages in free trade. In this case the value of a unit of imports (p_y) is equal to the cost of a unit of imports (p_y^*). Note also that if the country maintains a tariff, the TOT and VOT effects will generally work in opposite directions (one effect may be zero). If the foreign supply curve is upward sloping, a reduction in imports will lead to a positive TOT but a negative VOT. More advanced treatments of tariffs show, in fact, that the so-called optimum tariff discussed in Chapter 14 is simply the tariff rate that balances a positive TOT against a negative VOT.

Summary of Welfare Effects   The preceding discussion pointed out four distinct effects of factor movements. They can be summarized as follows:

1. The IMG is zero if the factor inflow or outflow does not change factor prices (the VMP_k curve in Figures 19.3 and 19.4 is horizontal).
2. The DRR effect is zero if the country maintains no factor import/ export tax.

3. The TOT effect is zero if the country faces a perfectly elastic foreign offer curve (the small-country assumption).
4. The VOT effect is zero if the country engages in free trade (it maintains no trade restrictions).

These results will now allow us to show some possible situations in which a country will definitely gain or lose from factor mobility.

3. CASES OF WELFARE GAINS OR LOSSES

The preceding four effects can interact in complex ways to determine the overall welfare effects of factor mobility. What we will do here is examine some simple situations that show how these effects can interact, and in particular, the circumstances in which a country could possibly lose as a result of factor mobility.

Case 1: Unambiguous Gains   Assume the following about the home country, country H. (1) Country H is small, such that it faces fixed world prices. (2) Country H engages in free trade. (c) Country H is very capital-scarce or labor-abundant, such that it is specialized in the production of the labor-intensive good. (d) Due to specialization, factor prices are not equalized by trade, and country H has a relatively low wage rate and a relatively high rental rate (see Chapter 8 for a review if necessary).

Now suppose that some foreign capital moves to country H or equivalently, that some domestic workers move abroad. Assume that in either case the mobile factor's earnings are fully repatriated. Since country H is specialized, either type of factor movement will raise the K/L ratio used in production, and thus the domestic rental rate will fall and the real wage rate will rise. Using the results of the previous section, the factor movements will have the following effects.

1. The inframarginal gains (IMG) will be positive for either capital imports (Figure 19.3) or labor exports (Figure 19.5 if we change the horizontal axis to labor).
2. The differential rate of return (DRR) will be positive if country H maintains factor import/export taxes, zero otherwise.
3. The terms-of-trade effect (TOT) will be zero, by the assumption that country H is a small open economy.
4. The volume-of-trade effect (VOT) is zero since there are no tariff distortions by assumption.

Points (1) to (4) thus add up to the fact that country H unambiguously gains from factor movements. The gain is simply the inframarginal gain shown in Figure 19.3 if capital is imported or in Figure 19.5 (with the axis relabeled L) if labor is exported. There may be a DRR gain as well, as shown in Figure 19.4.

Two qualifications should be noted. First, points (1) and (2) should not be taken to imply that it is always optimal to introduce a high tax on foreign factor earnings. While such a tax might generate a positive DRR, it will generally reduce the amount of factor mobility and thus reduce the IMG. Thus the net effect of the tax could be negative (welfare decreases). Nevertheless, more advanced treatments do show that some small tax on foreign earnings does generate a DRR that exceeds the negative effect on IMG. There will then exist some optimal factor tax (similar to the optimal tariff) that maximizes gains by balancing off a positive DRR against the negative IMG.[2]

The second qualification relates to labor outmigration. Suppose that the departing laborers do not repatriate any earnings. In this case the question of whether or not domestic welfare rises or falls turns on the question of whether or not the departed workers' welfare is still included in the national welfare function. If it is, then the results just presented are unaffected. If the welfare of the departed workers is *not* considered a part of national welfare, then overall welfare is reduced by an amount equal to the area under the *VMP* curve in Figure 19.5 (again, simply relabel the horizontal axis as L instead of K).

Case 2: Unambiguous Losses   Now assume that a slightly different set of circumstances prevails in country H. (1) Country H remains small, such that it faces fixed world prices. (2) Country H maintains an import tariff that raises the price of its import good (the capital-intensive good) above the world price. (3) As a result of the tariff, country H is diversified, producing both commodities. Since world prices and the import tariff are fixed, domestic prices will be unaffected by factor movements. (4) Due to the tariff, the domestic rental rate on capital exceeds the world rate, and vice versa for labor (this is the Stolper-Samuelson theorem, from Chapter 8).[3]

Now assume again that some foreign capital moves into country H or that some workers leave country H in response to the factor price differences. The effects of such factor endowment changes when a country is diversified were discussed in connection with Figures 19.1 and 19.2. With Y the capital-intensive import good, *either* an inflow of capital or an outflow of labor will shift production from X (the export good) to Y (the import good). This implies that the country will now import less Y and export less X or, in other words, will wish to trade less. The welfare effects can be summarized as follows:

1. The IMG effect will be zero. With fixed domestic prices and both goods produced, domestic factor prices will be fixed. The VMP_k curve in Figure 19.3 will be horizontal, and thus the IMG is zero.
2. The DRR will be zero if the country maintains no special tax on foreign factor earnings.
3. The TOT effect will be zero since the country faces fixed world prices.
4. The VOT effect reduces welfare. With the domestic value (price) of imports above their cost (the world price), the reduction in trade caused by the factor movements reduces welfare by the price difference times the decrease in imports $(p_y - p_y^*)\Delta I_y^h$.

Points 1 to 4 add up to the result that the factor movements unambiguously reduce welfare. This reduction is simply equal to the VOT effect shown in Figure 19.7. As we can see intuitively, inefficient domestic production of Y is replacing cheap imports of Y, whereas efficient domestic production of X and profitable exports of X are decreasing.

The only difference between Cases 1 and 2 is the underlying cause of factor-price differences. In Case 1 capital was expensive in country H due to a natural scarcity. In Case 2 capital was expensive in country H due to the tariff distortion. The tariff caused country H to produce too much Y relative to an optimum, but the capital inflow caused the country to produce even more Y, thereby leading to a further reduction in welfare.

There is one other way in which countries can gain or lose that is not captured in the preceding examples. If the changes in production and consumption induced by the factor movements cause a change in the terms of trade, then one country will gain a positive benefit while the other country will lose. It must be emphasized that unlike the IMG effect (both countries can gain) or the VOT effect (both countries can lose if they each have tariffs), one country must gain from the TOT effect while the other country must lose. The terms of trade cannot improve for both countries.[4]

The possible welfare outcomes can now be summarized as follows:

1. If factors move in response to factor-price differences that reflect a natural economic scarcity or abundance, countries will tend to gain even if foreign factors entering the economy repatriate all their earnings. It should be emphasized that, as in the case of commodity trade, factor trade of this type benefits both the factor-exporting and -importing countries as noted in Figures 19.3 and 19.5. It is definitely not true that one country gains at the expense of the other.
2. If factors move in response to factor-price differences created by tariffs or other distortions, a country's welfare may decrease. In

this case factor prices give incorrect signals about scarcity and productivity. Tariffs mean that prices are high for factors used intensively in inefficient, protected industries, and thus factor mobility serves to distort further production away from the country's pattern of comparative advantage.

3. Both points 1 and 2 have to be qualified by the possibility that factor movements could produce strong terms-of-trade effects. In Case 1 a strong negative TOT effect could lead to net losses, and vice versa for Case 2.

4. TERMS-OF-TRADE EFFECTS, THE TRANSFER PROBLEM, AND WORLD WELFARE

The purpose of this section is briefly to tie up a number of loose ends. The terms-of-trade effect mentioned in the preceding section may either harm or help a country depending on the direction of price changes. The analysis of this terms-of-trade change has often been called the "transfer problem" and is usually conducted with respect to a unilateral gift or transfer of money or commodities from one country to another, although the principle is exactly the same as in the case of factor movements. (The problem was originally discussed with regard to war reparation payments following World War I.)

Suppose that country F makes a gift of money or commodities to country H, or that some factors leave F to take up residence in H. Country H now has greater purchasing power and country F less purchasing power. Further assume that country H imports Y and exports X. The effect of this transfer on the terms of trade turns out to depend on the consumption response of citizens in each country (in addition to the production response in the case of a factor movement). Suppose that the residents of country H use their added purchasing power exclusively for the purchase of X, their export good. The demand for X will rise relative to the demand for Y in country H. Suppose also that residents of country F react to their reduced purchasing power by decreasing consumption of Y, their export good, while holding consumption of X relatively constant. The demand for Y will fall relative to the demand for X in country F. If we put these two effects together we will see that the world demand for X has risen relative to Y following the transfer. The price of X will rise relative to Y and country H will receive a secondary benefit due to a positive TOT effect.

The result is that if each country has a relatively high propensity to spend on its own export good, the TOT tends to move in favor of the country receiving the transfer. The receiving country thus ends up gaining more than the amount of the transfer and the sending country ends up losing more than the amount of the transfer. If each country has a high propensity to spend on its own import good, the opposite conclusion applies.[5]

From the point of view of the world as a whole, it turns out that the negative TOT effect experienced by one country exactly balances the positive TOT effect of the other country. Thus world real income is not changed due to terms-of-trade effects. The TOT effect can be expressed in terms of either imports or exports, so let us express it in terms of X. It can be shown that the TOT effect is approximately equal to the country's excess supply for X times the change in the price of X, $(X_p - X_c)\Delta p^*$, where X_c and X_p are the quantities of X consumed and produced, respectively. If X is exported, $(X_p - X_c) > 0$ and a rise in the relative price of X, $\Delta p^* > 0$, improves welfare. If X is imported, $(X_p - X_c) < 0$, and a rise in p^* decreases welfare.

In a two-country world the exports of one country must match the imports of the other country. Thus, if we add the TOT effects together for country H and country F, we will have a world TOT effect of zero:

$$(X_p^h - X_c^h)\Delta p^* + (X_p^f - X_c^f)\Delta p^* = 0 \qquad (19.1)$$

since $(X_p^h - X_c^h) = - (X_p^f - X_c^f)$. The consequence of this is that we can ignore the TOT when talking about the effects of factor mobility for the world as a whole.

From the point of view of the world as a whole the welfare effects are the same as those given in points (1) and (2) at the end of the previous section. If countries do not have distortionary tariffs or other taxes, factor movements are guaranteed to increase total world income by creating inframarginal gains for both countries. If on the other hand factor movements are prompted by distortionary taxation, then both countries may experience negative VOT effects and world real income may decrease. As we have seen several times in this book, distortions not only cause welfare losses in their own right, but they may also lead to further losses when combined with what would otherwise be welfare-improving policies (free trade in goods and factors).

5. FACTOR MOVEMENTS AND COMMODITY TRADE AS SUBSTITUTES

The previous several sections have focused on the welfare effects of factor mobility. In this section and the next we will focus on the ways in which factor movements influence the amount of world trade in commodities. If factor movements lead to a *reduction* in the amount of commodity trade, we say that factor movements and commodity trade are substitutes (i.e., the exchange of factors can substitute for the role usually played by commodity exchange). If factor movements lead to an *increase* in the volume of commodity trade, we say that factor movements and commodity trade are complements.

An important case in which factor movements and commodity trade are substitutes can be illustrated using the Rybczynski analysis of Figures 19.1 and 19.2.[6] Suppose that there are significant transportation costs between two countries, so that in each country the relative price of the country's export good is less than the relative price of that good abroad. Suppose Figures 19.1 and 19.2 represent the home country, which exports X and imports Y. Transportation costs imply that country H faces a world price ratio net of transportation costs, which is less than that in country F. Tariffs have exactly the same effect in that they make the domestic price ratio $p = p_x/p_y$ in country H lower than that in country F. Thus either tariffs or transportation costs will result in $p^h < p^f$, given X is country H's export good.

Assume that we have a Heckscher-Ohlin production technology in which X and Y are produced from labor and capital. Recall from Chapter 8 that, in such a model, factor prices can be equalized only if commodity prices are equalized by trade. If $p^h < p^f$ as in the present example, we also know from the Stolper-Samuelson theorem (Chapter 8) that country H will have a relatively high price for the factor used intensively in Y (the relatively expensive good) and country F will have a relatively high price for the factor used intensively in X (country F's relatively expensive good). Assume finally that X is relatively labor-intensive and Y relatively capital-intensive. We then have the difference between factor-price ratios given as follows:

$$p^h < p^f \text{ implies } (w/r)^h < (w/r)^f. \qquad (19.2)$$

Now refer back to Figures 19.1 and 19.2 and assume that Q and C are the initial production and consumption points for country H, respectively. With $(w/r)^h < (w/r)^f$, labor will migrate out of country H (Figure 19.1) and/or capital will flow into H (Figure 19.2) if factor mobility is allowed. The effects are shown by the Rybczynski analysis of Figures 19.1 and 19.2. An outmigration of labor will cause production to shift along the line segment connecting Q and A in Figure 19.1 at constant prices. Consumption will shift in from C to A. Thus trade is steadily reduced by the labor outmigration and is eventually eliminated when production and consumption come together at point A. Thus factor movements substitute for trade by making the labor-abundant country (country H) less labor-abundant, and vice versa for country F. Allowing the terms of trade to change complicates the story slightly, but the end result must be the same: Factor movements will eventually eliminate differences in factor endowments and trade will disappear.

Figure 19.2 shows the same process occurring for capital inflow. At constant prices the Rybczynski effect implies that production moves from Q toward A, whereas consumption moves from C toward A. The capital inflow reduces and eventually eliminates trade.

6. FACTOR MOVEMENTS AND COMMODITY TRADE AS COMPLEMENTS

Now consider a very different situation in which trade is caused by differences in production technology.[7] Assume that we have two economies with the following characteristics. (1) Countries H and F have identical factor endowments. (2) Countries H and F have identical technology for producing Y, but country H has superior technology for producing X. It is assumed that country H's X isoquants have the same shape as the X isoquants for country F, but that the former are renumbered so that more output is produced from the same inputs (this is called "Hicks-neutral" technical superiority, named after Sir John Hicks).

The situation is shown in Figures 19.8 and 19.9. Assumptions (1) and (2) imply that both countries have an identical Edgeworth box and identical contract curve in Figure 19.9. But their production frontiers differ, as shown in Figure 19.8. $\overline{YX^f}$ gives the production frontier for country F. Country H can produce the same maximum amount of Y but more X, so country H's frontier is given by $\overline{YX^h}$.

Suppose that Q^f in Figures 19.8 and 19.9 gives country F's production point in free-trade equilibrium. If country H allocated factors in the same way in Figure 19.9 (point Q^f), country H would be at point A in Figure 19.8, producing the same amount of Y but more X. This cannot be an equilibrium for country H because the marginal cost of producing X will be less in country H relative to country F. This is because beginning at Q^f in Figure 19.9, fewer factors are needed for an additional unit of X in country H relative to country F, due to H's superior technology. Thus, if $p_x^* = (MC_x)^f$ at Q^f in Figure 19.9, then we must have $p_x^* > (MC_x)^h$ at Q^f. The equilibrium for country H must be at a point like Q^h in Figures 19.8 and 19.9.

If the countries are producing at Q^f and Q^h in Figures 19.8 and 19.9, we can conclude two things. First, country H must be exporting X and importing Y (Figure 19.8). Second, the wage-rental ratio must be higher in country H (Figure 19.9) since the capital-labor ratios are higher in H. This is different from the case considered in the previous section, in that

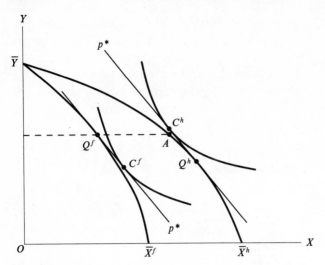

Figure 19.8

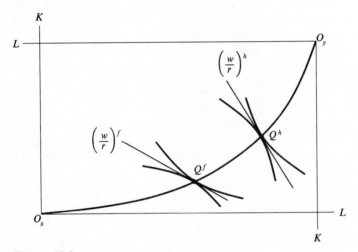

Figure 19.9

here each country will have a relatively high price for the factor used intensively in its export industry. If we permit factors to migrate, labor will flow into country H and/or capital will be exported, if we retain our assumption that X is labor-intensive. Similar comments apply, of course, to country F.

The result of this factor mobility is that each country becomes relatively better endowed with the factor used intensively in its export industry. This adds a Heckscher-Ohlin or factor-proportions basis for trade, which tends to reinforce the basis for trade caused by the difference in technology. Factor mobility can then lead to an increase in the volume of commodity trade. Country H will now export X not only because it has superior technology but also because it is now relatively well endowed with labor.

In this simple model of trade based on differences in production technology, it thus turns out that factor movements and commodity trade are complements. Although this may seem to be a very special case, it is in fact true that the complementary relationship holds for a wide variety of models in which the basis for trade is something other than differences in factor endowments. If trade is caused by such things as scale economies or imperfect competition, for example, factor movements and commodity trade are often complements.

7. CONCLUDING REMARKS

While international trade has traditionally focused on trade in commodities and assumed that factors of production are immobile, factor movements are, nevertheless, of considerable importance to many countries. Canada and the United States were, for example, developed with foreign labor and capital. In the latter half of the twentieth century, North American capital has in turn been exported. Major issues in recent Canadian international policy have revolved around factor movements (foreign investment) more than around commodity trade.

We showed in Section 2 of this chapter that the welfare effects of factor movements are quite complex. Yet despite this complexity, the bottom line seems surprisingly simple. The results show that countries will gain from factor movements (or factor trade) just as they do from commodity trade, provided that the prices that stimulate factor movements correctly reflect true economic scarcity and abundance. This is true even if the foreign factors working in the domestic economy repatriate 100 percent of their earnings. The only exception is when factor movements have a very adverse effect on a country's terms of trade.

If on the other hand factor movements are stimulated by price differences caused by distortions, a country's welfare may be reduced by factor movements. This is, of course, broadly consistent with the general principles we discussed in Chapters 10 and 11. In the presence of distortions, prices may incorrectly reflect a country's pattern of comparative advantage, and thus commodity trade or factor trade may serve to move a country away from, rather than toward, its optimal pattern of specialization. This was illustrated for commodity trade in Chapter 10, which showed how the distortionary effects of a production tax could imply that trade in commodities reduces welfare. The same principle was illustrated here by showing that factor movements stimulated by tariffs could cause a country to produce more of its import good (the good in which the country has a comparative disadvantage) and less of its export good (the good in which the country has a comparative advantage). Expensive domestic production is substituted for cheap imports. In the absence of a favorable terms-of-trade shift, the result is a welfare loss when the foreign factors repatriate their earnings.

PROBLEMS

1. In the situation shown in Figures 19.1 and 19.2 (constant terms of trade, no tariffs), how is per capita income of domestic citizens affected by the factor movements?

2. Gross domestic product (GDP) is defined as the total value of production in a country, whereas gross national product (GNP) is the income of domestic citizens. GNP thus equals GDP minus the repatriated profits of foreign investors plus the repatriated profits from investments by domestic citizens abroad. In each of Figures 19.1 and 19.2, discuss how GNP and GDP change.

3. In the Heckscher-Ohlin case of Figures 19.1 and 19.2 with fixed terms of trade, is there any inframarginal gain from factor mobility? (*Hint:* Remember the factor-price-equalization theorem.)

4. Suppose that the domestic economy exports a capital-intensive good but that most of the domestic capital stock is foreign-owned. With reference to the Stolper-Samuelson theorem, discuss the possibility that an improvement in the terms of trade could reduce the welfare of domestic citizens.

5. Refer back to Figure 11.1 (Chapter 11). Each of two identical countries is specialized in the production of one good. Let X be labor-intensive and Y be capital-intensive. Do you think factor prices will be equalized and if not, which country will have the higher (w/r) ratio? If factors are permitted to move, will factor movements and commodity trade be substitutes or complements?

NOTES

1. General algebraic treatments of this problem that identify these four effects mathematically are provided by Jones (1967) and Markusen and Melvin (1979).
2. See Jones (1967).
3. This is the case analyzed by Brecher and Diaz-Alejandro (1977).
4. Terms-of-trade changes, via their effects on factor prices, have further welfare effects if there is substantial foreign ownership of domestic factors of production (Bhagwati and Brecher (1980)). See problem 4.
5. See Samuelson (1952, 1954) for a formal treatment.
6. This result and the analysis are due to Mundell (1957).
7. This analysis is due to Markusen (1983) and Purvis (1972).

REFERENCES

Bhagwati, J. N., and R. A. Brecher (1980). "National Welfare in the Open Economy in the Presence of Foreign-Owned Factors of Production." *Journal of International Economics* 10, 103–115.

Brecher, R. A., and C. Diaz-Alejandro (1977). "Tariffs, Foreign Capital, and Immiserizing Growth." *Journal of International Economics* 7, 317–322.

Jones, R. W. (1967). "International Capital Movements and the Theory of Tariffs." *Quarterly Journal of Economics* 81, 1–38.

Markusen, J. R. (1983). "Factor Movements and Commodity Trade as Complements." *Journal of International Economics* 13, 341–356.

——, and J. R. Melvin (1979). "Tariffs, Capital Mobility, and Foreign Ownership." *Journal of International Economics* 9, 395–410.

Mundell, R. A. (1957). "International Trade and Factor Mobility." *American Economic Review* 47, 321–335.

Purvis, D. D. (1972). "Technology, Trade, and Factor Mobility," *Economic Journal* 82, 991–999.

Samuelson, P. A. (1952). "The Transfer Problem and Transportation Costs: The Terms of Trade When Impediments Are Absent." *Economic Journal* 62, 278–304.

——. (1954). "The Transfer Problem and Transportation Costs II: Analysis of Effects of Trade Impediments." *Economic Journal* 64, 264–289.

chapter *20*

Direct Foreign Investment

1. DIRECT FOREIGN INVESTMENT VERSUS PORTFOLIO INVESTMENT

Direct foreign investment is defined as an investment in which the investor acquires a substantial controlling interest in a foreign firm or sets up a subsidiary in a foreign country. Direct foreign investment involves ownership and/or control of a business enterprise abroad. For the remainder of this chapter, we refer to companies that engage in direct foreign investment as multinational enterprises (MNE), although they are also sometimes referred to as transnational corporations.

There are probably some economists who would maintain that investments made by MNE differ very little from the type of portfolio capital movements discussed in the previous chapter. Some might maintain that the effects on production, consumption, and welfare when an American farm machinery firm opens a Canadian plant differ little from the effects of some Americans buying an interest (noncontrolling) in Massey-Ferguson.

Most international trade economists now believe that there are important differences between direct and portfolio investments, although they differ as to their interpretations of the consequences of these differences. One relevant observation is that MNE often do not move substantial amounts of capital between countries (as is the case with portfolio investments) but frequently provide for many of their needs from the foreign capital markets. Thus the American manufacturer moving into Canada may borrow funds for plant and equipment from Canadian banks, or issue stocks or bonds on Canadian securities markets. A Canadian land developer operating in Texas or Florida may mortgage his properties with U.S. banks. The consequence of this observation is that direct foreign investments are not always caused by a difference in the general return to capital that prompts portfolio capital movements. The MNE arises as a result of specific business opportunities rather than (or more correctly in addition to) general levels of interest rates and returns to capital. To make a domestic analogy, a Denver land developer makes investments in the Houston market because the company sees profitable business opportunities, not because interest rates are different between Denver and Houston. These same business factors lead the developer to enter the Toronto land market.

A second important difference between direct and portfolio investments lies in the observation that foreign firms are at an inherent disadvantage in the domestic market. Thus if foreign firms are exactly identical to domestic firms, the former will not find it profitable to enter the domestic market. The MNE must, therefore, arise due to the fact that it possesses some special advantage such as superior technology or lower costs due to scale economies. This point also helps to explain the previous observation that MNE investments are often not primarily motivated by differences in returns to capital. They seem instead to be motivated by such things as the ability to exploit superior technical knowledge.

The inherent disadvantages of a MNE setting up operations abroad are numerous, and perhaps we can provide a convincing explanation of the point by a few examples. (1) Branch plants or subsidiaries in foreign countries lead to costs in communication and transportation not faced by domestic firms. These include the direct costs such as overseas phone calls and travel expenses of executives and also the time costs of delays due to mail, and so on. (2) Language and cultural differences between the home country and the foreign (or "host") countries inevitably create costs for the MNE that are not faced by domestic firms. (3) Similarly, the MNE at least initially does not have a close familiarity with the local business scene, tax laws, and other government procedures in the host country. Local laws often, in fact, tend to discriminate actively against the MNE. (4) The MNE faces risks such as exchange rate changes, expropriation, or other capricious government actions that are not as important to local firms. The MNE thus faces more uncertainty that, if the firms and their owners are risk-averse, constitutes a true business cost. (5) The MNE must frequently station managers and technicians abroad. Often these personnel can only be induced to live abroad by paying them substantially higher wages.

The point is perhaps clear. Due to these disadvantages, the MNE will only enter a foreign market if it has some compensating advantages over local firms. These advantages are thereby transferred to the foreign country (e.g., superior technology) and thus constitute an important potential gain for the host country. There may, however, be offsetting costs such as increased monopoly power. Some of the relevant advantages and costs will be discussed in the next three sections.

2. TECHNOLOGY TRANSFER

Perhaps the simplest and most obvious advantage that the MNE can possess is superior technology. Most MNE originate or have headquarters in the highly developed countries, where technical knowledge is most advanced. This technical advantage translates into a cost advantage, which allows the MNE to undersell rival producers, particularly producers from less-developed countries who employ more backward production methods.

Companies possessing superior technology have, of course, the choice of simply producing and exporting from their home country. In this case they are not MNE and the whole issue dealt with here does not arise. But there are a number of important factors that might lead a MNE to set up a branch plant or subsidiary abroad in preference to exporting. First, high tariffs or transportation costs in foreign countries raise the cost of exporting, relative to setting up a foreign operation. In the former case exporting involves paying the tariff and transportation costs. In the latter the MNE produces behind the tariff wall and saves transportation costs as well (we often use the metaphor "jumping the tariff wall"). Second, certain factor prices such as labor wage rates may be lower abroad. While factor price differences are not necessary for explaining MNE activity, as noted in the previous section, they certainly do contribute. Obvious cases in which factor price differences are important include situations in which the MNE produces abroad for export back to the home market (e.g., textiles and electronic goods in Southeast Asia). Third, the MNE may feel that its advantages are temporary and that it should preempt possible foreign rivals and set up foreign plants while it still has an advantage. This will be the subject of Section 4. Fourth, some countries, particularly developing countries, offer the MNE favorable tax treatment if it sets up (and particularly if it exports) from their country. Fifth, setting up a foreign operation may for some reasons be less risky than exporting (or importing). A firm may feel, for example, that a foreign government in financial difficulty is less likely to disrupt a branch plant than it is to impose import tariffs or quotas. Similarly, a company that buys a product abroad (e.g., a steel company purchasing iron ore) may feel more secure if it owns the foreign source of supply. This argument can, however, cut the other way, insofar as foreign subsidiaries run the risk of expropriation.

In any case, suppose that a firm with technical superiority in the production of some good sets up a branch plant in another country. The firm may, of course, move factors of production such as capital and labor, with resulting welfare effects as analyzed in the previous chapter. To concentrate on the issues at hand, let us, therefore, assume that the firm moves no physical factors but, rather, hires capital and labor in the foreign factor markets. The only thing that moves internationally is the intangible technical knowledge. This type of investment is thus often referred to as "technology transfer."

What are the advantages of this investment from the point of view of the host country? Because of its superior technology, the MNE can produce more output from the same resources or the same output from fewer resources relative to a domestic firm in the host country. The new technology thus shifts out the production frontier of the host country. The host country's GNP or total output will increase as a result of the MNE entering the country. In countries with substantial unemployment the new jobs created by the MNE may provide a further increase in income.

What are the possible disadvantages of the MNE from the point of view of the host country? Due to the fact that the MNE possesses some technical advantage, it seems likely that the MNE will tend to enjoy a monopolistic position. This will lead to some resource misallocation and to the repatriation of profits by the multinational, profits that might otherwise have gone to domestic entrepreneurs in the absence of multinational activity. If the MNE profits are greater than the increase in the value of output due to the MNE, then it seems possible that the host country could be worse off with the MNE.

A technical analysis of this trade-off between increased efficiency and monopoly power is postponed until Section 5 of this chapter. Perhaps it is sufficient to note here that if the MNE is to drive out domestic firms in the host country, it must sell at a price that is sufficiently low (or pay real wages that are sufficiently high) to make production unprofitable for domestic firms. This limits the exercise of monopoly power by the MNE and, as just noted, forces the MNE to pay a real wage higher than that offered by domestic firms. Indeed, there is a certain irony here, in that if a MNE monopoly replaces a competitive industry, it must be making the host country better off. The reason is that since the MNE is paying a higher real wage (selling at a lower price), the total increase in the value of production cannot all go to the MNE in the form of profits. Some of the increase must be captured by the host country in the form of higher real factor payments.

If, on the other hand, the MNE replaces a domestic monopoly, then there will be a transfer of profits from the domestic monopoly to the MNE. Thus even though total profits must rise by less than the value of production due to increased real factor payments, the increased profits plus the transferred profits may exceed the increase in production. By capturing profits that would have gone to the host country, the MNE may possibly make the host country worse off.

Before moving on, we should note that the topic of technology transfer, as in all discussions of MNE, is a complex and at times a controversial one. There are propositions put forward that the MNE "undermines" domestic industry and transfers "inappropriate" technology. The unfortunate thing is that most of the authors who put forward these notions do not carefully develop the logical structure of their ideas, which are thus difficult to assess. The notion of "inappropriate" technology (e.g., too capital-intensive) is a case in point. As we noted earlier, any technology transferred by a MNE must be sufficiently appropriate to allow the MNE to compete successfully with domestic firms. True, there may be even better technologies that could be developed to exploit the host country's cheap factors (e.g., new labor-intensive technologies for less-developed countries), but it certainly does not follow that the technology that is transferred is inappropriate relative to what is currently in use.

3. MULTIPLANT ECONOMIES OF SCALE

Recent studies of multinationals have given us a fairly clear picture of the types of industries that tend to attract MNE. The studies show that the level of multinational activity in a particular industry is closely related to the importance of "intangibles" in that industry's overall operation. These intangibles involve activities that are not directly related to the physical production of goods, such as research and development, advertising, marketing, and distribution. Thus industries in which research and development are very important are more likely to be dominated by MNE than industries in which they are unimportant. Similar comments apply to industries in which advertising, marketing, finance, or other nonproduction activities are important.[1]

Intangibles in turn seem to be closely related to the concept of economies of multiplant operation. By "economies of multiplant operation" we mean advantages possessed by the owner of two or more production facilities over independent owners of the same production facilities.

The great body of research on Canada, in particular, seems to emphasize repeatedly economies of multiplant operation, in explaining the incidence across industries of American MNE operating in Canada.[2]

In explaining economies of multiplant operation, we need to distinguish between firms and plants. A plant is a production facility, and thus a firm may be composed of many plants plus one or more nonproduction facilities (e.g., offices, research labs, etc.) that carry out nonproduction activities. Industries in which firms typically have many plants spread out domestically or internationally are said to be characterized by multiplant economies, and it is in these industries that we often tend to find the MNE.

Multiplant economies often arise from the fact that the firm's nonproduction activities are "joint inputs" into physical production, or perhaps there are simply scale economies in these activities. Some examples are as follows:

Research and Development (R and D)   Suppose a firm invents a new product or a new production process. The cost of developing that new product or process is independent of the number of plants. Further, the product or process can be incorporated into any number of plants without diminishing the usefulness of the innovation to any single plant. The innovation can be jointly used by all the plants (hence the term "joint input"); thus the average cost of R and D is reduced in proportion to the number of plants. Multiplant economies thus arise from avoiding the duplication in R and D that would exist in single-plant firms.

Advertising, Marketing, and Distribution   Expenditures on market research and fixed costs of advertising (e.g., producing a commercial) share a related property. Once certain initial expenditures are made, new geographic areas can be added for a marginal cost at most, which is significantly less than average cost. These economies are thought to be extremely important in consumer industries such as beer brewing.

Management Services   There is some evidence that there are economies of scale relating to management services. Large-scale operation permits a greater degree of division of labor. Second, when the various plants are producing the same goods (a "horizontal" MNE), there are probably scale economies in certain management areas. For example, cost accountants may be able to monitor two identical plants for less than double the resources needed for a single plant.

Capital Market and Other Financial Economies There is likewise some evidence that large-scale operations permit the firm to acquire capital and other inputs at lower cost. This gives the two-plant firm another advantage over independent one-plant firms.

If there are high tariffs or transportation costs in the world, it will be inefficient or unprofitable to supply all countries with a good produced from a single production facility in one country. In the absence of multiplant economies of scale or technical differences as discussed in the previous section, we would simply expect to find independent firms in the various countries producing the good, since there would be no particular role for the MNE. But with multiplant economies, a firm can gain a competitive advantage by establishing a large number of plants, thereby lowering its average costs, as noted previously. By maintaining plants in a number of countries, the MNE spreads out its fixed costs and thereby achieves lower costs relative to single-plant firms in each country. If this cost advantage is very significant, the MNE may drive local competition out of the market, as discussed in the previous section on technical superiority.

Multiplant economies mean that the MNE can at least potentially increase the welfare of both the home and host countries. The MNE achieves greater technical efficiency by eliminating costly duplication of R and D, management, marketing, and so forth. This frees more resources for actual production and thus can lead to a welfare improvement.

The possibile hitch is the same one discussed in the previous section. The efficiency captured by the multiplant firm may be at the expense of increased monopoly power. Thus, although the MNE is more technically efficient than independent national firms, it may exert more monopoly power, resulting in ambiguous welfare effects. Research on this trade-off is still in its early stages but there have been several simple models in which the efficiency gain of the MNE outweighs any increase in monopoly power. The condition for the MNE home country to gain is that the MNE makes more profits than would be made by a strictly domestic firm. If this were not the case, the firm would not become a MNE in the first place and the whole issue would not arise. If the MNE sets prices in the host country to prevent entry by domestic firms, which assume the MNE prices are fixed (called "Bertrand behavior" in oligopoly theory, after the French economist Joseph Bertrand), then the host country must be better off as well.[3] It is not clear if this result will generalize to more complicated forms of behavior, but as noted in the previous section, the threat of entry places important constraints on the ability of the MNE to price in a monopolistic fashion.

4. APPROPRIABILITY AND PREEMPTIVE ENTRY

A somewhat different version of the technology transfer argument is called "appropriability" or "preemptive entry." Suppose a firm in one country gains technical superiority over its rivals. Unlike the situation considered in Section 2, however, suppose that tariffs, and the like, are low enough that the firm would in general prefer to produce and export from its home base rather than set up branch plants abroad. In such a situation a MNE might never arise. We would simply observe domestic firms exporting goods in which they had a technical advantage.

Now consider a dynamic context in which the firm believes that its advantage is temporary. That is, the firm believes that sooner or later foreign firms will master the new technology and the former's advantages will disappear. When this happens, even relatively small tariffs or transportation costs may mean that the firm's foreign markets will disappear, since it is now the original exporting firm that will be at a disadvantage.[4]

The idea is that the original firm can prevent this scenario by "appropriating" or "preempting" the foreign competition by setting up subsidiaries in the foreign country before indigenous firms have the chance to develop. The result is that foreign firms may never bother to develop competing technology or, even if they do, the original firm may suffer much less of a loss in foreign markets since it has competition in place when new firms enter. Defensive behavior on the part of leading firms thus leads to the creation of foreign operations and the MNE.

This theory of the MNE seems more sinister than the previous theories presented. The benefits to the home country seem less clear since the theory assumes that domestic firms would have eventually caught up. Nevertheless, in the long run the MNE must still in some sense outperform potential domestic rivals if it is to retain its position. Like the previous theories, this theory has not yet been developed in a rigorous analytical context, and thus a better understanding of the welfare consequences of the MNE must await further research advances.

*5. THE WELFARE EFFECTS OF MNE ON HOST COUNTRIES

The purpose of this section is to present a technical analysis of the effects of a MNE investment on a host country. Since the effects of superior technology are somewhat easier to analyze than the effects of multiplant economies or preemptive entry, we will use technology transfer as the basis for the MNE investment.

Figure 20.1 shows the initial situation for the host country. $\overline{YX}_n$

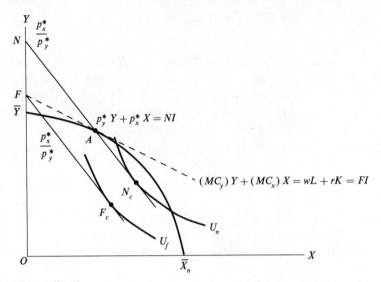

Figure 20.1

gives its production frontier. X is arbitrarily assumed to be the import good, and the X industry is assumed to be imperfectly competitive. Thus the initial free-trade production point is A, where $p_x^* > MC_x$. The Y industry is assumed to be competitive so that $p_x^* = MC_y$. Total national income (NI) is given by the budget line passing through A and the consumption point N_c. If marginal costs are equal to average costs, the value of payments to factors of production (FI) is given by the tangent to A, since the slope of the production frontier is equal to the ratios of marginal costs. We have

$$NI = p_x^* X + p_y^* Y \tag{20.1}$$
$$FI = wL + rK = (MC_x) + (MC_y)Y. \tag{20.2}$$

Suppose we measure NI and FI in terms of good Y in Figure 20.1. Point N on the vertical axis gives NI, and point F gives FI as shown. We can then show the division of NI between factor payments (FI) and profits by drawing a budget line with slope p_x^*/p_y^* through point F. This gives the consumption possibilities open to factor owners, who will choose point F_c to maximize their utility. The difference between total consumption N_c and consumption of factor owners F_c represents profits in the X industry. Since the X industry is domestically owned by assumption, these profits are part of domestic income and contribute to domestic welfare even though they may be very unevenly distributed.

Now suppose that a MNE enters the domestic X industry and drives out all domestic producers. In Figure 20.2 the production frontier shifts

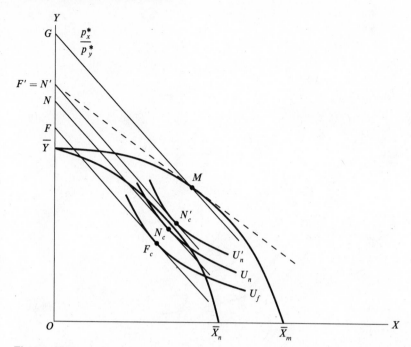

Figure 20.2

to $\overline{YX}_m$ by virtue of the fact that the MNE has transferred superior technology. Suppose arbitrarily that prices do not change (this assumption has no importance) and that the MNE monopoly chooses to produce at M in Figure 20.2. The total value of output that we could call GNP is given by the budget line through M and therefore by point G if measured in terms of Y. Payments to factor owners are again given by the tangent to $\overline{YX}_m$ at M (if marginal costs equal average costs) and therefore by point F' if measured in terms of Y. But now FI and NI are the same thing since there are no profits going to domestic citizens. Thus point F' in Figure 20.2 also gives the new level of NI, which we can denote N'. The national budget line is given by drawing a line with slope p_x^*/p_y^* through point F' $= N'$. Consumption by domestic citizens will be given by N_c' on indifference curve U_n' in Figure 20.2. As drawn, the host country is unambiguously better off with the MNE, despite the fact that the MNE is earning and repatriating profits (equal to $G - N'$ in Figure 20.2). Factor owners are significant gainers since they capture the entire increase in welfare from U_f to U_n'. Owners of the domestic X industry will be worse off due to their fall in profits.

Figure 20.3 illustrates an alternative outcome in which FI rises with the MNE but NI falls (the loss of domestic profits is greater than the increase in domestic factor payments). The MNE produces at M, which

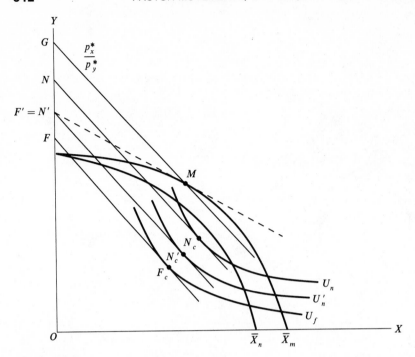

Figure 20.3

results in a $NI = FI$, shown by $N' = F'$ in Figure 20.3. The amount $(G - N')$ again gives the MNE profits. Domestic consumption and welfare are given by N'_c and U'_n, respectively, which represent a fall in NI but a welfare improvement for factor owners.

Is it possible that factor owners could be worse off with the MNE (FI decreases)? As noted earlier, research on this problem is still in its early stages, but it does appear that at least for some models, the MNE must result in an increase in FI. In these models the fact that FI must rise is a logical consequence of the assumption that the MNE must price in such a way that domestic firms are deterred from entering. In fact, under what is known as "Bertrand behavior" on the part of potential entrants, the MNE will have to price in such a way that NI rises as well as FI. Thus in at least some situations the MNE is assured of increasing welfare in the host country.

6. CONCLUDING REMARKS

In this chapter we have tried to distinguish the determinants of direct foreign investment from those of portfolio investment as discussed in the previous chapter. Portfolio investments seem to be basically motivated by international factor-price differences and therefore can be analyzed using the traditional tools of international trade theory. Direct foreign investment seems to be determined more by the characteristics of individual firms, and thus the traditional microeconomic theory of the firm seems to provide more appropriate methods of analysis.

The basic notion as discussed previously is that firms are at a certain disadvantage in competing with the indigenous firms in a foreign country. Thus for a firm to become a multinational it must have certain compensating advantages over foreign firms. Three possibilities were discussed. First, the MNE may have technical superiority that allows it to undersell its foreign competitors. Second, in industries characterized by economies of multiplant operation, the MNE that can establish production facilities in many countries captures a cost advantage over strictly national firms that maintain only one or a small number of plants. Third, the MNE may arise due to strategic considerations. If a firm has a temporary advantage that it feels will be eroded over time, it may decide to set up branch plants in order to appropriate or preempt those markets before foreign competition arises.

The welfare effects of MNE on host countries seem to be a complicated trade-off between increased technical efficiency and the possibility of increased monopoly power. Such a trade-off is not, of course, inevitable, since we could probably find cases in which competitive MNE entered a country in which a product was either not produced or produced by an inefficient domestic monopolist. But even when a monopoly MNE enters and drives out a competitive industry, the MNE must set prices sufficiently low or real wages sufficiently high to keep the domestic competitors out. Under certain assumptions this pricing to prevent entry guarantees that the host country will be made better off.

There is, of course, a wide variety of other arguments both for and against the MNE. Most of these are long, complex, and often vague, and thus cannot be dealt with here. Perhaps we can mention a few without commenting on their validity. In addition to the point about technology transfer, supporters of the MNE argue that these corporations have a valuable role to play (particularly in developing countries), in teaching modern organization, and management and technical skills in the host countries. This learning-by-doing in the host country then has a positive external effect on the entire economy, which adds to any direct income effect. Those opposed to the MNE talk about "exporting jobs" from the home country and about "cultural and economic imperialism" from the point of view of the host country. They talk about the MNE creating an "international division of labor," which seems to mean that high-paying white-collar jobs are located in the home country, whereas low-paying blue-collar jobs are located in the host country. While this may in some sense be true, it must be remembered that all international economic activity creates a division of labor, and it is indeed from this division of labor that we get mutual gains from trade. Similarly, an international division of labor certainly does not imply that the host country is worse off.

It is interesting to note that we hear arguments against U.S. firms locating manufacturing plants in Canada from both sides of the border. Americans accuse the U.S. firms of exporting jobs. Canadians fear the export of profits and the loss of domestic control over the Canadian economy. It seems that they believe that both home and host countries are made worse off by the MNE. We reject this point of view. It is, in fact, far easier to construct cases in which everyone gains from the MNE than to construct cases in which one or both countries lose.

PROBLEMS

1. "American multinationals are bad for Canada because they transfer profits abroad." Evaluate this argument.
2. "American multinationals are bad for Canada because they undermine economic independence." Evaluate this argument.
3. "American multinationals are bad for the United States because they transfer jobs abroad." Evaluate this argument.
4. In Section 3 we noted that multiplant economies imply that the MNE is potentially welfare-improving, due to the avoidance of duplicating R and D and other activities. Yet some regard the (possibly) lower level of R and D in Canada due to MNE as welfare-reducing rather than cost-saving. Try to evaluate the argument that reduced R and D is a harmful effect of the MNE.

NOTES

1. See Caves et al. (1980), Eastman and Stykolt (1967), Gorecke (1976), and Scherer et al. (1975).
2. Eastman and Stykolt (1967) presented the first convincing evidence.
3. See Markusen (1984) and Horstmann and Markusen (1987).
4. This idea is due to Magee (1977).

REFERENCES

Caves, R. E., M. E. Porter, and M. Spence (1980). *Competition in the Open Economy: A Model Applied to Canada.* Cambridge, Mass.: Harvard University Press.

Eastman, H. C., and S. Stykolt (1967). *The Tariff and Competition in Canada.* Toronto: Macmillan.

Gorecke, P. K. (1976). "The Determinants of Entry by Domestic and Foreign Enterprises in Canadian Manufacturing." *Review of Economics and Statistics* 58, 485–488.

Horstmann, I., and J. R. Markusen (1987). "Strategic Investments and the Development of Multinationals." *International Economic Review* 28, 109–121.

Magee, S. P. (1977). "Applications of the Dynamic Limit Pricing Model to the Price of Technology and International Technology Transfer." In K. Brunner and A. Meltzer (eds.), *Optimal Policies, Control Theory, and Technology Exports,* pp. 203–224. Amsterdam: North-Holland.

Markusen, J. R. (1984). "Multinationals, Multi-Plant Economies, and the Gains from Trade." *Journal of International Economics* 16, 205–226.

Scherer, F. M. et al. (1975). *The Economics of Multi-Plant Operation: An International Comparisons Study.* Cambridge, Mass.: Harvard University Press.

chapter 21

Growth and Dynamic Trade

1. INTERTEMPORAL GAINS FROM TRADE AND FOREIGN INVESTMENT

Preceding chapters have viewed trade as taking place in a timeless or static environment. Yet many important issues such as growth and foreign investment take place in a dynamic or intertemporal context. To understand these issues properly, therefore, requires that we use an explicitly intertemporal framework. The purpose of this chapter is to provide such an analysis.

The first issue we examine is international borrowing and lending, with particular emphasis on the gains from trade. Consider a very simple situation, in which there is only one commodity (corn) but two time periods. To simplify matters further, initially assume that we get a fixed endowment of corn each period, so that there is no production or investment. The situation is shown in Figure 21.1, where C_0 and C_1 are current and future period consumption, respectively, and E is the endowment point.

Individuals in the economy have identical preferences defined over current versus future consumption, as represented by the indifference curves in Figure 21.1. In the absence of the ability to trade, the economy's consumption in each period must equal the endowment; thus, autarky consumption is C_{0a} and C_{1a} in the two time periods. The economy attains welfare level U_a in autarky.

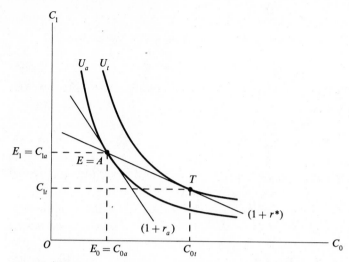

Figure 21.1

The important point is that the slope of U_a at the equilibrium E in Figure 21.1 is a type of price ratio involving people's willingness to substitute between current and future consumption. The slope of U_a is simply the consumer's marginal rate of substitution between C_0 and C_1, and will in equilibrium be equal to the market "price ratio" of C_1 in terms of C_0. This price ratio involves, of course, the rate of interest, but is not actually equal to the rate of interest. Suppose that the rate of interest is 10 percent. If I give up a unit of corn today (lend it to someone else), next period I will get back my unit of corn plus 10 percent. A unit of consumption foregone today gives me $(1 + .10) = 1.10$ tomorrow. More generally, the return on foregone consumption is $(1 + r)$, where r is the rate of interest. Algebraically, we have:

$$\Delta C_1 = (1 + r)(- \Delta C_0) \quad \text{or} \quad - \frac{\Delta C_1}{\Delta C_0} = (1 + r). \quad (21.1)$$

The equilibrium price ratio tangent to U_a at $E = A$ in Figure 21.1 is thus $(1 + r_a)$, where r_a denotes the autarky rate of interest.

Now suppose we can trade at a world rate of interest r^*, which differs from our autarky rate. r^* is arbitrarily assumed to be less than r_a in Figure 21.1. As in the static case, this difference in intertemporal prices is a source of gains from trade. In Figure 21.1. the economy can now attain point T and utility level U_t. It does so by borrowing an amount $(C_{0t} - E_0)$ (which is like an import) in the current period and paying back an amount $(E_1 - C_{1t})$ (which is like an export) in the future period. If instead r^* was greater than r_a, the country would be a net lender in the first period. The difference between r^* and r_a thus determines the direction of international capital flows, just as the difference between autarky and world commodity prices determines the direction of commodity trade in the static model.

Figure 21.1 shows the country attaining a higher welfare level through foreign borrowing, but it must be pointed out that this may be misleading. Just as trade may significantly redistribute income among factor owners in the static model, so also can there be significant redistribution and even welfare losses for some groups here. Suppose, for example, that the two time periods are very long, so that a significantly different set of individuals is alive in each time period. The first generation in Figure 21.1 greatly increases its consumption and welfare by foreign borrowing. The future generation must, however, pay back the loans, and so has lower levels of consumption and welfare than it would have had in autarky. Moreover, the future generation is powerless to prevent the current generation (or its government) from going on this type of spending spree at the future generation's expense.

The situation shown in Figure 21.1 does not allow for the possibility of productive investment. Figure 21.2 adds a transformation curve, which shows the country's ability to transform current output into future output through investment. In our example, corn can be planted instead of consumed, thereby yielding higher future output and consumption by sacrificing current consumption. Point E in Figure 21.2 continues to represent the endowment point, whereas the curve IE shows the transformation curve or investment opportunities.

The autarky equilibrium in Figure 21.2 is given by point A, where

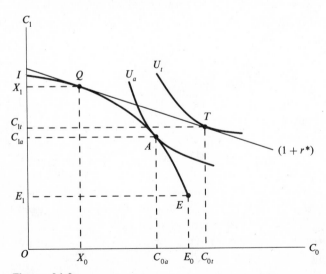

Figure 21.2

U_a is tangent to IE. At A, an amount $(E_0 - C_{0a})$ is invested in the initial period. The payoff from this investment is the increased consumption $(C_{1a} - E_1)$ in the future period. Investment opportunities thus allow the country to increase future consumption by sacrificing current consumption.

Now suppose that the country can borrow or lend at the world interest rate r^*. This means that the country faces a world "price ratio" $(1 + r^*)$ as shown in Figure 21.2. The production optimum for the country is to invest (plant corn) up to the point where the marginal return is just equal to the world rate of interest (the return from lending the corn to foreigners). This production optimum is given by point Q in Figure 21.2, where $(1 + r^*)$ is just tangent to IE. An initial period investment of $(E_0 - X_0)$ returns an amount $(X_1 - E_1)$ in the future period.

The country's consumption optimum is given by point T in Figure 21.2. The country borrows an amount $(C_{0t} - X_0)$ in the initial period and repays $(X_1 - C_{1t})$ in the future period. The ability to invest and borrow internationally raises welfare to U_t.

Note a very important difference between Figures 21.1 and 21.2. In 21.1 current consumption can be increased only via foreign borrowing at the expense of future consumption. But when productive investment opportunities exist (Figure 21.2), foreign borrowing used to finance investment can lead to increased consumption in both periods and thus to an unambiguous welfare gain for both "generations."

The policy implication is that there is nothing wrong with foreign borrowing per se from the point of view of future generations. The question is, rather, whether the funds are used simply for current consumption or for productive investment. In the latter case the ability to borrow from abroad may benefit both current and future generations.

2. FACTOR ACCUMULATION

In this section and the next two we examine some of the specific causes of growth for an economy and analyze the consequences of growth on such variables as total income, per capita income, and income distribution (factor prices). Perhaps the most obvious source of growth is the accumulation of factor supplies.[1]

In order to examine the effects of factor accumulation, let us use the simple two-good, two-factor Heckscher-Ohlin model first developed in Chapter 8. We assume that good X is labor-intensive and good Y capital-intensive. Since most of the interesting questions arise in the context of uneven growth in the supplies of the two factors, let us assume that the economy has accumulated labor relatively faster than capital. To keep the example very simple, suppose that the rest of the world has not grown at all over the period in question.

The situation is shown in Figure 21.3, where $T_0 T'_0$ represents the country's initial production frontier. The world price ratio is p_0 and production and consumption are at Q_0 and C_0, respectively. We know from the Rybczynski analysis of Chapter 8 that a faster accumulation of labor relative to capital causes a biased outward shift in the production frontier, in the direction of X (the labor-intensive good). The production frontier in Figure 21.3 thus shifts to $T_1 T'_1$.

The effects of this biased growth depend in important ways on what has happened to prices. Suppose first that we are a small country in a nongrowing world, such that prices remain fixed at p_0. Production and consumption shift to Q_1 and C_1, respectively, in Figure 21.3. Total income rises but in this simple case the distribution of income remains fixed. Recall from Chapter 8 that if the country is diversified in a Heckscher-Ohlin model, factor prices depend only on commodity prices (the factor-price-equalization theorem). The unit-value isoquants for X and Y remain fixed at constant prices, and thus the wage-rental ratio remains fixed at w_0/r_0 in Figure 21.4. The distribution of income does not change, and since the wage remains constant, so does labor income. But since there is now less capital per worker due to the biased growth, per capita income (wage plus rental income per worker) must have fallen. If instead there had been a relatively greater growth in the capital stock, exactly the same conclusions would apply, except that per capita income would have risen. Per capita income is thus more likely to grow when accumulation of nonlabor factors exceeds the growth of the labor force.

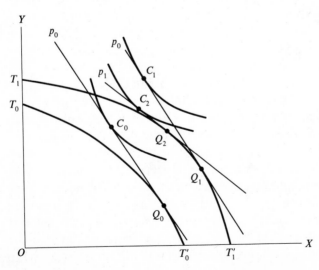

Figure 21.3

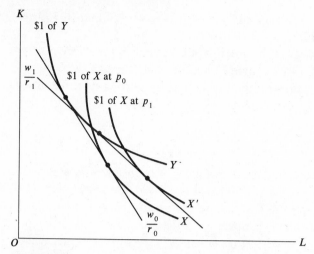

Figure 21.4

This simple and intuitively appealing relationship can be either strengthened or weakened by price changes. In the example of Figure 21.3 accumulation is heaviest in the factor (labor) used intensively in the export industry (X). This causes the country to increase its trade offer at the initial price ratio p_0 ($C_1 Q_1$ exceeds $C_0 Q_0$). Biased growth in the direction of the export industry means that the country wishes both to export more and import more. In the absence of changes in the rest of the world, this will generally drive down the price of exports and/or drive up the price of imports. The country's terms of trade deteriorate to p_1 in Figure 21.3. Growth in total income and growth in per capita income are less (or the fall in per capita income is greater) than they would have been if accumulation had been biased toward factors used intensively in import-competing production.

The effect on factor prices is shown in Figure 21.4. With the price of Y constant (using Y as the *numeraire*), the price of X falls so that it now takes a greater physical output of X to generate $1 of revenue. The unit-value isoquant thus shifts out in Figure 21.4 and the factor-price ratio falls from (w_0/r_0) to (w_1/r_1). We know from the Stolper-Samuelson theorem of Chapter 8 that the real wage falls and the real rental rate rises. If on the other hand there had been a strong bias in accumulation in favor of capital (used intensively in import-competing production), the country would have wished to trade less and so improved its terms of trade. We know from the Stolper-Samuelson theorem that this would in turn raise the real wage and lower the real rental rate. Thus in either case biased factor accumulation does lead to a factor-price change, which works against the increasingly more abundant factor. This effect acts to stabilize the economy and regulate growth. Rapid accumulation of capital, for example, eventually leads to a depressed return to capital and to a lower rate of investment and capital accumulation.

In summary, then, growth in per capita income is relatively greater when (1) accumulation is more rapid in nonlabor factors and (2) accumulation is more rapid in factors used intensively in import-competing industries.

3. TECHNICAL CHANGE

It is widely believed that technical change has been a major source of growth in the world economy over the past two centuries. Technical change is difficult to analyze for the simple reason that it takes many different forms. Rather than attempt to provide an exhaustive list of types and their consequences, we therefore consider only a single type, which we feel captures many of the issues.[2] In particular, we examine "neutral" technical change in one sector, defined as an equiproportionate decrease in the factors needed to produce that good. Geometrically, neutral technical change means that the isoquant for some particular output of the good moves inward along a ray from the origin.

Figure 21.5 depicts a situation in which neutral technical change occurs in the export sector (X) of the economy. Maximum possible production of X increases while that for Y does not. The production frontier thus shifts from $T_0 T_0'$ to $T_0 T_1'$ in Figure 21.5. At constant prices, total income increases as does per capita income, since the labor force is held constant by assumption. But unlike the case of factor accumulation at constant prices, factor prices do change in this case. This is shown in Figure 21.6, where the unit-value isoquant for X shifts in at constant prices p_0 due to the neutral technical change (t_0 and t_1 denote technology parameters before and after the change). The wage-rental ratio increases from (w_0/r_0) to (w_1/r_1) indicating a rise in the real wage of labor, the factor used intensively in the production of the good experiencing the improvement.

As was the case with factor accumulation, this result is however modified and possibly reversed by price changes. The technical improvement in X shown in Figure 21.5 leads to an increased trade offer and hence to a deterioration in the terms of trade unless the country is very small. As was the case in Figure 21.4, this fall in the relative price of X will shift the unit-value isoquant for X back out in Figure 21.6 and may result in a wage-rental ratio lower than (w_0/r_0). In summary, neutral technical change in a sector raises per capita income and the price of the factor used intensively in that sector for the small country, but terms-of-trade effects complicate the situation for the large country.

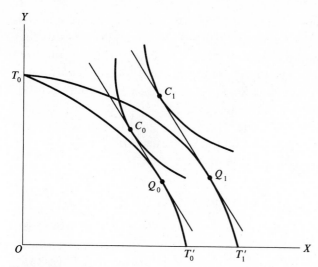

Figure 21.5

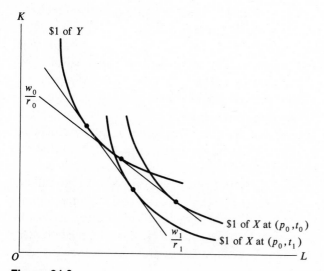

Figure 21.6

Other forms of technical change are often more complicated. Suppose, for example, that the technical change takes place in labor, so that workers become more productive in each industry (sometimes called "factor-augmenting" technical change). The direct effect of this is that wages should increase. But note that this increased labor productivity is in a sense like having more workers of the old low-productivity variety. As explained in the section on factor accumulation, this may act to depress the wage rate. The overall effect of labor-augmenting technical change thus depends on the relative strengths of these two effects.

This last example is perhaps sufficient to illustrate the complicated effects of technical change. It seems that the most general statements that can be made reduce to the following: (1) Technical change will improve per capita income for the small economy since total income increases without an increase in the labor force. (2) If technical change is concentrated in import-competing sectors or in factors used intensively in these industries, favorable terms-of-trade changes may generate further gains in per capita income. (3) The income distribution effects of technical change are complicated even in the absence of price changes.

4. SCALE ECONOMIES AND INCOME ELASTICITIES

Economies of scale have likely played an important role in raising per capita incomes over time. This contribution occurs for two reasons. First, as supplies of factors such as capital and labor are accumulated over time, scale economies mean that output can grow more than in proportion to the increase in factor supplies. Doubling factor supplies in the presence of scale economies more than doubles output.

Second, the development of the world economy has involved gradual but significant improvements in transportation and communications systems and, at least over the past 40 years, a reduction in trade barriers. These changes have meant that potential market sizes for firms have significantly expanded, allowing firms greater sales and reduced costs through the capture of scale economies. Lower tariffs and transportation costs thus lead to lower production costs and ultimately to higher per capita incomes.

There is one point here that may be of some significance in understanding the historical development of Canada and especially the United States. It has to do with the fact that scale economies may lead to a strongly biased pattern of growth and trade even if the underlying determinants of growth such as factor accumulation and technical change are neutral.

The point is illustrated in Figure 21.7, where Y is produced with constant returns and X is produced with increasing returns. $T_0 T_0'$ is the initial production frontier that shifts in a biased fashion to $T_1 T_1'$ when there is neutral or equiproportionate growth in all factors. At the constant world price ratio p_0, the optimal initial pattern of production and trade is to specialize in Y (point Q_0) and trade Y for X to reach the consumption point C_0. After growth the reverse pattern of specialization and growth is optimal and the country should produce at Q_1 and trade to C_1 in Figure 21.7. If the country grows faster than the rest of the world, its capture of scale economies may imply a fairly radical shift in its pattern of production.

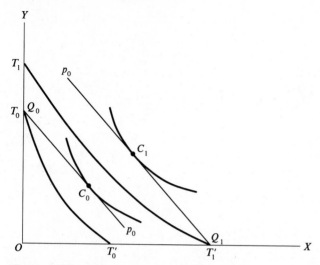

Figure 21.7

Figure 21.7 may shed some light on the development of the United States, which shifted from being a manufacturing importer in the eighteenth century to a manufacturing exporter by the late nineteenth century. High growth levels within the American economy relative to Europe and the large free-trade internal market meant that U.S. firms could capture scale economies earlier than their European counterparts. As in Figure 21.7, it thus may be that the pattern of comparative advantage in the United States shifted during this period toward goods produced with scale economies.

While speculating on questions of economic history, we find it of interest to discuss a determinant of biased growth that has been of great concern to economists studying developing countries. For most of this book we have assumed that utility functions are homogeneous. It is a property of such utility functions that income elasticities of demand for all goods equal 1. That is, a 1 percent increase in income results in a 1 percent increase in the demand for each and every good. Graphically, this means that an increase in income leads consumers to move out along a ray from the origin.

A different assumption is illustrated in Figure 21.8. Suppose that Y is food and X is manufactures. Suppose also that the production frontier shifts out in a neutral fashion from $T_0 T_0'$ to $T_1 T_1'$ due to technical change. The number of people is thus constant and per capita income increases. Assume finally that the income elasticity of demand for food is very low and for manufactures very high. Most of the increased income per capita will thus be spent on manufactures at constant prices. This last assump-

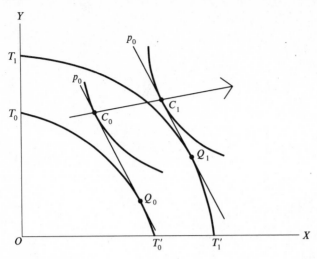

Figure 21.8

tion is illustrated in Figure 21.8 by the fact that consumption shifts in a biased fashion from C_0 to C_1 at constant prices p_0.

This biased growth in demand will have terms-of-trade effects. Figure 21.8 has been drawn such that the country actually decreases its trade offer ($C_0 Q_0$ exceeds $C_1 Q_1$) after growth, despite neutral change on the production side. Demand is channeled in the country's own export good (X) while few additional imports (Y) are demanded. In Figure 21.8 the increased production of Y actually exceeds the increased home consumption demand, whereas the increased production of X falls short of the increased home demand. Export supply and import demand both decrease with growth.

The opposite conclusions would apply to a country that had a comparative advantage in Y. Neutral growth on the production side would lead to increased export supply (since increased home demand for Y is low) and increased import demand (since increased home demand for X is high). If you then put these two countries together, it must be the case that the terms of trade improve over time for the country exporting X (the high-income elasticity good) and deteriorate for the country exporting Y. Neutral and equal growth in production for the two countries would translate into unequal growth in per capita incomes. The country exporting X would experience a higher rate of growth in per capita income due to the terms-of-trade effects.

This simple idea has been applied to the analysis of economic development, where it has been asserted that highly developed countries export the high-income elasticity goods (manufactures in our example) and less-developed countries export the low-income elasticity goods. The consequence of this is that the developed countries' terms of trade improve with time and less-developed countries' terms of trade deteriorate. Thus the rich get richer and the poor fall further behind. Empirical tests of this proposition seem to offer some, although not totally convincing, support (Prebisch 1964, Singer 1950).

5. TERMS-OF-TRADE EFFECTS, DISTORTIONS, AND IMMISERIZING GROWTH

A recurring point in preceding sections was that if a country's growth results in an increased desire to trade (e.g., growth is concentrated in the export sector), then growth will lead to a deterioration in the country's terms of trade unless the rest of the world is growing at the same rate or faster. This raises the question of whether the resulting deterioration in the terms of trade could be so severe that the country is actually made worse off by growth. The answer is that this can indeed happen—a phenomenon that is referred to as "immiserizing growth."[3]

An example of immiserizing growth is shown in Figure 21.9. A technical improvement in the export sector shifts the production frontier from $T_0 T_0'$ to $T_0 T_1'$. At the initial prices p_0, the country would wish to trade more, supplying more exports of X and demanding more imports of Y. This causes the country's terms of trade to deteriorate (the relative price of X to fall) and, as shown in Figure 21.9, the deterioration can be so large that welfare is reduced. This is illustrated in Figure 21.9 by a fall in consumption from C_0 to C_1 and a reduction in welfare from U_0 to U_1 at the new price ratio p_1.

This possibility of being made worse off by a technical improvement seems paradoxical. The important fact to realize about the situation shown in Figure 21.9 is that the country obviously has monopoly power in trade. The country's increased export supply and increased import demand affect prices in a substantial way. We also know from our discussions in Chapter 14 that when a country has monopoly power in trade, free trade is not the optimal policy. A tariff should be instituted to move the terms of trade in the country's favor.

The source of the welfare loss in Figure 21.9 has to do with the fact that the country with monopoly power is engaging in free trade rather than optimizing its trade with a tariff. This absence of an optimizing policy means that as growth occurs, trade policy is not being adjusted in an optimal way. This results in the possibility of immiserizing growth as shown in Figure 21.9.

Immiserizing growth cannot occur if a country follows an optimal trade policy. That is, when growth occurs, the country can always increase

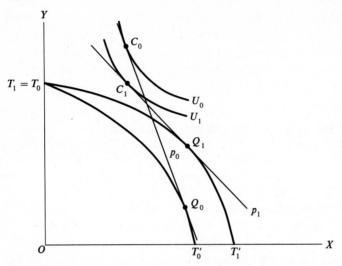

Figure 21.9

its import tariff (or export tax) so as to leave the country's trade offer unchanged at the old prices. There will then be no deterioration in the terms of trade and no welfare losses. In general, the country can do even better than this arbitrary policy.

The failure to have an optimal trade policy is a distortion in a certain sense and it is this distortion that leads to the possibility of immiserizing growth. Other types of distortions can similarly lead to welfare losses from growth. Figure 21.10 shows a small economy facing the fixed world price ratio p_0. Production is distorted by a production tax on X (or a production

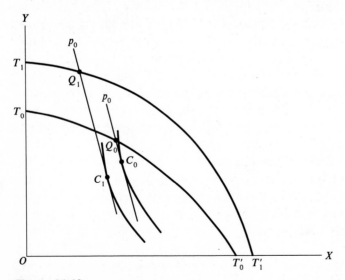

Figure 21.10

subsidy on Y), which raises the price ratio above the marginal rate of transformation. Initial production and consumption points are Q_0 and C_0 in Figure 21.10, respectively. Suppose now that growth is heavily biased toward the import-competing sector Y. Production must shift to a point on the new production frontier $T_1 T_1'$, which has the same slope as point Q_0. This may be a point such as Q_1, which results in lower consumption at C_1 and thus immiserizing growth.

The economic reasoning behind this result in Figure 21.10 is as follows. Due to the distortion, the economy is initially overproducing Y at Q_0. Biased growth in favor of Y causes the economy to produce even more Y, effectively increasing the degree of distortion. You could draw another diagram to show that biased growth in favor of X would effectively decrease the distortion and thus lead to an unambiguous increase in welfare. [4]

6. EXPORT-LED GROWTH AND THE "STAPLES THESIS"

The determinants of growth that we have discussed to this point are what we might term *internal* determinants. Factor accumulation and technical change as we have discussed them are events happening *within* a country, events that have varying consequences for the economy depending on the response of world prices to the changes in domestic excess demands.

Growth may, however, be induced from abroad, and indeed external sources of growth are thought by many to be of significant importance in explaining early American and Canadian development. Although there may be several sources of externally induced growth, the most common type is thought to occur via increased foreign demand for domestic exports, either directly or through lower transportation costs, and is therefore referred to as "export-led growth."

One particular view of the process of export-led growth is referred to as the "staples thesis," staples being defined as products having a high natural resource content. The ideas behind the staples thesis were first formulated by W. A. Mackintosh and H. A. Innis, in an attempt to explain certain common features of successive phases of Canadian development. [5] It was observed that the development of the Canadian economy was initiated and extended by the exploitation of a series of exportable, natural resource-based products. It was assumed (and apparently never convincingly demonstrated) that each successive phase was induced by external factors such as demand changes. The view that growth depended on the exportation of resource-based products has come to be known as the staples thesis. Successive staples important to

Canadian development were, in rough chronological order, fish, fur, timber, wheat, and minerals.

The staples thesis as described by Marr and Paterson (1980) consists of four principal elements, describing each phase of development.[6] First, there occurred a new or increased foreign demand for some staple. As noted earlier, this can happen either because the *foreign* demand actually increased or because falling transportation costs meant higher domestic prices and demand at constant foreign demand. Second, the natural resource base needed to produce the staple existed domestically. Third, technical change in production and the development of internal transportation facilities frequently helped make exploitation profitable. Fourth, "linkage effects" helped spread the growth due to staple exploitation into other sectors of the economy.

Linkages are simply economic interdependencies; there are backward, forward, and lateral linkages. Backward linkages have to do with the demand for inputs by the new industry. Transportation systems needed to move the staples production might be a simple example. Forward linkages occur when it is profitable to process further the basic raw materials of staples production into semifinished or finished goods. Timber processed into lumber or paper, wheat into flour, or nickel ore into refined nickel ingots are examples. Lateral linkages include the demands for food, housing, and services by the workers in the new industries.

While the staples thesis does provide an interesting description of development, it does not provide a theory in the usual sense of the word. In particular, early writers did not specify the precise mechanism by which changes in external demand were translated into substantial economic growth.

To see the importance of this, consider the simple international trade model with fixed factor supplies that we have used throughout this book. In such a model, a change in foreign demand results in a favorable terms-of-trade shift with, of course, a resulting improvement in per capita income. But such an improvement should be modest, as total resources are fixed. Production increases in the new staple sector but only at the expense of production in other sectors, from which resources are "bid away" by staples production. This is shown in Figure 21.11, where the production frontier is $T_0 T_0'$ and initial production, consumption, and prices are given by Q_0, C_0, and p_0, respectively. An improvement in the terms of trade to p_1 leads to increased production of the export sector (X) and to increased welfare, but it would be stretching the point to claim that anything really dramatic happens. It is, in other words, hard to believe that a theory of development can be built upon terms-of-trade improvements in this sort of simple model.

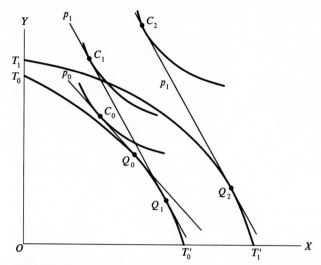

Figure 21.11

One alternative is to attempt to construct a model based on *Keynesian multipliers,* a concept familiar to most readers of this book. In a Keynesian macroeconomic model an increase in exports constitutes an autonomous increase in expenditure, and hence has a multiplier effect on production and income. This could be the basis of a fully specified theory if it were not for the fact that most macroeconomists no longer regard these multipliers and their underlying models as generally valid. The problem is that the Keynesian model ignores supply, or alternatively, assumes that output is completely demand-determined. It would seem to be a serious mistake to attempt to build a theory of development on such a concept. [7]

Another alternative we can suggest has to do with international factor mobility. Although little formal research has been done on this idea, it seems clear that much of North America's development was associated with inflows of foreign labor and capital. The Western boom of the late nineteenth century was, for example, built in part on inflows of foreign settlers with their financial and human capital.

Suppose that the staples sector (e.g., wheat) requires inputs of labor, capital, and raw land, and assume further that raw land is for all practical purposes a free good (it does not constrain output). Also assume that capital and labor are internationally mobile. Assume finally that the economy is initially in equilibrium in Figure 21.11 at production point Q_0 on production frontier $T_0 T_0'$.

Now suppose that the terms of trade improve from p_0 to p_1 in Figure 21.11 due to increased foreign demand or lower transportation costs. The initial changes as described previously are to shift production and consumption to Q_1 and C_1, respectively. But these changes increase the productivity of at least one factor in the production of the staple and so raise its return. But since this factor is mobile, we get an inflow of it, which begins to shift the production frontier out. Further, since the mobile factor is being added to essentially free land, there is little of a diminishing-marginal-product effect that might otherwise bring the factor inflow quickly to a halt.[8] With land in free supply and the other factors mobile, the supply curve of the staple is extremely elastic. A small improvement in the terms of trade not only shifts internal resources (the movement from Q_0 to Q_1 in Figure 21.11), but also induces a factor inflow that may have a far greater effect on export production. This effect is shown by the shift in the production frontier to $T_1 T_1'$ in Figure 21.11 and the shift of production from Q_1 to Q_2.

With internationally mobile factors, export-led growth does therefore seem to be a possibly valid source of development. Whether or not this description is closely consistent with the North American experience is unclear at this time; more thorough answers await empirical examination.[9]

7. SUBSIDIES FOR HIGH TECH

In recent years the governments of many developed nations have decided that they should become more directly involved in the growth and development of the economy. Governments have, of course, always been somewhat involved through subsidizing education, modifying the tax system to encourage investment, providing research grants, and occasionally assisting in a specific large project. But usually this involvement has been fairly indirect in the United States relative to Europe in particular, leaving the specific allocation of resources to private market forces.

More recently, governments in North America, Europe, and Japan have felt pressure to support directly domestic industry in a nebulous class of industries and products called "high technology." Governments seem to have the attitude that their countries will not have a high growth rate and will fall to second-class status unless they produce goods that are technically sophisticated. Unfortunately, every other Western nation seems to have the same view, which makes one wonder who the inevitable losers will be (perhaps everyone will lose money).

The rationale behind government involvement in developing new industries seems to be that private markets do not make socially optimal investment decisions, and thus governments should become involved. There are at least four possible reasons for which private firms may not make socially optimal investment decisions. (1) Private firms are not so clever at predicting the future as the government is. (2) The private discount rate is higher than the government's rate. (3) There are externalities in investment activities that are not properly internalized by private firms. (4) Governments have noneconomic objectives such as national prestige.

There is no evidence that (1) is true. There are many examples to the contrary. Reason (2) may be true because corporate taxation requires that pretax rates of return be high if private business is to invest. The solution to this, however, is to reform taxation and not to involve the government directly. Given appropriate tax policies, private firms and governments should evaluate projects using exactly the same criteria. Reason (3) may be true for a limited range of activities. Research activities producing knowledge as their principal output are a case in point. It is hard to protect the ownership of knowledge (although there are patent laws) and if the innovators cannot capture the full value of their investments, an externality or external benefit is conferred on society. But firms will underinvest since they know they cannot capture the benefit of the innovation. This reasoning has been behind government sponsorship of education and research. Reason (4) is a justification for government intervention if such objectives represent people's preferences.

Whether or not recent government projects are justified under any of these headings is a matter of opinion.

8. CONCLUDING REMARKS

In this chapter we have moved the analysis of international trade from a static framework to a dynamic one. It is only in such a context that important issues such as growth and foreign investment can be dealt with.

The first topic we discussed was international borrowing and lending. We asked in what sense the ability to trade across time (as opposed to across goods) could lead to gains from trade and in what sense current international borrowing could impose costs on later generations. The answer to the first question is that there certainly are intertemporal gains from trade, although the incidence of these gains falls unequally on different groups (e.g., generations) and some groups may actually be worse off. But this is not a new problem; we have noted many instances throughout the book in which the aggregate gains from trade are accompanied by strong redistributive effects. The answer to the second question was shown to depend on whether the borrowing was simply used to finance increased current consumption or to finance productive investment.

The next several sections considered various determinants of growth such as factor accumulation, technical change, and scale economies. We showed that an important determinant of the overall effects of these sources of growth was their effect on international prices. Growth that is strongly biased in favor of the export sector should, for example, lead to adverse terms-of-trade changes that dampen the gains from growth. Section 5 pointed out that it is, in fact, possible for the resulting deterioration in the terms of trade to be so strong that the country is actually made worse off by growth. We noted that this is simply an example of how an otherwise favorable change (growth) can, in the presence of a distortion, have an unfavorable effect, and we presented a second example of how a distortion can generate such a result.

Section 5 examined the idea of export-led growth. We suggested that this idea has not been developed in a satisfactory fashion and offered a possible interpretation based on international factor mobility. Section 6 concluded our discussion by expressing reservations about governments' attempts to displace private decision making in guiding development. Recent preoccupations with "high tech" may prove to be a case in point.

PROBLEMS

1. In light of Section 1, contrast the effects on future generations of two types of borrowing from the U.S. (a) The American government borrows to finance current expenditures on public goods. (b) General Motors borrows to finance construction of a new plant.

2. Redraw Figures 21.3 and 21.4 for a biased growth in favor of capital.

3. Consider the case in which all factor supplies grow in the same proportion or technical change occurs in both sectors at the same rate. (a) Show the effect on the production possibility curve. (b) If the rest of the world does not grow, is it likely that the country's terms of trade will deteriorate?

4. Draw a diagram corresponding to Figure 21.8 for a country that exports Y. Putting your diagram together with Figure 21.8, try to show that equal growth in both countries must cause a rise in p_x/p_y.

5. With reference to Figure 21.10, show that if growth instead leads to an increase in the production of X, then welfare must increase.

NOTES

1. A good general survey is provided by Findlay (1984).
2. Chacholiades (1973) provides a comprehensive treatment in his Chapter 13.
3. See Bhagwati (1958).
4. Bhagwati (1968) and Johnson (1967) discuss growth in the presence of domestic distortions.
5. Innis (1930) and Mackintosh (1923).

6. Marr and Paterson (1980).
7. See Isard (1960) for a critical examination of Keynesian multiplier growth models.
8. The existence of a specific factor like land is important to this argument. In the Heckscher-Ohlin model a change in prices would raise the return to the mobile factor in all countries.
9. Dales (1966) reported that import tariffs had a similar effect of causing mobile factors to flow into import-competing sectors.

REFERENCES

Bhagwati, J. N. (1958). "Immiserizing Growth: A Geometric Note." *Review of Economic Studies* 25, 201–205.

———. (1968). "Distortions and Immiserizing Growth: A Generalization." *Review of Economic Studies* 35, 481–485.

Chacholiades, M. (1973). *The Pure Theory of International Trade.* Chicago: Aldine.

Dales J. H. (1966). *The Protective Tariff in Canada's Development.* Toronto: University of Toronto Press.

Findlay, R. (1984). "Growth and Development in Trade Models." In P. B. Kenen and R. W. Jones (eds.), *Handbook of International Economics.* Amsterdam: North-Holland.

Innis, H. A. (1930). *The Fur Trade in Canada: An Introduction to Canadian Economic History.* Toronto: University of Toronto Press.

Isard, W. (1960). *Methods of Regional Analysis.* Cambridge, Mass.: MIT Press.

Johnson, H. G. (1967). "The Possibility of Income Losses from Increased Efficiency or Factor Accumulation in the Presence of Tariffs." *Economic Journal* 77, 151–54.

Mackintosh, W. A. (1923). "Economic Factors in Canadian History." *The Canadian Historical Review* 4, 12–25.

Marr, W. L., and D. G. Paterson (1980). *Canada: An Economic History.* Toronto: Gage.

Prebisch, Raul (1964). *Towards a New Trade Policy for Development, Report by the Secretary General of UNCTAD.* New York: United Nations.

Singer, Hans (1950). "The Distribution of Gains between Investing and Borrowing Countries," *American Economic Review* 40, 473–485.

Watkins, M. H. (1963). "A Staple Theory of Economic Growth." *Canadian Journal of Economics and Political Science* 29, 141–158.

Index

ISBN 0-06-044212-3